Dying Well

The Resurrected Life of
Jeanie Wylie-Kellermann

Bill Wylie-Kellermann

D1523021

Cass Community Publishing House

For more information and further discussion, visit
ccpublishinghouse.org

For her grandchildren,
Wylie-Eggarts and Wylie-Faheys all
Whom she loves even now;
For Denise Griebler
Who found her way to me and to Detroit
By way of Ched's memorial homily;
and
For The Detroit Peace Community,
Dearly beloved,
Who embraced, in living and in dying,
Jeanie Wylie-Kellermann

Teach Me
(November 12, 2005)

after this length of warm days,
          undeserved, unexpected
a leaf nods thanks,
          turns at its node
     to catch the wind's rude pull
and sails abrupt toward
          ash or humus

a life becoming of the earth

does it really know when to let go? or how?
must it be so roughly compelled?
or does the will to hold
          turn slowly in an instant
     to nature's grace?
or even are one—beginning to end?

beneath our feet the world
          reels and tilts
     toward dusk
          we find our footing
in the rustle which is the path at hand

in my own, my turning
my eyes are fixed
on you who know
          from whence this prayer

teach me, Jeanie, forever

Contents

Acknowledgments

This book is verily an event of community. Thanks be to God for contributions, helps, and love—in the book and the life it tells. Great gratitude ...

First to Joyce Hollyday, not only for family pastoral care, anniversary retreat leadership and the epilogue recounting it, but for a major editorial overhaul—which is to say, you should have seen this before she put her elegant hand to it. Or maybe not.

To Daniel Berrigan (now gone to God) for a kind letter about the book (even "sighting a unicorn"), but gently averring it wanted the edit that Joyce accomplished.

To Steve and Christine Clemons, donor activists, for generously supporting that edit;

To other readers in whole or in part, Julie Lyons, Elena Herrada, Liz McAlister, Irene Elizabeth (Rene Beth) Rodgers, Denise Griebler, and Ched Myers, for encouragement, admonition, and suggestions.

To the Collegeville Institute for a writers' week in early 2006 that jump-started the work.

To Dorothy Bass and Valporaiso Institute, for envisioning the book as "dying well" in their series of basic Christian practices; for a grant shaping it so and a community retreat to seal the deal;

To the query/discernment group—Marianne Arboghast, Deb Choly, Martha Chevalier Dage, Elaine Enns, Ched Myers, John Zetner … and eventually Ed Rowe, for good hard questions, attentive discernments, and all sort of other supportive gifts;

To Deb Choly for organizing care coverage when I was away; to Beth O'hara-Fisher for taking the update calls when we were too overwhelmed; to Sr. Connie Supan for local child therapy;

To the serial intensive pastoral care team, Ched Myers and Elaine Enns, their bodywork emissary—Elaine Emily, Will O'Brien and DeeDee Risher, Josie Winterfeld, Joyce Hollyday, Liz McAlister, plus Tom Lumpkin and Ed Rowe;

To Rose Berger for leading the ritual of transition in Minneapolis with a deft and poetic hand, and the L.A. Worker for the communal hospice quilt;

To *The Witness* staff, Julie Wortman, Marianne Arbogast, Gloria House, and Marietta Jaeger, and to the Board for support, spiritual and financial;

To Dave Frenchak and Dody Finch (both now of blessed memory), Carol Ann McGibbon and all at SCUPE (sadly also of blessed memory) for gracious allowances in my work life through those seven long years;

To some of the attending doctors, who proved themselves remarkable human beings: Susan Rice, Jack Rock, Rigdon Lentz, Bernd Barthel, Wilma Agnello, Greg Caircross, Laslo and Eva Csastary, Ralph Cushing, plus nurse friends, Deb McEvoy, Peggy Gavagan, and Debbie Mast;

To Laura Markham and Ron Williams for the capital gains gift to Central Methodist which supported some of the more unorthodox treatments;

To the Detroit Peace Community, so called by Jonah House during the 1980 year of weekly witness at the Pentagon, for living into the name;

To artists who created with Jeanie or otherwise healed her soul—Ange Smith, Susan Horvath, DeeDee Risher, Lucy Wylie-Kellermann, Mary (Wylie) Carter, Nancy Cannon, MaryAnn

Angelini, Dierdra Luszwik, John August Swanson, Betty Laduke, Virginia Macsymowicz, Tom Lewis, Liz McAlister;

To photographers Herb Gunn, Daymon Hartley, Rudy Simon, for being present and granting permission to use their work.

To poets cited—Rainer Maria Rilke, Emily Dickenson, Jacob Mersberger, Connie Supan, and to those who have allowed their work to be published with permission, Daniel Berrigan, DeeDee Risher, Michael Lauchlan, Jim Perkinson, and Lydia Wylie-Kellermann;

To musicians who so often held the space and carried the day—Julie Beutel, Bob O'Brien, Katie Carter, Barbara Sale, Mary, Misty, and Babs Lee Carter, Jacob Mersberger, Andie Gaines and her chanting crew, Bobby Thompson, Ange Smith, Charlie King, Andrea Ayvazian

To Simone Sagovac, beloved transition manager for organizing and convening of the point-of-death team; to Jacob and Jeannie for the handmade casket, Ed Bobinchak for the coffin window ramp, Laura Silveri for the gorgeous cloth stretcher, Pat Hartsoe for the deadlift, the Kellerman brothers for the crematorium run, and all who stepped up in that deep moment;

To Julie Lyons for green burial encouragements and to Paul Buchanan and Generations Funeral Home in creating a wide berth for alternative practices;

To Ched Myers for his memorial sermon and permission to reprint it; to Noah Strosahl Kellermann for production of Jeanie's video; and to all other memorial participants ... Lydia and Lucy, Coleman McGehee, Ed Rowe, Tom Lumpkin, Rose Berger, Pio Celetino, Jim Wallis, Maureen Taylor, Joyce Hollyday, plus drummers, chanters, singers, poets, dancers, altar builders, readers and lectors, and the feastmakers to follow;

To the Wylie and Kellermann clans for extending the kindom with their love irrepressible;

And to Bea Wylie for imagining that God may have wanted her and Sam to have another child, the blessed intuition herein confirmed.

The last picture. The Wylie-Kellermanns, feast of Stephen, December 26, 2005. Credit: Family collection.

Foreword

by Lydia Wylie-Kellermann

We were stuck between the bathroom and bedroom. Dad was holding her up on one side while I picked up one leg at a time to help her walk. This time our choreography wasn't working. She wasn't helping and we couldn't do it. We looked at one another, realizing that this was it. Her body was shutting down and she could no longer move. Just that morning we had set up the hospital bed in our living room next to the Christmas tree. It was time. Dad looked at me with tears in his eyes and said "Tomorrow. I want one last night together in our bed." One more night to feel her skin rest against his, to feel the movement of breath running through her body, and to wake up next to one he had every morning for 20 years. A final night to hold her and weep, before the loneliness of that hollowed bedside.

I give thanks for my parents' marriage. Their love was one of quick wit, physical passion, liturgical grounding, theological imagination, feet on the street, and love letters in jail. Their marriage was not always easy, but it was beautiful. They shared openly the dirty, messy, hard stuff between them, teaching my sister and me to embrace and honor our own anger. And on afternoons that they "kicked us out" to play in the woods while they made love, we learned about the joy and celebration of loving another.

In my mom's dying, I witnessed the parts of marriage you don't plan on or expect. Seven and a half years of round-the-clock caregiving. Of life-and-death decisions. Of losing her in a grocery store only to find her at the front of a long line searching her empty pockets with a Butterfinger bar on the counter. Of graciously responding when she announced she was a vegetarian after the chicken had been prepared or eating her weird concoctions when she decided to "cook." Of daily injections and nebulizers and handfuls of pills and changing her sterilized dressing. Of getting her dressed in the morning. Of waking to that haunting sound of seizures with the look of panic in her eyes. Of surgical waiting rooms. Of endless research of alternative medicine and newfound hope. Of waking up, realizing he can't stomach skipping Western medicine's radiation. Of lighting candles and singing prayers. Of vigiling. Of creating a space filled with light and angels for the years of dying time.

If I were being merely objective, I would have to say my mom was brilliant! And my dad knew that, too. And, suddenly, the woman who always had the right words could no longer finish a sentence. My dad lost his partner years before she died. In the midst of his marriage, there was loneliness and loss. It is hard to grieve and articulate the little deaths in the midst of daily rejoicing that she is still alive! As her mind deteriorated, a sweet, gentle strength immerged filling our house with smiles and hugs. But the partnership in mind was gone.

My dad was amazing. And I don't think I tell him that enough. My mom's dying was a long, imperfect, human journey. But he loved her so tenderly through every second of it. And in her dying, she could trust that. It was a sacramental, marital call that he rose to with love.

This is indeed a book about my mom, about community, and about dying in a culture of death. But it is also a very real story about the ones who care for the dying—who walk beside in all the ups and downs, laughter and tears, living and dying.

Reading these pages, the love will jump right off the page. It's been over a decade since my mom died, and the act of carefully crafting this book has been another way for my dad to love my mom.

This is a gift you hold in your hands, a love letter, a story. I give thanks for all those who love the dying—some of the most important and courageous work there is. And so often lonely, thankless and long. I hope that within these pages, we all find a bit of your own story and a friend on the journey.

Thirteen winters have passed, I have fallen in love, made my own sacred commitments, and birthed two kids of my own. I have known the awe and joy of marriage and family. I ache for my dad in a new way imagining that loss. In those years, I learned both about dying in the arms of your partner and also how to love and care for your dying partner. I trust that whatever unexpected moments happen in my own family, and whatever side of that I am on, we will walk along with one another and love each other tenderly 'til that final day.

Dad, thank you. Thank you for falling in love with Mom, for standing before God and community and giving your lives to one another, for teaching us about love through arguments and laughter, for making decisions about life and death for and with her, for loving your daughters, and talking to us about death at such an early age, for grueling decisions made with the help of community, for finding joy in the darkness, for entrusting the dying to a loving God, for holding her hand during her final breath, for the courage and creativity of sending her home by another way, and for the love of writing it all down here. I love you.

Jeanie and Bill in the Cass Corridor, 1985. Credit: Family collection.

Introduction: The Sort the Wind Moves

What kind of book is this, anyway? Well, it's not the first book I've written unintended. It's a bit of a "found object"—or several. Like "found art." Pieces picked up along a certain distinctive path, or even the flotsam and jetsam harvested from a narrow strip of beach, then balanced and strung like a mobile for the breeze, or simply arranged, framed, and hung. I present it to you thus, dear friends and passersby.

The heart of it, the main find and bearing beam, is a series of letters updating family and friends about my wife Jeanie Wylie's illness and death. She began them herself when first struck down in 1998 with a most aggressive brain tumor. They originally alerted her readership at *The Witness* magazine, where she was editor and publisher, but quickly morphed into a regular posting, for the sake of curiosity or prayer, called "How's Jeanie?"

As her energies and then her capacities slowed, I picked up the responsibility (and you'll see where one of our daughters, Lydia, felt called to put her own hand in). Posted on the website, batched electronically, and commended to the snail mails, the letters summoned a progressively wider community, by whose intercessions we substantially lived. And very soon people began to say, "I save them. Have you noticed you're writing a book?" So this is the book.

It is a book about healing and prayer, community, and intercession. The story of finding our freedom and keeping control of the medical decisions is told in its stumbling discernment. At the same time, and perhaps more so, this is a book about dying well—which Jeanie did, learning and teaching us as she went.

I figure to make sense of the letters, you're going to need to know something about her. About her passions, and the look in her eye, and the shape of her life in this world. Dying well is probably inseparable from living well, so there's a bit of biography necessarily slipped into these pages.

Jeanie was stunningly beautiful, howsoever transfigured in the end. Of course, I came into her life at a certain point, so I can't help it if this book turns into something of a love story. In fact, I've decided to begin the tale with our romance and engagement, just so you know.

A writer friend looking over the first draft commented, "You hardly ever mention love, but it's on every page." That makes me happy. I loved her so.

One Christmas early in our marriage, I gave Jeanie a blank book, bound and beautiful. Into it I had transcribed a first clutch of poems for her. I would add to it a page at a time, generally re-presenting it as a gift, wrapped and delivered, but often just writing one in and hoping she'd come upon it by surprise.

I plan to insert a few love poems into these pages, to fill in some blanks to which she and I alone were privy. At the time she died, the book remained incomplete, empty pages beckoning. Who knows? Perhaps I'll fill them yet …

Which is to say, I love her still. I've already had to pause twice for tears in making these notes, filling this page. So if this is not a book about grieving, it is nonetheless a book that is an act of grief. Putting down these words is a ritual of mourning. It answers my ache.

You'll also need to know something about our family. About our daughters, Lydia and Lucy. And our extended family. So you'll find pieces of history from, and tribute to, the families out of which Jeanie and I were birthed, and the one we gave birth to. As well as the mentors who shaped us along the way in life and faith. Since I'm holding the primary narrative voice, this may turn into something of a spiritual memoir—at least in glimpses, fits, and starts.

And, perhaps every bit as important, you need to know our community. In the letters are references to the particulars of our life together: our politics, our worship life, the landscape of our neighborhoods in Detroit and beyond, a short topography of characters, our times even (or how we read them)—all in all the practices of our commonlife. This is inevitably a book about living and dying in community. In all of it, I'll strive to be starkly and lovingly honest about us all.

So now you're probably thinking, he doesn't really know what kind of book this is. Perhaps not. Maybe it has a life and identity of its own. But one I'm growing to love in the finding and the making.

Oh, one more thing. Apart from the letters, I've written this almost entirely in the first year of griefwork. Despite several edits since, my own and others, it retains that tenor, moment, and perspective. Now as it goes to press a decade hence, I am inserting a paragraph here or there, seamlessly like this one, to bring things up to date.

It does, to be sure, have parts moving in and out of one another, much like that image of the literary mobile that I inadvertently swiped right from our life. After Jeanie published her first letter about her illness, a package arrived in the mail. It was from someone we didn't know, a priest on the East Coast,

I think. When we opened the parcel, a pile of driftwood sticks and seajunk tangled with fishline presented itself with a simple note of love and care.

We nodded thanks, but I don't know if we ever replied. The gift was initially under-appreciated, as they say. Some time later, perhaps months, one of us pulled it from the box. It wasn't tangled in the least. It righted itself almost magically, and with a perfect, delicate balance.

The note was gone and so too the record of whom properly to thank. We hung it over Jeanie's altar (more on that to come), and it delights to this day, moving with the barest breath of a wind. It was a blessing from the nethermost parts of the sea. A prayer now anonymous, but among the constant.

I would be glad if this book of flotsam found could hang together with half its grace. And gladder still should it be set moving by a wind of breath, mine or yours or, above all, Jeanie's. The breath of the Spirit. Of life. And my gladness would compound ever so slightly if, among you readers, that artful pray-er and mobile maker, who stands anonymous for you all, would finally hear this thanks.

Jeanie at the Monastery of Gethsemani on the day of their
engagement, 1984. Credit: Bill Wylie-Kellermann

My Wake-up Call

Gethsemani

Carefully testing the steps, and helping one another over the missing slats of stair, Jeanie Wylie and I climbed the weather-worn frame of the fire watchtower. The Kentucky hills were warm in the winter sun. A church bell called the start of prayer in the noon office. Pushing up and through the trapdoor, we suddenly had a view of the abbey below, where the monks of Gethsemani were even then lifting the psalms in Gregorian and interceding for us all. Thomas Merton had once requested this abandoned lookout for a hermitage, but the abbot put him off just then.

"So, are we here to decide something?" Jeanie asked. A rhetorical question. Our hands touched on the rusting metal ledge. I had spent a month with the monks, ostensibly weighing a choice that was really a done deal when I arrived.

I had hitchhiked from Detroit, and Jeanie drove down to pick me up, bearing, at my request, rubber boots for the February mud and two leather shoe thongs. The latter mysteries were for stringing each of us a single bead of a fossil—actually a reed segment from the days that this bioregion was lush with wetland grass. These had been dredged from a streambed and spread with the gravel of the monastery's farm lanes, and I'd found them in my walking meditations through the hills. They would be, for us, engagement rings.

"Yes," I replied, pulling out one of the homemade lanyards and placing it round her neck. I handed her the other, and she did the same to me. We kissed and lingered in the holding, then turned back toward the view. So close we could nearly have touched it, a hawk hovered before us on the rolling-under-neath-him steady air.

Later that evening, as we walked across the monastery field, grasshoppers clicked their heels and leapt. In the east, a full moon rose. And ever after we would celebrate any full moon as our engagement anniversary.

The decision to marry Jeanie Wylie was the easiest I'd ever made. I just knew it, "balls to bones." Or better—we knew it together. From our earliest conversations, she and I understood this commitment to mean working out our salvation within the vocation of marriage. I suppose I am still, even with these words.

I never second-guessed. And that was no small matter for me, since for years I'd been crippled in my capacity to make clean and straightforward decisions. I would settle and swing, backtracking and self-doubting. I could name the crushing moments of incapacitation in my upbringing, when I'd been left to guess the life-hinging, one "right" choice. I could rehearse the moments when my freedom was pretended, but stolen. But not this time. In that decision my freedom was reclaimed—or received as gift. In my "yes" to Jeanie was a kind of healing.

It was true for her as well, though perhaps in a different way. Jeanie once told me that on that same trip, she had sat before the abbey's famous statue of Jesus in the Garden of Gethsemane, stretched upward in the bloodsweats of prayer while the sleeping disciples drowsed together just downhill. In those days, the sculptures were surrounded by a stand of cathedral-like white pines. Jeanie wept and wept uncontrollably. Over something for which she'd almost given up yearning: a marriage partner, to be

Monastery, Trappist, KY, where Jeanie and Bill were engaged.
Credit: Abbey of Gethsemani

sure, but even more for the concrete experience of God's love for her.

As we both knew, the sculptures are dedicated to Jonathan Daniels, an Episcopal seminarian who was killed by a shotgun blast in Lowndes County, Alabama in 1965 after he was released from jail in connection with a voter registration project. A Detroit friend of ours, Gloria House, working the same project was actually with him at the time.

I remember finding those sculptures myself years before. It was on my first visit to the monastery, for a month then as well. Daniel Berrigan, Jesuit priest, poet, and peacemaker—one of my theological mentors—had sent word in advance and opened the gatehouse door for me.

My first marriage had fallen apart. My marriage? Hell, my community, my ministry, my life ... The monks seemed to think I was exploring a vocation. In the choir stall with the sweet strains of Compline washing over me, I began to wonder myself.

Father Alan had mentioned the statues, reporting in detail his own first visit to them, how he had struggled to climb up and kept falling back. So I went looking. I was certain they had to be on one of the higher hills, so I set out on my first trek for the tallest. The last bit was indeed a struggle, so I was convinced this was the place, but no.

I knew it wasn't the fire watchtower hill, since I'd already been there, so I tried a knoll further north. Disappointment again. You may begin to surmise by now. In the end, I stumbled upon the statues quite close to the abbey on a gentle pine rise. The steep struggle that Alan had described had nothing to do with hills.

In my own prayers there, I always linger longest with the sleeping disciples. Peter, James, and John curl and lean against one another in drowsy solidarity. I'm with them. My own personality type suffers that same trance, sleepwalking through life. Jeanie Wylie was my wake-up call. Even gone to God, she still is.

A penny for your suicidal thoughts

I should step back and confess the level of despair that I suffered prior to that earlier Gethsemani visit—when my life was completely ashamble. As the song says, "At that time my heart was all broke/ I looked like ashes and smelled like smoke." An intentional community in which a group of friends and I believed with all our hearts had gone up in flames. My marriage, not the least, with it.

I know that in the darkest days of that time, my tears would barely come, but I considered alternatives, bleak or worse. In the course of that despair, I wrote a little meditation. I present it to you thus:

A Meditation on Personal Suffering

Sit in the half-lotus position with legs crossed and one foot upon the opposite leg. This should be a little painful at first. If not, try the full lotus. This will really hurt. Close your eyes and begin to focus attention on your gags and sobs. Say to yourself, "Now I am crying a horrendous sob." In this way you will be brought fully into the present moment. If you think only about future misery, you will never be able to experience completely the misery which is here and now. If your mind is full of distracting thoughts, let them bounce around until they crescendo into a dull ring which sounds ominously like the German word Weltanschauung.

Now imagine your being, your whole consciousness, to be like a penny that someone has left on the railroad track. Let your whole weight rest upon the cool steel of the tracks and feel the first faint vibrations of the oncoming train. It may help to repeat a phrase in your mind such as "Casey Jones a steamin' and a rollin'." As the vibrations build, think to yourself: "This train is coming just for me. I am here just for this train."

As the earth shakes and the whistle screams and the lead wheels come down upon you, feel yourself spread and flatten and become one with the track itself. Now you are in deep meditation and may imagine as long a train as you choose. Fifty to seventy-five cars are probably sufficient for the beginner. However, even the experienced practitioner should avoid overexposure to this method. Let's say three hundred cars tops. Now feel the caboose go by and lie peacefully resting for a few moments.

Many people find this exercise more relaxing than death itself.

I hope you find it funny. At least a little. Even now, 30 years later, it makes me laugh out loud. Embracing the humor of its absurd intent may actually have saved my life.

You might recognize it as a parody in the style of Vietnamese Zen master Thich Nhat Hahn, who writes wonderful meditations for peacemakers and activists. In a certain sense, he helped pull me though this time. When my life and marriage came apart, there was a period when I couldn't bring myself to read Scripture. Nhat Hahn mediated my way back. I was in such incapacitated disarray that I really needed to learn all over again how to breathe and walk and eat—the very things that Nhat Hahn taught one how to do, all while being awake, mindful, paying attention.

I published the meditation in our little community newsletter. A cry for help, you say? Perhaps, indeed. I don't recall for certain, but it may, in fact, have been that very issue that prompted Dan Berrigan to arrange for my stay at the abbey. My walking meditation took to the Kentucky hills. My meals were set at a monastic table. My breathing tasted incense in a church filled with Gregorian psalms. I was making my way back to the Book.

When I finally came through, I found myself in Detroit, taking tentative new steps back toward community and relationship.

'Not triumphantly, but somehow ... '

Jeanie and I met when she moved into the Catholic Worker neighborhood in Detroit. The Catholic Worker is the movement of hospitality house communities founded by Dorothy Day in the 1930s. The "Worker neighborhood" is a phrase that means much the same in cities across the country: a marginal community, fragile and abandoned, a gathering place for the homeless and cast-off, a spot where spreading the table of a soup kitchen would be most welcome. That people find one another in such locations and marry had become a venerable Worker tradition.

Truth be told, Jeanie was probably moving into the "Little Brothers of Jesus neighborhood"—but that turns out to be much the same thing. It certainly was in Detroit. The Little Brothers are a contemplative order embracing poverty and simplicity, founded in Africa by a Frenchman, Charles de Foucauld. Little Brothers from around the world had often visited Jeanie's home when she was growing up—a special connection her father, Sam Wylie, nourished.

Sam had good instincts. And he loved all things French. He maintained a similar connection with Taizé, the community in southern France that pioneered liturgical renewal and summoned youth on pilgrimage from around the world. He became friends quite early on with its founder, Frère Roger. Jeanie spent several months there as a child, attending a one-room school, delighting the monks, tending the community's farm animals, and lingering long in a tiny stone chapel that became forever a room in her psyche.

It was at Taizé that Jeanie first became a vegetarian, living mostly on fresh yogurt and vegetables. It was the animals that did it. She looked into their faces and knew them by name and could not eat them. Except for the turkeys. They were so stupid, she was willing to make an allowance against them.

In those days Sam had just become dean of the General Theological Seminary on the Lower West Side of Manhattan. Jeanie knew all the crannies and towers of the close, walking the low wire fences like they were her own personal tightropes and being the darling of the seminarians. Sam was beloved by them as well. He had a gift for holding the heart of the Gospel firm, hand in hand with a great openness that appreciated the cultural, political, and theological experimentations that they dared in the late '60s and early '70s.

Picture a dining room table where a procession of students and theologians, scholars and other intriguing visitors were fêted with food and conversation, to which Jeanie listened and occasionally spoke. Even with only the family at hand, Sam loved and convened lively table talk. And even as the youngest, Jeanie became one who could hold her own.

Her mom, Bea, tells the story of a meal with the Archbishop of Canterbury, who was proving an opaque conversant. Bea is amiably engaging, but to her every overture or opening comment, he would reply dryly, "Yes, yes, yes, yes, yes." Not necessarily rude, but off-putting, certainly not taking the conversation anywhere. But after the meal, Bea came upon the archbishop in the living room, thoroughly entranced and actively engaged by the Jeanie girl.

In her middle school years, Jeanie attended a private Anglican school on the Upper West Side, St. Hilda's & St. Hugh's—a slightly harrowing experience she thought her parents never quite understood. This was when I began studying theology, just blocks away at Union Seminary. We always liked to imagine that we had sat next to each other on the bus, or shared the grip of a pole against the bone-wrenching sway of the IRT Broadway local.

Jeanie was born Beatrice Jean Wylie (though she never used her first name) in Providence, Rhode Island. She was late, born after Bea wondered aloud to Sam if God wanted them to have another child, and he failed to say he thought not. Perhaps he simply agreed. In any event—surprise—Jeanie arrived, younger than her sisters and brother by more than seven years.

Her mom had been a missionary kid in China, venturing boats and trains in troubled times—though her memories of it all are placidly idyllic. Bea was no theological slouch herself. She and Sam met as seminarians, and she can still take her New Testament straight, in Greek.

Sam had served Episcopal churches in Providence and Boston and then, just as Jeanie was about to begin high school in New York City, he accepted election as bishop of the Diocese of Northern Michigan in the Upper Peninsula, so she attended Menominee High instead. Friends and colleagues thought this a bad career move for her dad, but he loved it. A huge cut in salary was involved (which, at his initiative, he made even deeper on the premise that the disparity between bishops and clergy should be minimized).

The obscure, seemingly non-viable diocese of tiny, struggling churches was ripe for Sam's visionary imagination, for improvising new forms of lay ministry. Among his published books, he's probably best known for a little pamphlet called *A Celebration of Smallness*. The Little Brothers surely smiled.

Once, years prior, over family table discussion, perhaps considering the vocational direction of things, Sam reversed an evangelical commonplace, saying, "No, not triumphantly, but somehow … " They giggled uncontrollably and made it a family dictum of sorts. Years later, on her altar, Jeanie had a little painted glass representation of the motto, made by one of her nieces.

Menominee proved good for her, by all reports. One really excellent teacher, Jack Hynek, recognized in Jeanie a kind of pedagogical match. He pushed and pulled and prodded and provoked, mostly with questions, and she rose to him. Boyfriends were harder to come by. She was drop-dead gorgeous (I've seen the photos)—but so smart as to be off-putting to most.

She was elected to Girls Nation—a weeklong mock government in Washington, D.C., sponsored by the Daughters of the American Revolution (DAR), for learning legislative and political skills. As a "senator," Jeanie shepherded through Congress an amnesty resolution for resisters of the war in Vietnam. But she really made her mark by refusing to shake hands with President Richard Nixon, which left the DAR ladies scandalized and aghast (though her folks back home beamed quietly at the various telephoned reports).

Engaged journalism

After earning her master's degree at Columbia University School of Journalism (her thesis was a feature article on the relationship between a wealthy Upper East Side parish and another in the South Bronx), Jeanie moved to Detroit to work for the Associated Press. Her tenure there was short. When she covered the Arab community in Detroit (largest anywhere, outside the Middle East), she wrote not only about the tastes and aromas but about how the community was under surveillance first by SAVAK, the security apparatus of Iran's Shah, and then by the FBI. When she reported on the Republican National Convention, she took her notepad to the street, interviewing demonstrators and arrestees, and fell in with a couple of folks making a film on deindustrialization in Detroit.

That proved momentous. That summer of 1980, General Motors (GM) announced their plan to build a new Cadillac plant in Detroit, using eminent domain to clear a neighborhood called Poletown. This was not the first time, nor the last, that a Detroit neighborhood was destroyed wholesale. Thriving communities like Black Bottom and Mexican Town had been decimated by "urban renewal" and expressway projects. But it was the first time it was done to a white majority neighborhood and it was the first time eminent domain was used to clear space for a profit-making corporation. The film turned into that story, and Jeanie turned into its writer. I always think of her as an "engaged journalist," one not only with a perspective, but also a commitment to struggle.

Jeanie was making the film, but also making the history. She took her first arrest occupying a neighborhood church slated for demolition. She and her co-producer, George Corsetti, learned how to make a film as they went. That in itself is a wonderful tale with turns and reversals aplenty. In the end, the neighborhood was destroyed, and the film *Poletown Lives!* won first prize for a documentary at the American Film Festival.

I didn't yet know Jeanie and, strange to say, given my own commitments, I never went over to see what was going down. I suppose I swallowed the official narrative served up in the newspapers, of old ladies in babushkas in the way of economic necessity for a city on the ropes. In fact, there's a scene in the film (I use it still in teaching and have to make my confession repeatedly) in which the Poletown residents are stamping letters,

Graduation from Columbia School of Journalism, 1979.
Credit: Family collection

trying to get the word out to the wider community. I always wince. I know my name is on one of those envelopes.

After we were married, Jeanie wrote a book with support from consumer advocate Ralph Nader, telling the story in detail. She typed it all on an early Radio Shack computer, a TRS-80, generally called a "Trash-80" by informed users. I was on the phone at my parents' house with another of my theological mentors, William Stringfellow (you'll hear more about him as we go), when an operator broke in with an emergency interrupt. It was Jeanie in tears. The computer had crashed and she'd lost the entire book.

Before rushing off to her side, I called Stringfellow back to report the situation, so he wouldn't worry beyond need. Known for his writing on the demonic in America and the power of death in technocratic imperialism, he quipped dryly, "It needs an exorcism."

We saved the book. A computer-savvy friend got it to print everything on its small drive, but things were mixed and out of order. The book's last chapter ended confusingly with a snippet from our wedding service: "O Lord, I am not worthy to receive you, but only say the Word and I shall be healed." Stringfellow retorted upon report, "See, it's begging for an exorcism."

Poletown: Community Betrayed was published by the University of Illinois Press. When it came out, GM officials thought they ought to make a public response, so they invited Jeanie to an open conversation with a well-prepared public relations officer bearing documents. General Motors did the presswork (though Jeanie may have supplemented, for all I know) and provided the buffet spread for the reporters—designed so that they would subliminally identify with the gracious host.

Jeanie was nervous going in, but no need. It ended up being a moment of glory. She knew her stuff and left the poor public relations man backpedaling and temporizing the whole session. It was a press coup, but not for the corporation. More like free publicity for the upstart author. I don't know if he lost his job, but the PR guy left the room with his tail down. Jeanie Wylie carried the day and loved every minute of it. I sat in the back scarfing finger food from our gracious hosts and beaming her encouragements.

There were many consequences of the Poletown event. Expanded use of eminent domain on behalf of corporate forces was one. Another, perhaps even more notorious, was the mad inflation of a Detroit phenomenon called Devil's Night.

Arson was heavy in Poletown. Jeanie's research discovered that demolition contractors found it easier and cheaper to level and haul off a burned-out hulk than a fully standing home, so they were paying kids $10 a pop to set fires in houses slated for demolition. The smoke and threat had the further political advantage of driving out residents who were still trying to remain and fight off the destruction of the neighborhood.

For all the arson, not a single person was ever caught or prosecuted. This "officially sanctioned" devastation jumped the boundaries as a spark. The night before Halloween had long been a mischief night in Detroit. After Poletown it became Devil's Night.

In 1984, 800 house fires were set on this night, with upward of 500 being common each year in the decade following Poletown. Some of these, to be sure, were fires set by kids in dumpsters that spread. But in the early days most were insurance fires, set by landlords ready to get out of the market, taking their assets in insurance disbursements while masking them and overwhelming the arson squad. The rest of us paid in fee increases and smoke.

"C.F. the White Witch"

When Jeanie and I met, I was living with friends at Bonhoeffer House, a small household in the Worker orbit named after the German theologian and pastor executed by the Nazis for his resistance to Hitler. She would come to parties there—in the days when there was among our community a kind of free-floating sexual energy in the air.

Both of us had romantic partners, but neither was part of the community. Jeanie and I talked, but our relationships were always out of sync—hers good when mine was strained, or vice versa. When the waves finally harmonized, with both relationships on the rocks and clearly washing out, the way opened.

But first I had to overcome a bit of male turfiness. Jeanie had begun not only to join us in public witness actions—at the Pentagon and at the headquarters of a local weapons manufacturer—but to write about them in *On the Edge*, our local Worker rag. There she was writing on the political moment, quoting Bonhoeffer and Merton. And I'm saying, who the hell is this? And what does *she* know?

Then one day, I was about to hitchhike to an annual retreat of nonviolent types, to discern the signs of the times at Kirkridge, a retreat center near the Appalachian Trail in Pennsylvania's Pocono Mountains. Jeanie generously offered to drive me down to the I-80 turnpike, potentially shaving hours off my journey.

En route it dawned on her more precisely where I was headed and she announced, "That's close to where my sister Mary lives. Why don't I just drive you there?" Whereupon a great U-turn for Detroit, a quick stop for her clothes and a toothbrush, and (here's the twist) her undergraduate thesis on T. S. Elliot and a copy of *The Lion, the Witch, and the Wardrobe*, from C.S. Lewis' *Chronicles of Narnia* series.

Jeanie studied Elliot at the University of Michigan (1974-78), where she had severe trouble convincing certain professors that *Hollow Men*, *The Waste Land*, and *Four Quartets* traced any sort of spiritual trajectory or conversion. But she knocked them on their asses with her analysis and graduated with honors.

Safe to say, she knocked me over, too. I drove while she read. Suddenly it dawned on me that maybe I should be listening to her on Merton and Bonhoeffer, too.

The *Chronicles of Narnia* have a longer history with her. She got her first set of the volumes in England and read them curled up on the rug before the roaring fire in the Bishop of Lincoln's manse. She may have grown up in Boston, New York, and Menominee, but she was formed and nurtured substantially in Narnia.

Recent cinematic events have raised the cultural currency of the *Chronicles*, but she knew them by heart before they'd become commonplace. Every once in a while, I'll be reading along in some heavy theological tome, such as my copy of Stringfellow's *An Ethic for Christians and Other Aliens in a Strange Land*, and

Jeanie arrested in front of Immaculate Conception Church during the Poletown struggle, 1981. Credit: Family collection

come across a marginal note in Jeanie's handwriting: "C.F. the White Witch," or some other Narnia reference.

Once at the University of Michigan, accosted by an enthusiastic Crusader for Christ with his "four spiritual laws" in hand, Jeanie was proving a tough sell, though she made clear she was a Christian. In exasperation, he finally said, "So, if you wanted to convert someone, what would you do?" Replies she, "I'd give them the *Chronicles of Narnia* and tell them, after reading, to come back if they want to talk." I don't think he did.

The *Chronicles* are not without critical shortcoming: Children wielding swords in war and a substitutionary view of the atonement come readily to mind. But the act of imagination, along with the summons to faith, make them eminently worthwhile. Through the years, they became for our family standard fare for reading aloud.

I read to Jeanie when she took her turn at the wheel. At the poignant climax in *The Lion, the Witch, and the Wardrobe*, when the young characters Susan and Lucy turn round in the resurrection of the lion, Aslan, to see their hearts' desire face to face, we were both in tears. So I turned to her and declared, "Jeanie Wylie, I think I'm in love with you." I suspect she was not surprised—and if anything thought me a little slow on the uptake.

Jeanie with Bill in front of Oakland Co. Jail after fasting and being released from civil contempt charges, 1985.

2

Carried on Love Kites

Our romance grew in jail. That Advent—to this day our family's favorite season—our community joined in a series of nonviolent direct actions at Williams International, the cruise missile engine manufacturer in Walled Lake, a Detroit suburb. Each day, affinity groups took candles to the gates to kneel and pray and sing, and also to block the entrance to workers and executives. Our group included Maurice McKracken, then an 82-year-old Presbyterian pastor and renowned community activist from Cincinnati. He was, to be sure, a genuine inspiration, but Jeanie and I were paying more attention to each other.

We faced a kind of double jeopardy, having done a misdemeanor trespass to be prosecuted in Federal District Court, but also having violated an injunction in Circuit Court—under which theoretically we could be held until we promised not to block the entrance again. No such doing, of course. This meant that we were constantly being ferried from the jail to one courthouse or the other. Normally a pain, this was fine with us, as Jeanie and I arranged ourselves to be handcuffed together.

Separated in jail, we were keeping up a syncopated conversation on sex, romance, and the Holy Spirit. I say syncopated because, searched coming and going, we could not pass notes in transit, and we were forbidden to send mail prisoner to prisoner. Consequently, we were reduced to jailhouse "kites." That's the term for notes passed from a cellblock, hand to hand.

We devised elaborate connections for kiting correspondence to one another, schemes generally involving the chaplain or some use of the common educational facilities. But we were often out of sync (yet again), responding to letters two or even three exchanges back. Plus some of them got intercepted—one captured verily at the point of delivery and thrown into the trash can, just out of tantalizing reach.

But the jail got full, the press got bad for the cruise missile manufacturer, and before we knew it, we were unceremoniously released in time for Christmas Eve ceremonials. Jeanie and I walked arm in arm in the falling snow of freedom, and soon I was headed for the thought-laden retreat at Gethsemani, and the two of us toward marriage.

Shortly after our wedding, a surprising connection came from the campaign at Williams. It was building so successfully that, to quell it, the corporation and the prosecutors decided to bring conspiracy charges against a number of us, including Jeanie and me. It was admittedly conspiracy to commit a misdemeanor, which sounds a little silly, but it did up the ante from a 30-day to a one-year jail sentence.

Though a few people secured lawyers, most of us were defending ourselves. We often found it humanized the whole courtroom process. Jeanie was amazing and clearly could have had a career as a lawyer. She had the mind for it. At one point during a recess, the prosecutor came up and joked about offering her a job.

Just prior, she had been cross-examining me. She had asked an open-ended question about the history of police infiltration (undercover cops had already testified to being among us during the campaign's advance planning and prayer). The prosecuting attorney rose to object. But Jeanie replied that she believed he had "opened the door to this" by asking me in direct examination about historical instances of violence among anti-war demonstrators that undercover police might, in effect, control.

The magistrate, looking over the top of his glasses with a faint smile, turned back to the prosecutor, who withered as he declared: "Objection overruled." Whereupon I launched into a short discourse on surveillance and entrapment for the jury's edification.

Jeanie and I grew to like this magistrate. He was respectful of everyone and accommodating to defendants arguing *pro se*. A practicing Catholic layperson, he allowed that the explication of conscience had a place in the courtroom. He ruled with a light touch and occasional humor. He seemed a good human being, doing his best in a hard job.

He was even tuned in to the fact that Jeanie and I were in love and newly married. We had decided not to acquire a marriage license for our church wedding two months prior. A minor bit of ecclesiastical disobedience was involved, but we wanted no confusion of state involvement in a sacramental act of worship. And we wanted the sacrament to have precedence over any legalities.

Though we later came to question the privileges involved (especially when gay and lesbian folk were denied such rights), at the time we had no real objection to the civil contract as such and eventually decided to enter into one. At that point, we thought of our good magistrate. He was flattered, and though it was not his day to do marriages, he readily agreed. It was November 1, 1984, Feast of All Saints, which became our second, "legal" anniversary. We went out in the company of two amazing women, both nuns, who had agreed to serve as witnesses.

One was Kit Concannon, a Loretto sister with a long history of work among the poor of Latin America. In Detroit she had organized a kind of "underground railroad" for getting political refugees, at that time mostly Salvadorans, through the state and across the bridge into Canada. In the course of this, she founded what became Freedom House, a refugee community going stronger now than ever. Her death in 1987 touched our community deeply.

The other was Liz Walters, an IHM (Immaculate Heart of Mary) sister, who was one of our anti-nuclear compatriots. She has the distinction of having stood on the tracks and single-handedly stopped the "White Train," which carried nuclear warheads from Texas to the Trident submarines based in Georgia. This was all the more courageous, since a similar train had refused to stop some months earlier for anti-nuclear activist Brian Willson, whose legs were crushed and severed in the process.

So, anyway, powerful women. When Jeanie and I wondered aloud if the civil ceremony would be traditionally patriarchal—where I was to "honor" and she to "obey"—the sisters simply pressed their way into the "No Admittance" area and returned with a copy of the ritual. It was cleanly mutual, as it turned out, and we were relieved.

In the courtroom before the bench, the magistrate was very sweet. He said he knew that we were already informed and thoughtful about these matters, but that he was just going to plow ahead and give his ordinary remarks. He offered several words of wisdom. Such as, we couldn't each give 50 percent to the marriage; if it was going to work, we each had to give 100 percent. He asked the questions, we pledged our troths, he signed the papers and headed back into his chambers. But just before he disappeared, he popped his head back out and advised, "Don't tell the prosecutor."

Doing the right thing

Our September 1 wedding two months earlier at Cass United Methodist, the inner-city church I was pastoring, had been a sacramental amazement. Eucharistic, with complicated provisions for Catholics and teetotaling Protestants. Bishops from three traditions were present, mingling with colorful Cass Corridor street characters and a crew of developmentally disabled friends who had come over on a bus from Grand Boulevard. A wide assortment of Detroit and distant politicos, some of whom had deigned to cross a church threshold for the first time in years, was on hand. Feminists and felons, organizers and ordered religious, poets and pastors, journalists and janitors made up the crowd—plus, of course, family and friends.

Ed Rowe, still one of my pastors, began. Mel Hall, dearest friend and co-pastor, preached.

Another dear friend, author and activist Jim Wallis of *Sojourners*, presided. His role was entirely appropriate, since he was present at Gethsemani with us when we got engaged. He'd come for the conclusion of my retreat (and perhaps to scope out this woman). I recall Jeanie's spirited, and even contentious, political conversation with him over lasagna and red wine late into the night at the solar house in the woods. Walking back to the abbey beneath the full moon, Jim turned to me and said, "She's a good one." And next evening at a rib shack in Bardstown, he took us each by the hand and blessed our life together.

Our friends Katie Carter, Bob O'Brien, and Julie Beutel sang a Malcolm Dalglish song, "Shake These Bones:"

I'll show you who I'm loving, Lord, in the night
And when the door is open, Lord, and filled with light,
And when the door is open, Lord, and filled with the
morning light
We'll hear the child who calls to us out of sight.

I'll show you what I'm feeling, Lord, every day
I'll shake these bones and shout and sing my life away
I'll shake these bones and I will shout and sing my life
away,
For it won't be long until these bones turn to clay.

Perhaps you can see why our friends would reprise this at Jeanie's memorial service. Another reprise was Widor's "Toccata"—perhaps the finest piece of organ music ever written.

Susan, Julie, Katie, Bob singing "Shake These Bones" and "Ancestor's Breath" at the memorial, January 8, 2006. Credit: Family collection

It was played at Bea and Sam's wedding, and Sam's funeral, too. So freighted with depths.

Since our vows come up later among the letters, I won't recite them here. They reflected concretely not only our commitment to one another, but simultaneously the life to which we were joining ourselves: to fidelity, community, nonviolence, simplicity, and hope. I recited them again at her memorial in thanks and benediction.

My brother Stevie juggled and squeaked together balloon animals at the cakey church reception, but the party was venued at a Catholic hall for later evening. Lots of Motown music and great communal dancing. My friend John Bach, mentor in leaflet-writing and direct action, who was glad the date coincided with the Montreux Detroit Jazz Festival, had hitched out from Connecticut. He came forward, took the mic, and told a brief tale of his hitch, coming down to an amiable trucker who had picked him up. He had explained to this guy where he was headed and how he knew me and what was up. At the conclusion of which the driver asked, "So, is your buddy doing the right thing?"

And John replied, "Yeah. Yeah, I think he is." And then, pausing a beat to hoist his glass in a simple toast: "To Jeanie and Bill, for doing the right thing."

A burial blessing

Using sleeper-car train tickets that were a wedding present from Jeanie's brother Johnny to get there, we honeymooned on Block Island, Rhode Island, at Stringfellow's place. So, here is just a bit more about him.

William Stringfellow was a Harvard-trained lawyer who graduated in 1956 and went straight to East Harlem to do street law, before there really was such a thing. From there he was led into the freedom struggle and the anti-war movement. His autobiographical account of those years, *My People is the Enemy*, was something of a hit, and established his voice as a theologian.

The people of Harlem, he claimed, put him onto a lifelong project of understanding the "principalities and powers," or the "rulers and authorities"—those political spirits and structures of power identified in the New Testament. It was the way, he said, that people talked about "the Man," or the cops, or the mafia, or the welfare bureaucracies, the charitable foundations, or the utility companies—as though these were predatory creatures arrayed against the community—that sent him back to the Scriptures. He became notorious for reading the current political moment through the biblical lens of the powers.

Reading Stringfellow in high school was like a light going on for me: I thought theologically for the first time. I heard him speak when I was in college. He was, at the time, desperately ill and spoke seated at a table, a microphone amplifying his dry, faint voice. But he blew his audience away, as if he were booming out the truth—especially the black students, who had never in their lives heard a white person speak as he did.

Then I met him in seminary. Dan Berrigan (my mentors were themselves close friends) introduced him to a group of us in connection with their idea of an "underground seminary"—with echoes of Bonhoeffer's resistance seminary Finkenwalde in the back of their minds. In the course of the resulting anarchistic Bible study weekends, Stringfellow became a mentor, and eventually a friend.

Stringfellow was also known to Jeanie's dad. They had crossed paths in the Episcopal denomination's Church Society for College Work. So, it occurs to me as altogether possible that Jeanie sat politely, or talkatively, with him at the deanery dinner table and never knew it.

As Jeanie put it, Bill Stringfellow's home may not have been the shrewdest place to celebrate our honeymoon. Block Island is quaint and beautiful, with beaches and bluffs, cedar-shake hotels and lighthouses. But it had drawbacks.

We actually stayed in Dan Berrigan's little cottage, perched on a cliff at the edge of Bill's property, trying to sleep in his single bed. In those days, written high on the wall in Dan's distinctive hand was a wonderful poem dedicated to the place.

> At lands end
> where this house dares stand
> and the sea turns in sleep
> ponderous, menacing
> and our spirit fails and runs
> landward, seaward, askelter
>
> we pray protect
> from the laws clawed outreach
> from the second death from envy's tooth
> from doom's great knell
> all
> who dwell
> here

Wylie family portrait—Mary, Sam, Jeanie, Bea, Rene
Beth, Johnny. Credit: Family collection

The blessing, of course fell upon us. But beneath it was a roster of nonviolent resisters who had been given refuge or retreat there—almost entirely male. Jeanie was beginning to tune into the vibes of the persistent male ambiance in the whole scene.

She went into a major state of rebellion, as she later put it—even dreaming about some woman named Isis rising up in a rage. We had to look it up later to confirm our suspicions that this was in fact a powerful, even stormy, Egyptian warrior goddess. So Jeanie's psyche was busy and well-honed.

Add to this Bill's dogs—a couple of much beloved, if yappy and snippy, terriers—who had a bad case of fleas. Probably the cat, too. We would come back to the cottage after dinner in his home, scratching the bites on our legs and trying not to bring anything jumpy or foreign into the bed.

There were, however, even more gifts in it as well. Just the Palm Sunday previous, we had been in New York with Bill, where he was spending a few months at General Seminary. It was there we shared with him our plan to marry. He nodded that this could be a good decision, even though Saint Paul had eschewed it. Bill had not so long before lost his own beloved partner, Anthony Towne, and written his most beautiful book about the experience of mourning. So he had a sober admonition for us: "Never imagine that you can't live without each other." He was commending freedom in the face of death.

Consequently, his blessing of our marriage on the island had a familiar ring. He opened the Episcopal *Book of Common Prayer* ceremoniously and read a passage of Scripture: "May the One who raised Christ Jesus from the dead quicken your mortal bodies also." But he read it noticeably from the "Service for the Burial of the Dead." There was a certain ambiguity: Was this a deft theological observation, or a wry comment on the status of our new estate? Only since Jeanie's illness and death has it seemed more prescient and prophetic.

A means of grace

Jeanie's father had died just before she graduated from high school in 1974. Nobody saw that coming. Sam had made a return visit to General Seminary, to speak in a series on personal spiritual journeys. He preached a resurrection sermon, went back to his room, and succumbed suddenly to a heart attack.

Jeanie was called out of class and down to the school office, as I recall, where her priest and his wife passed the news. Together, they went searching for her mom, who had yet to hear. So Jeanie was present for her mother's shock: "I don't want to hear that. I can't hear that." My memory, which is really secondhand hers, is that the moment was gathered up immediately in the *Lord's Prayer*.

Jeanie's mom was a disciplined intercessor. Even to her death in 2016 she was looked upon as a sort of wise woman elder in the Society of the Companions of the Holy Cross, a prayer order of the Episcopal Church. She first tutored Jeanie in prayer at bedside.

One night following a long chain of family prayer links—"Bless Mom, bless Dad, bless Rene, bless Mary, bless Johnny"—Jeanie interrupted herself to ask her mom if it would be all right to bless God. At first this seemed like a theological conundrum, but then Bea remembered the prayer book and certain psalms: "Bless the Lord, O my soul, and all that is within me bless God's holy name." So she ended up commending it, in a formula suggested by the Psalter.

On another occasion, Jeanie was praying for one of her dolls, a more questionable practice, when she asked if her doll would be with her in heaven. Bea paused. Long. Then she replied, "If you still want your doll when you're in heaven, it will certainly be there." That's what I call theologically adept.

For all the nuance of her political and theological sophistication, Jeanie envisioned the heavenly landscape in a most unabashed and straightforward way. Years later in the hospital, when we got the news of the final tumor growth and knew immediately that this was the turning time, I crawled into the hospital bed with her and wept. But she comforted me with her vision: "Oh, Billy, it's sad, but not all that bad. I'll get to see my dad and my brother and your folks."

Jeanie's relationship with her dad was complicated. He certainly shaped her in the delights of dinner table converse, where opinions were welcomed, tested, and enjoyed. With Bea, he tutored her in travel, on the several trips to Europe and another to Haiti. And he encouraged freedom, a certain rebellion even, smiling on it secretly—though she intuited the secret.

As a child, in the days when Sam was a rector on Boston's Beacon Hill, Jeanie and her best friend, Michelle, were the two and only charter members of the "Bad Lessons Club." Its sole rule was that you had to do a bad deed every day—none of which was secretly approved, mind you.

One example was sneaking off to cross a busy boulevard, in order to take forbidden rowboats on a lake in the park—which

actually counted as two bad lessons. The young girls were
capable of joining older brothers in pranks, such as talking to
strangers in random phone calls or summoning cabs to a nonexistent address across the street. Jeanie could slip down a church
basement manhole with her brother and explore the recesses of
the undercroft by flashlight or candle.

Stealing candy from the drugstore was a standard—and
may even have been the club's *raison d'etre*. If I'm not mistaken,
the whole operation eventually folded on a liturgical confession. Here's an account of that in Jeanie's own voice, slow and
detailed.

> *Sunday after Sunday the priest would turn to us, arms
> outstretched, palms foremost. With solemnity and quiet
> love his words would reach us: "Christ our Passover
> has been sacrificed for us." The priest robed in woven
> gold and royal red, clouded by incense, immediate in
> sanctity, was my father.*
>
> *The same hands that offered to the church the
> Eucharist served us our meals at home. The same voice
> that pronounced the liturgy said grace before we ate.
> The same man demanded of us dignity and servitude.
> He waited only for the day when we would be old
> enough to reason, to choose and voice beliefs, to read,
> to appreciate music, to travel, to reach out to others in
> a spirit of eager questing, wine glasses pushed to the
> side forgotten, eyes lit with excitement, foreign tongues
> confused in the vigor and joy of man in search of God,
> my father. But I was only eight.*
>
> *One Sunday in particular I remember … I found
> myself on my knees with the rest of the congregation,
> immersed in the confession: "We confess that we have
> sinned against you in thought, word, and deed …
> Have mercy upon us … The remembrance of them is
> grievous unto us, the burden of them … "*

I paused, dizzy with the weight of this next word. This word that I had never heard or spoken elsewhere, whose very meaning I had learned from the uncertain fear I felt now. "The burden of them is intolerable." Five thick syllables of judgment, of weight, a cross upon my back.

Gary's Drugs had fluorescent lights and high ceilings. The men behind the counter wore white jackets and never let us lie on the floor and read through the comic books.

Two or three of us at a time would mount an attack. We'd walk right in, talking, laughing, friendly, as kids are supposed to be. Then we'd move around, inspecting the bags of rubber bands and boxes of staples, jars of vitamins, funny pink and yellow birthday cards that spun on the rack, the razors and cigars, until at last we were face to face with the candy.

With two bars up the sleeves of our jackets we'd walk calmly, laughing and talking, out the door, then race for the alley and our feast.

"The burden of them is intolerable. We are heartily sorry for these our misdoings. Have mercy on us, most merciful Father, for the sake of thy dear son, our Lord Jesus Christ."

Two nights later I cried so hard I could barely breathe. I twisted my face into my pillow and sobbed. Hot and wet, my face smothered in soft cushioning, I tensed myself in rage, and shame …

I stood beside my parents' bed. The hallway beyond the open door loomed dark and silent, huge. My feet were cold upon the rug.

"Mommy," I whispered. I patted her arm softly. "Mommy." I had to keep my voice low. If Daddy woke up, he'd be angry that I was waking her ...

"A nightmare, sweetheart?"

I couldn't answer. I pushed my face into her waist and muffled my cries. Her fingers ran through my hair, quiet and good, much like a slow river tugging hair at the roots, billowing it outward on a lazy summer day.

"Mommy," I gasped quickly, "I stole!" Tears rose again. I fought them just long enough to cry, "Caaaaandy!"

She found out all the essentials: From where? When? But more important, she knew that I was sorry, that I wouldn't do it again. She thanked me for telling her. We would go tomorrow to say I was sorry to Mr. Gary.

I lay in bed, my face against the damp pillow I had just left. My mother sat beside me, waiting for me to sleep. Like vomit, the tears rose again. I doubled up in shame and anger, clawing at the pillow. I screamed my sorrow, muffling my voice in the hot dampness.

We went and stood before my father, who was now awake. My mother was speaking. She had told the whole story to him. My tears were tight inside me. He would be angry.

"She doesn't understand that she's forgiven," I heard my mother say. "Sam, give her an ecclesiastical absolution."

My father leaned forward, his eyes grave but his hand gentle. He reached out from under the troubled blankets and put his hand on my head.

Words that I'd never heard poured over me. The somber majesty of Sunday was around me and for me. I was absolved.

With my mother's hand resting on my shoulder, I fell asleep.

Jeanie's dad could be the very means of grace, but in her experience hinted above, he could also be emotionally volatile. There was in him some recess of anger (I can imagine it just from the pieces I know of his childhood), which could well up. He only once struck her in anger, but it was a wound that stuck, and remained untouched by the quick reversal of his regret and apology.

Jeanie suspected that she may have enflamed his anger because she stood up to him. Toe to toe. He liked it much in theology and politics, but perhaps less so in emotional engagement. Perhaps it was a surprise coming from his youngest child—though she was late enough to be almost an only child.

If you know the Enneagram, a personality typology of mysterious origin (some say Sufi) used in spiritual direction, it numbers nine personality types. There's no test for the typing, you just self-identify. You start reading about each type and, suddenly, you find one that rings true and say to yourself, "Oh, shit, they've got my number!"

Jeanie was an Eight. She was the champion, the fighter, the world changer, the force to contend with. She thought that likely came, to oversimplify, from standing up to Sam. I, on the other hand, am a Nine—the peacemaker, balancer, reformer, moving (at worst) with a sleepwalking inertia.

We were side by side on the gut-oriented, angry side of the personality circle. Difference is, I stuff my anger and she voiced hers. We were a potentially volatile mix: the irresistible force and the immoveable rock. Nines, or at least this one, don't usually fight fair. I'm the go-cold-and-silent, passive/aggressive type that drove Jeanie nuts. She insisted I come out of my shell, put up my dukes, and fight. She threw things. She couldn't believe I wouldn't yell back. She did teach me. I actually learned. Sort of.

Relatives in a book unwritten

Jeanie was the littlest in the family, but she perceived herself as standing up on occasion for her older sisters and brother. She adored her siblings. Rene Beth (Irene Elizabeth) is the oldest. She thought of herself as timid, but she was politically active and brought back tales as a student from the Selma march during the civil rights era. She was Jeanie's idol in musical tastes as well, savoring early, then late, out of season freedom songs, Motown, the Beatles, and the classics of folk.

Mary is an artist, a painter of light, freer than Jeanie in her growing-up days—even a little wild. Like Rene Beth, she went to Brown University, but with a different emphasis. If she got it sideways from Mary, Jeanie's own eye for beauty blossomed late. It was there in her editorial work at *The Witness* magazine, and it was prominent as a contemplative impulse in the dying years.

Johnny left the house early for boarding school, before college at Haverford. His taste in records tended to include the comic and quirky, which never fully took with Jeanie. He was obsessively organized and he loved all things train-wise—schedules and routes and mechanics—plus he was a smart-minded computer programmer. But he also had a habit of doing a housecleaning swoop, putting random items and papers in a box in a closet, and if he didn't need anything from it in six months, the whole thing got dumped. It was an interesting freedom. He died unexpectedly of pancreatitis during Jeanie's illness.

I was myself related to Jeanie Wylie, and I don't mean just by our marriage. Just weeks prior to our wedding, my folks returned from a Lisle family reunion in Washington County, Pennsylvania. They were all excited by the character of the clan, largely Presbyterian church folk and teetotalers, it seemed.

This was news to me, as my mother was a Zachman. I'd always thought us basically German. But the patriarch, Robert Lisle (*l'isle*—"the island"), who was Scots-Irish, had come over at the time of the American Revolution and even taken up arms against the new government in the Whiskey Rebellion. The first in a sequence of ironies.

When Jeanie heard Washington County, she exclaimed, "That's where my family's from!" As it turned out, my folks came bearing a genealogical book with a level of detail that made my eyes fog. But Jeanie devoured it like a novel, sensing narrative along every line. On the first reading, she turned up five connections, the main one of which was that my grandmother's grandmother's brother was married … well, Jeanie could say it and somehow see it. I could hardly follow its thread.

"Of course!" I thought. Marrying her felt like a homecoming. I hadn't realized how close in rewoven roots the home really was.

Opening that book was a journey begun for Jeanie Wylie. It became a project, a fascination, if not a minor obsession. This was in part because the line went back through her mama's mama, Irene Cowen, who had been a schoolteacher in western Pennsylvania, specifically Washington County. She had experienced a call to mission work overseas in China and became engaged to a Presbyterian who had the same call.

Not long before departure, however, he jilted her for another woman. He wrote the Mission Board that he would still be going to China, but that his wife would not be Irene Cowen, but this other. The board wrote back, bless their wisdom: No, Irene Cowen will be going to China, but not with you.

So, against plan, she launched out on her own. The boat to China took its time, as they say. On the way, she fell in love with another Presbyterian missionary, George Brown, and by the time they set foot ashore, she had a lifelong partner in marriage and ministry.

Through Bea and her brothers, we had access to Irene's letters home, and Jeanie began absorbing the saga. It was a compelling and adventurous missionary tale. Then Jeanie began collecting and studying old family photos farther back, noticing faces more aboriginal or African in feature.

These became mysteries to track down, and household census data was acquired to supplement the lineage book. An epic poem, really the scandalous confession of a saddlebag pastor in the line, came to light. A piece of the puzzle tracked the

passage of one family member by prison ship from England as
an indentured slave to the West Indies. When he finally arrived
in the States, a new account emerged, concerning his secretarial
assistance to island royalty.

Jeanie was determined to make a pilgrimage to Washington
County with her mom. As they went out the door, she grabbed
one of the family photos off the wall and called over her shoulder to the rest left hanging in the hallway, "Help me, guys."

When they arrived in the county, looking for shelter in a
motel, all rooms were filled due to a dog show in the area. They
pressed on to the very town and found a bed-and-breakfast
open. On the wall before them as they walked in the door was
the framed marriage license of the couple in the photo she bore!
This seemed a good omen.

The next day, they tracked down the family historian, living
in a house trailer lined with musty books and stacks of paper.
When Jeanie described the marriage that united our lines, he
smiled and said, "Those were my great-grandparents." He was
most generous in sharing judiciously from the documentary
piles. He subsequently rode along with her, as guide to the
family homestead and various farms pertinent.

At one such address was an intriguing story of a murder
unsolved, which had cast a shadow. Another involved a family
scheme to sell wool for Army uniforms during the Civil War.
When the war ended and the bottom dropped out of the uni-
form market, taking other small investors down, the family was
forced to skip town, at least for a time.

Jeanie and Bea went to the local cemetery, looking for head-
stones. Inside the church, they opened the archives. It turned
out that one of Jeanie's relatives had saved the congregation by
taking a barge-load of something (grain or wool) down the river
all the way to New Orleans, walking home with the proceeds to
replace the roof and pay a pastor.

In tracking the aboriginal features, Jeanie was led not just
to the Jamaican prisoner, but to the Leni Lenape, a tribe of the
Delaware Indians, who had lived in this region claimed and

surveyed by General George Washington. The Scots-Irish were Indian fighters and regarded themselves with pride for holding the frontier—a task for which the pacifist Quakers, as they thought, were too squeamish.

Ironically, the Leni Lenape had themselves special peacemaking vocations within the Delaware nation, with which Jeanie became knowledgeably intrigued. The same line of research led to the discovery of a massacre of Moravian Indians, in which she was beginning to suspect she may have had relatives on both sides, shooters and victims. This, in turn, put her in correspondence with the current Delaware leadership and her proposal for a marker, indeed a liturgical act of repentance, at the site. She and I made homage to that place together.

Jeanie's avid interest in family history made my dad sit up and take notice. By gum, he had history too! He wrote some letters and discovered a Kellermann family tree going back to Darmstadt, Germany in the 16th century, which was a big surprise.

We'd always been told that we had come from Alsace-Lorraine. In Ontario during World War I, being from Germany was a deficit. So our family portrayed itself as almost French, from that blurry border region where you could go either way— one of those classic fictions of family denial. It was a smaller version of the mythic fictions indulged in our collective historical memories, such as the belief that early settlers found empty wilderness—where genocide, in fact, prevailed.

Jeanie was dragging us all into the light. She wasn't just tracking information, she was reading the larger history. Clearly a book was forming in her, one with a genre more hybrid even than this one. It would be a genealogical book, narrated as an unfolding story, a sleuthing family tale of culture and identity, all told while letting it open out on good, solid, historical perspectives from the underside.

The collected papers and books of her research fill several shelves which I've not yet had the heart to delve or disrupt. The newly bound and updated Lisle genealogy volume sits there.

Jeanie and I are in it together—as are Lydia and Lucy. But Jeanie's genealogical work trailed off into illness. The family history is a book unwritten.

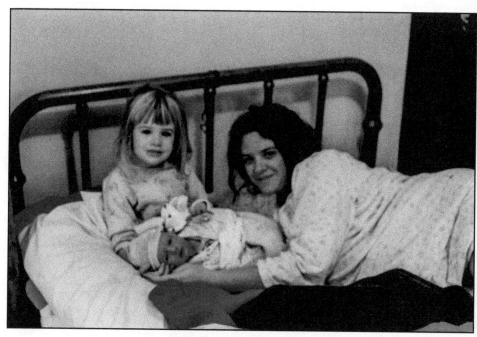

Jeanie with Lucy and Lydia in the brass bed where the birth had
taken place, December 4, 1989. Credit: Bill Wylie-Kellermann

Birthing in the Face of a Dragon

We discovered we were pregnant with Lydia while camping in the Black Hills of South Dakota. The trip in our little red Toyota was in celebration of our one-year anniversary. Jeanie wanted to take me there, since she'd spent several weeks during a college summer at Yellow Thunder Camp, the political reoccupation of the Hills by the American Indian Movement under the leadership of Russell Means. It was to her, as to the Lakota, a sacred space.

We'd come by way of the Badlands and first noticed the changes in her while climbing along those arid ridgebacks. She'd been short of breath and searching constantly for the slightest cleft of shade (so few and far between). Jeanie was accustomed to pushing herself physically, but her body was rebelling in protective double duty.

It gradually dawned on us that we should get a test. So we left our pined campsite by the stream and headed into town, a place called Afton. We were practically pacing out the end wait and this doctor, a wise old practitioner, could tell we were anxious (though such anxieties can cut both ways). "I have good news," he ventured. "You're gonna have a baby."

For so long I'd thought I never would have kids. I was even attracted to women who couldn't, or wouldn't, and that seemed fine. Childlessness was a kind of political expedience, second only to celibacy in leaving one responsibly unencumbered for jail time or the risky life. But with Jeanie, I just knew it was part of the deal. I guess we spoke of it. I remember we did, but mostly it was a knowing unsaid. Something implicit, like never thinking twice.

Back at the campsite, we sat together by the stream bank and held one another, suddenly three. As the afternoon cooled, we took to climbing the small boulders around which the waters spilled, working our way upstream toward the source. The brush thickened and eventually turned us back, but not before I found a prize, a memento of the hour: a gnarl of pine that looks so much like a crucifix that it hangs on my study wall to this day.

Pregnancy worked its way into Jeanie's writing, but not in conventional terms. For Advent, when expectation reigns, she found herself reflecting on the 12th chapter of Revelation—on the Woman Clothed with the Sun, who gives birth in the face of a dragon, crouched and ready to devour. Once in a while the image is associated with the birth narratives of the Gospels, but rarely. It fully comports with Caesar Augustus' surveillance and taxation census, or even more with Herod's Massacre of the Innocents, in the brutal attempt to rid his world of messianic upstarts.

But generally (except for Mexican *indígenos* who seize upon it as an image of Our Lady of Guadalupe), it is deemed too apoc-alyptic for comfort. Best left cosmic and obscure and certainly off the holiday map. Jeanie, however, was brooding over what it meant to give birth in a culture of death. Of bringing a child into the world at a time, between nuclear weaponry and environmental collapse, when the future seemed so uncertain. Crouched to devour.

We compounded these broodings, or enacted them, by taking Lydia in utero to Nicaragua on a Witness for Peace delegation. Jeanie was toward the end of her second trimester. The Contra

War funded by the United States against Nicaragua's Sandinista revolution was at full bore.

Witness for Peace was a project begun a few years earlier, when a delegation of North Americans visited the Nicaraguan *campo* as part of a prayerful direct action and fact-finding trip. What they noticed was that everywhere they went, Contra activity quieted—presumably to hide the illegal war, but perhaps even more to keep *los norteños* safe from politically volatile harm. So an idea dawned: What if we kept a constant presence of North Americans in the countryside? Would it mitigate the U.S.-sponsored attacks against the Nicaraguan people? Would it function politically to bring the truth of the hidden war home?

And so began an organizing project facilitating a continuing sequence of short-term delegations, meeting first with Nicaraguan church people, union folk, and political leaders in Managua, then making for the countryside to spend some time with *campesinos* under attack, hearing their stories and, perhaps, to some small degree, sharing their risks, if not their fate. Maybe even mitigating it a bit.

Say it flat out: the Contras were trained terrorists, financed by the United States and supported by the CIA. You may recall that when the U.S. Congress cut off funding for the war, the Reagan administration continued to finance the covert operation through elaborate subterranean schemes, some involving cocaine, but most notoriously by redirected funds from a secret arms sale to Iran, already by then an avowed enemy. Think Oliver North.

There are many stories from our two weeks in Nicaragua, but the most important to mention would be our accompaniment of Juana Francesca back to her home for the first time since her husband and two of her children had been killed there by the Contras. Recognize in that the face of the dragon. She wept and wailed as peasant neighbors gathered around and we stood awkwardly by, hands in pockets.

Eventually our delegation circled to pray the *Lord's Prayer* in English and in Spanish simultaneously. With priestly assistance, we scattered holy water to reclaim the space for life. It had involved some group discernment, but Jeanie, who thought her body strong enough for any such venture, rode the rutted path to stand with this mother at her home, *La Cruz de las Piedras* (Stone Cross). The holy water crossed Jeanie's brow, as all of ours.

Say, too, that we danced beneath the stars by Lake Managua. And that's how we describe to Lydia her gestation: in one another's arms on the roofless veranda of a downtown club. Jeanie refrained from the rum to mitigate unnecessary risk.

Lydia Irene was hospital-born, in a birthing center. The labor was long, as she kept turning her head and more or less refusing to come out. We had gone to the hospital prematurely, though not before Jeanie's water broke. By the time we got there, my breath coaching in the car had her hyperventilating.

Our family doctor calmed us both down and sent us back home to do the labor properly and in our own space. How's this for a house call? Dr. Susan Rice came over at 3 a.m. to check the dilation, then sat with us for two hours as Jeanie labored and I read aloud to her from *The Wind in the Willows*, another Wylie family favorite. Jeanie was becalmed and distracted, and Susan drowsed 'til 5 a.m. work, while Mole discovered the world of the river and made fast friends with Rat, all the while learning those joyous freedoms of a boat.

At Jeanie's memorial service, we read one of her most remarkable pieces from this period: a baptismal meditation suitable to the feast day on which we gathered, but focused on her qualms about baptizing Lydia.

Jeanie labored hard over it. She didn't really balk at baptizing Lydia, but she did count the cost. And she measured it against her own protective instincts, even in utero. As a sacramental sign, infant baptism is pure grace. A child is welcomed into the community of faith and is embraced by the fullest freedom of our God, without lifting a finger. Nor could she if she tried.

And yet, this be no cheap grace. In baptism we, her parents, set her on the road to discipleship. Welcome, we say: this way goes the cross. Costing not less than everything. I beg your pardon? We say: join us, sweet child, in a life of risk and freedom.

Within a Communion of Children

This is how she wrote it in 1986 for Detroit's Catholic Worker paper *On the Edge*:

I didn't want to baptize Lydia.

My love for her took me off guard. I'd only been able to see her and touch her for a few hours and already I wanted the world for her. I studied her while she lay in my arms to eat and she stared back. I cried often. I was overwhelmed.

In a quick constrictive moment, I wanted to draw a circle in the dirt around Bill and Lydia and me. I envisioned a brick tower rising on the circle and securing us from intrusions which might not honor the bond of love and satisfaction that held us together. I never wanted her hurt. I cried when she cried. In the flush of raging feelings which came with the afterbirth, I became anxious and impatient if nothing could be done to calm my child. Having entertained the thought, "Even if she dies tomorrow it will all have been worth it, just to know her," I was terrified that she would die. Die, leaving a void like my father had when I was seventeen. Sacrificed on an altar to a God who routinely asks too much. I was simultaneously struck by the magnificence of what God could create and singularly disinterested in hearing the voice of that God again.

And then came the question of baptism. Water, words, community. Offering our child back to God. We would stand with Abraham at the sacrifice. We would give her to a God who models the cross. We would invite her to listen for a voice calling in the night, to vigil, to put herself at risk, to leave family and friends, to speak clearly a truth for while one can be executed. We would thereby invite her into the risks we have already elected and, by God's grace, still will elect to take with our own lives. In the act of baptism we would wash away the possibility that our concern for her might justify a diminishing of our own obedience to our Lord's perverse ethic of vulnerability and gain through loss.

Bill and I like our lives. Not to aggrandize the risks we do take nor to minimize that much more compelling risks taken by those living the gospel in places like Guatemala, we are nonetheless sometimes frightened. We are sometimes pushed to our limits. For the most part, I think we find the way we live exhilarating. However, this sense of freedom does not extend to any harm of long-term separation overtaking Lydia.

It's a challenge to resist the impulse to open an IRA for her college education. We're still planning to put her in a public school, but we are already filling out forms in an effort to determining which one.

The temptations are many.

The neighborhood. Is a home that's been adequate for us, despite the multiple times that we've been broken into, adequate for her? There have been seven fires in as many months in what we believe is a deliberate policy of neglect and abuse which will open up land for development. One of our neighbors is in jail for raping a child. And then, a furnace man told us two years ago that our furnace has to be replaced. At worst, he said, it could explode. One question we can postpone for several years: Where will Lydia play?

Tax resistance. Is it reasonable? Certainly it leaves us wide open at all times to the intrusion of the state. And we don't really know the stakes. We're willing to surrender our property, but would they jail Bill? Me? What would become of Lydia? Surely she has a right to her parents.

But then we ask ourselves what it means if the introduction of one child changes the way we understand all that we do. If this child reorders our priorities, who then will we be?

When entertaining the alternative of baptizing Lydia into this life, I finally found some resolve. I pictured her raised in the suburbs, sheltered, provided for with life insurance and college savings. Nonetheless, it was still not within our power to insulate her from nuclear threats, or cultural violence, or a society coming apart at the seams. In fact, in this scenario, I would have denied her the company of God, the only companion promising hope that all this can be redeemed.

Another alternative that falls between suburban security and our current life also seems to me to eventually promise the same thing for us. Bill and I could get, or keep, movement jobs and responsibilities. We could move to a safer neighborhood with good schools. We could pay our federal taxes, but make our concerns known to our elected representatives. We could send money to various special interest groups and teach Lydia about global relationship and the need to have respect for other cultures, for the environment, for peacemaking.

And there is nothing wrong with such a life.

But when I picture it for us, I am sad. The sadness stems from the knowledge that, whatever rationales we could offer, we would be setting limits on what we were willing to offer to God. Our child's welfare and security would be sacrosanct and other commitments would slide. I could imagine that some of those securities would come to lay a claim on us and endure even after Lydia was grown.

But is it too strong to say, as I just did, that altering our lifestyle to provide more money, comfort, beautify, and security would be denying Lydia the company of God? Perhaps—in that nothing we do can separate her from the love of God. But I do believe that it would distance us as a family.

At our marriage Bill and I repeated John Wesley's Covenant Prayer:

Lord God, I am no longer my own, but thine. Put me to what though wilt, rank me with whom thou wilt; put me to doing, put me to suffering; let me be employed for thee, exalted for thee or brought low for thee; let me be full, let me be empty; let me have all things, let me have nothing; I freely and heartily yield all things to thy pleasure and disposal.
And now, O God ... thou art mine and I am thine. So be it. And the covenant which I have made on earth, let it be ratified in heaven.

It is something that we want very much to live. Individually, Bill and I had discovered some areas where we felt particularly vulnerable to God. Many of them overlapped—like our experience that the Bible makes very clear sense to us while in jail and our feeling that there is a (perverse) value in having to wonder if your house has been broken into or if everything you have accumulated has been burned to the ground. To insulate ourselves would be to shield ourselves from times and places where we have heard God's voice. It would make us less able to share with Lydia and to demonstrate to her the nature of our faith.

So, we baptize her into the risks we've elected for our lives. We take her, in utero, to Nicaragua. We share with her this broken, violent world. We baptize her into the communion of saints who have been crucified in every possible way. We baptize her into the grueling decisions at Gethsemani and into Easter hope. We lay her on the altar before a God who rejects our carefully laid plans and takes her life into His/Her own.

And in so doing, we smash an idol.

The child is no longer a reason to flee from the voice of God. Instead, we carry the child, with our hearts, toward the one who utters us and calls us into being. We claim our lives in that voice and entrust each other's to it. We loosen our hold, our desperate grip, on each other's presence and well-being.

With Abraham, we can—at God's suggestion—find back our claim to descendants as numerous as the stars. It is enough, it is more than enough to be loved by God. Our child is safe in covenant with our God who is neither predictable nor always comfortable, but she will find there a hand that wipes away her tears, an end to her thirst and a wind that sets her loose.

On June 13, Lydia Irene was baptized with water and the spirit. She was sealed as Christ's own forever. She, and we again with her, died in Christ.

Recently we learned that a picture of Lydia is pasted to a prison wall in Fort Worth, Texas. Ardeth Platte, who is serving six months for trespassing, leafleting and praying at Wurtsmith Air Force Base, writes:

Lydia is now pictured in the midst of the many children of all races posted above my bunk. At night, the birthing of peace leaps throughout me as I glance at them, the future justice and peace creators. In the middle of the children's pictures is the eight Day Center's photo of a child releasing a dove at the bombs stretched behind Eisenhower's statement:

"Every gun that is made, every warship launched, every rocket fired signified, in the final sense, a theft from those who hunger and are not fed, those who are cold and are not clothed. This world in arms is not spending money alone. It is spending the sweat of its laborers, the genius of its scientists, the hopes of its children."

Lydia is in good company. I can guarantee you that this tac board display provokes my thoughts, challenges my commitment and dedication and keeps us praising God.

* * *

A high school friend of mine, a Chicago stockbroker and a mother, recently visited us. She was appalled by our block, felt unsafe in our home and was angry at us for raising Lydia here.

Last night Lydia sat in her high chair fingering rice cereal and Bill asked, "Will your feelings be hurt when someone steals your bike?" and I asked, "Will you be hurt when someone steals your bike?"

We can't say with certainty which decisions we'll make in the years to come. We know they are hard and will grow harder as she grows older.

A year ago, a group of us met to discuss such issues. The meeting was prompted in part by my fear that various families would decide to move without consulting each other and that we would end up hopelessly scattered.

Jeanie at prayer vigil outside Wurtsmith AFB, 1983.
Credit: Family collection

An alternative that I saw then, and that I still hope for, would be for us to move closer together. I'm sure that if we moved onto one or two blocks, we could offer strong community for our children and also stay in the city. We would be offering each other's children peers that are also being taught not to steal, not to lie, not to believe that fighting is impressive. We could rely on our friends to keep an eye on the children playing outdoors. And we could visit each other, without having to get everyone into assorted car seats, when we needed a break from solo childcare.

There are many things that make choosing to raise Lydia in this neighborhood sane. We'd like her to be familiar with the soup kitchen and to understand with her heart the object lessons that are apparent in hunger and charred, vacant homes.

But one of the greatest gifts we feel she can receive is a life in this community: we want her to know and feel the love of people who are alive, who don't give a damn about money and who are willing to do with their lives what they think God is asking.

At the last Detroit Peace Community retreat, in the midst of conversation about fear—of violence, of crime, of risk—Kit Concannon said she lived the way she did because "I have all of you."

I can't think of a better gift. We give thanks for this community now and in the days to come.

The flesh of an apple

When Lydia was 2, I did a 60-day jail bit for trespass at a SAC base (Strategic Air Command) in northern Michigan. I'd done my first action there on Easter in 1982, and Jeanie had covered it for social critic and filmmaker Michael Moore's *Michigan Voice*. But now I was several subsequent violations further along, and the sentences were increasing.

Two things of note. First, I made a discipline of writing a poem for Jeanie each day. It was those that first went into the incremental poetry book with which I presented her. Each of them was framed by the window in my cell. Around it, or of it, or through it, things seen and imagined.

The second note is best introduced by one of the poems. Herewith:

1.

for days my eye upon it,
the sun resting
on a sabbath horizon.
i prepare my thoughts
and wash.
against the weather and the odd chance

my prayers go up.
for rest and spirit and the inner
elements of a car.
setting my coffee on the casement,
I watch for its single eye

2.

my name, a muzzled bark
from above.
the click of the door
and the slow flop
of asian rubber sandals
which are kept from running
but would rather fly.

3.

not news or topics,
those are taken up or scattered
like wood beads and toy keys.
this and nothing more:
your eyes are your eyes.
your voice
not disembodied or strained
by the long distance line.
I kiss the very word
upon your lips.

4.

the window steams
with late kisses.

sweetpie and the little girl
in the lamplight
wave and wave.

5.

the window and the eye
grow dry.
over again
the long haul wait
and the searching prayer.

It was a hard bit for all three of us. I admire friends and
mentors with kids who have done much longer stretches. Jeanie
and Lydia would come for a visit, and though there was no wall
or glass partition, contact was forbidden. Try explaining that to
a 2-year-old who sees her daddy on the other side of the table.

She would squirm and fight and cry, confused. Outside they
would wave to my window. Then Jeanie would have to make the
night drive home with Lydia kicking and wailing in the car seat
most of the way.

The two of us took different tacks to the dilemma. Jeanie
made Lydia a children's book for bedtime reading, with photographs of me behind bars, explaining in the simplest terms what
jail meant and why—and why it meant I loved her. It's even now
in Lydia's box in the attic. Stashed beside it are my letters to her,
explaining the same thing in more adult terms, speaking to the
child as a woman (and so to the child in that woman). To my
knowledge, she has yet to read them, but I figure they may come
in handy one day with a therapist.

We almost lost Lydia, or so it seemed to a panicked father.
Geez, did everything happen when she was two? She and I were
home alone, me chopping vegetables and she standing beside
on a chair. Her nose was stuffed and running, which became an
issue when she popped a carrot in her mouth and began to chew.

When she inhaled through her mouth, the carrot was taken in and stuck. She couldn't breathe.

I freaked, but had the presence to remember what I could of a baby Heimlich maneuver, placing her face down on my leg and forcing the wind out with a push to the back. A piece came, but she was still wheezing heavily. I scooped her up and ran outside, looking for a neighborly car (Jeanie was gone with ours to work). Nothing in sight.

I raced back in with Lydia in my arms and called friends at a distance who made haste, but had ground to cover. I went back outside pacing my panic while the kid labored her breathing hard. Jeanie pulled up unexpected and miraculously welcome. Most amazing was her centered calm, which she conveyed to me as I drove, and to Lydia by singing quietly to the girl in arms.

The ER triaged her straight in and a surgery was arranged— basically going down her windpipe with orthoscopic tweezers. We had to sign away our rights to allow the anesthesia, and then say goodbye to her as if our last. She came through without a hitch. And I held her all that night as she slept, singing quietly and praying my thanks.

Between the girls lie two miscarriages. Make no mistake, these are deaths, and griefs, and wounds to the heart. The hidden consequence of that, call it an odd gift for Lydia and Lucy, was their closeness. A gap of three and a half years some- how surpasses or supplants sibling rivalry. Those two have been stormless best friends all their lives. If it could be planned, I would plan it. But not the way it happened.

The first miscarriage is a blur in my memory. We were not far along, just enough to know but already living in the joy. The medical doings are what's vague. They escape me now. I recall better the main event of our grieving.

We planted an apple sapling in the backyard and prayed around it, commending ourselves and the unborn child to God. Because we also poured libations upon it, watering the roots with our grief, we continued to do so when occasion warranted. It became a carrier of the sacred.

Jeanie covering the Lambeth Conference, Canterbury, England, 1998.
Credit: Bill Wylie-Kellermann

Years later, when we moved some blocks west, we balled and bagged that little tree and hefted it onto the lift of a U-Haul truck for replanting in the new yard. Then, in a rash of neighborhood arson, our garage was burned to the ground. The tree stood close and the side facing it was, if not ignited, completely charred nonetheless. I doubted its survival, but trimmed dead branches and sprayed bark sealer on the long open wound of its trunk. Now the garage slab has passed from basketball court to a raised-bed garden and the tree is threatening the power lines with its reach. Spring blossoms were thick, and it looks to be a good crop coming in this year.

The other miscarriage was in England, in Canterbury, no less. Jeanie was covering the Lambeth Conference, the once-a-decade gathering of Anglican bishops from the worldwide communion for consultation and conversation. I was along semi-officially as photographer, and Lydia, two and a half, came for the European ride.

I could guess causes, the strain of travel and certain particulars of accommodation, but these are largely beside the point. Jeanie entered the hospital of socialized medicine with nothing more than a signature at the door. Consider that. The medical accommodations were industrially quaint but adequate. The hard part was compounded simply by being separated and so far from home and, for Lydia and me, on foot.

Lydia watched her mother get wheeled off on a disinfected gurney. Then she let me carry her on my shoulders the 15 blocks to where we were staying 'til the morrow. I'm sure I come nowhere near in knowing Jeanie's motherly grief.

Her sense of ritual addressed it yet again. Several days after, we walked into a nearby apple orchard. At her behest, I climbed another tree heavy with fruit and pressed the needle of a Canterbury medallion deep into the bark for hidden memory. To this day, I still feel that wood as flesh my own.

On a train to heaven or hell?

Just a word about the trip and its continuing itinerary. We stayed on several weeks to travel Europe, but we made it an ordeal of our own doing. We got Eurail passes. It was as if we imagined ourselves college students hopping the train with our rucksacks and a blanket, but instead we had a toddler and all her paraphernalia in tow: diaper bag and stroller and maybe even a portabed. People looked at us in astonishment, their eyes saying, "Rent a car, for God's sake."

It was nevertheless a wondrous trip. At Stonehenge, Lydia ducked under the fence and ran blithely into the forbidden center of the ring. Of course, it required both of us to chase her down and share the view. In Scotland, we got off the bus in Kilmacolm without a clue as to where we might stay. We found a bed-and-breakfast with a sweet couple eager to watch Lydia while we went to the inn for supper.

More important, perhaps because it was said to be haunted, they knew the precise location of the Lisle castle ruins. Down a two-track lane and over several sheep fences to a river cliff. They knew its history too, better than we. One story involved an angry prince dragging a cannon out from Glasgow and blowing in the front wall when Robert made off with his mistress. (So he went to America and made whiskey, we surmised, taking along his single malt recipe, no doubt.)

In Ireland, we pursued the Wylie lineage face to face, though Aunt Harriet, slightly enfeebled, had forgotten to mention our correspondence to her children. Our arrival was unexpected and their hospitality doubly gracious. The visit included day trips to the small family plot called a farm, along with churches and graveyards still sacred.

To France, by an overnight boat full of college kids crashing with their rucksacks and blankets on the deck. In Paris, walking along the Seine to Notre Dame Cathedral, we stopped by the Louvre, but with Lydia in the stroller we never got past the courtyard (she remembers the pigeon flocks rising when she ran at them). It was as close as we got to 10,000 masterpieces.

By train and bus and foot to Taizé, to chant with the crowd in candlelight and feel the stone cool of Jeanie's little chapel. And finally, to Germany for a visit with friends, to Darmstadt, no less (though ironically, I didn't yet know my roots were there). It was a wondrous ordeal and, apart from the miscarriage, I'd do it all gladly again. Indeed, in memory, I do as I write.

Perhaps one further word. Our hosts in Darmstadt, Peter Grieb and Monica Wissert, were both part of *Aktion Suhnezeichen* (Action Reconciliation), a German postwar project, still going, which does service work abroad in the lands with which Germany fought, and at home preserves the memory of the Holocaust. Both of them had done hands-on work restoring the concentration camp site at Dachau and making it prayerfully accessible to visitors.

They took us there on tour. We saw the place of the famous gate (*Arbeit Macht Frei*: "Work makes you free"), walked among the stone foundations and the reconstructions, looked upon the furnace, prayed in the chapel, and slowly read though the history panels in the museum. I recall being particularly struck by one of the early newspaper clippings, a public threat, really, published on June 2, 1933. Here's the translation:

> *Warning!*
>
> *On May 30, two persons were observed trying to look over the wall surrounding the concentration camp in Dachau. They were of course immediately arrested. They explained that they had been curious to see what the camp looked like inside. In order to give the opportunity to satisfy their curiosity, they were detained overnight. It is hoped that their curiosity has now been satisfied, in spite of this unforeseen measure.*
>
> *We wish to still the curiosity of all those who might ignore the warning by informing them that in the future they will be given the opportunity of studying the camp from inside for longer than just one night.*

All inquisitive persons are hereby warned once more!

In Charge of the Supreme S.A Command

Special Commissioner Friedriche

Who, in heaven's name, were these two people, lifting the lid on a culture of denial (and having it slammed shut on their fingers)? I imagine someday writing a short story about them and contriving my own open-ended conclusion.

Our friends told us at the time of our visit that even now, families often leave town for the birth of their children. This was so the birth certificate wouldn't read "Dachau." Another form of denial.

The impact of our visit on Lydia was indirect, to say the least, but certain in my estimation. As a senior in high school, she did a directed study with a small circle of friends on literature of the Holocaust. Her reading included a novel on Bonhoeffer and a signed copy of Elie Wiesel's *Night*, which Lucy's godfather, Tom Fentin, had secured as a gift.

Healthy haunts of childhood

In preschool, Lydia's favorite book was *The Clown of God*, written and illustrated by Tomie dePaola, a Franciscan artist. "Favorite" may be a bit of a misnomer, since she approached it with that mix of fascination and fear that is appropriate to any children's book about a death. "Favorite" may apply more aptly to the preference Jeanie and I had for it among the picture-book tales.

Gorgeously illustrated, the story concerns Giovanni, a young boy in Sorrento, Italy, who was gifted at juggling, particularly vegetables. He is picked up by a circus and begins a long career of fame and sideshow fortune, with his own most famous trick of adding different colored balls until the seventh, "the golden Sun in the heavens," is the apex. In the course of his travels, he meets two Franciscan mendicants with whom he shares his bread and from whom he hears the story of their begging ordered life.

When he grows old, his talent fails him, the crowds boo, and the circus abandons him by the side of the road. Eventually, starving and in rags, Giovanni remembers the friars and heads "home" to the monastery. Exhausted, he collapses there in a heap at the back of the chapel. He's wakened by the candlelight procession on Christmas Eve. Each in the community, one by one, places his gift before a statue of the Madonna and Child. To him, both look stern.

After the crowd is gone, with no gift of his own to speak of, he paints his face and performs one last time the Circle of Seven, successfully adding the climactic heavenly ball. And then he collapses. The monks belatedly rush in to stop the "sacrilege" but find him dead—while in the hands of the now-smiling Child, miraculously, is the golden ball.

It seems one of those tiny mysteries of providence that such a book should form the young psyche of one who would face her mother's death. But then, we all face death, and that is the formative point of such a child's book as this.

I was going to say, I can't think of many children's stories that deal straightforwardly with death, but immediately several in our own collection pop to mind. Shel Silverstein's weird and wonderful *Giving Tree*. And Robert Munsch's *Love You Forever*, which traces the lifecycle of a boy through his aged mother's death. It contains a refrain that Lydia and Lucy would sing to one another: "I'll love you forever/ I'll like you for always/As long as I'm living/ My baby (Mommy) you'll be." When Jeanie read it to the girls, she would make up music to go beneath it. Haunts my memory even now.

Made in Bethlehem

Lucy. We knew precisely when and where she was conceived. It was in dense fog on a Florida beach, during an Eastertime visit to my folks. They were babysitting Lydia that night. For much of the pregnancy, Lucy's nickname was Starfog. Here's another poem from my jail series:

is there already another?
a prayer with a question mark,
an unnamed assent intricately wrought,
someone in the sacred cry begun?
i lie in my jail bunk
staring at this thick sky
and imagine the chances,
the hint and sparkle
of a billion hidden suns

Lucia Jeanne was born at home in the brass bed that belonged to my Grandmother Lydia. Weirdly, she remembers the day. We had intended the birthing center again, but instead of the hyperventilating Lamaze classes, we took our training from some midwives. They didn't set out to convince us of anything, but there we were, sitting in the circle beside folks preparing for homebirths and it suddenly made too much sense to do otherwise.

With the midwives over my shoulder, I caught Lucy myself and cut the cord. It's a whole different thing to labor and birth in your own bed, your own room. You can see it in Jeanie's face in the photos immediately after. Glowing and gorgeous. Even Lucy seems to be smiling. What she actually remembers is being taken into the tub and submerged in an herbal bath with leaves and flowers floating around her. Not a bad way to start your first day on the planet.

As it happened, we took Lucy along to Israel and Palestine on a human rights delegation when she was seven months old. We weren't really looking to take the girls. It just seemed Lucy was too young to stay at home apart from us.

We'd been invited into the group by Stew Wood, the new Episcopal bishop. Jeanie was then editor of the diocesan newspaper. We took counsel with one another and agreed to go, but appeared at the first meeting of the group with an infant in arms. There was, needless to say, some consternation and considerable discernment. But in the end, Lucy herself won them over, and we were embraced as a threesome.

Worth pulling back to mention the fourth of our 'some. I packed up Lydia for the drive to Grandma Bea's in Menominee. Grandma was so beloved, Lydia was more than happy with this arrangement. Plus there were trains that ran nearby, whose cars could be counted, and a bakery on the corner with smiley-face cookies.

On the way home I made a tape, speaking directly to Lydia in the present. We were going to Gaza. It's nothing like the air-struck and bulldozed and rubbled desolation of today, but there are always risks of such travel. I wanted Lydia to have an explanation in my own voice if something happened to us.

She has, I know, listened to this recently and appreciated it much. I pause now to wonder if she needed to hear it at the time, whether the effect wouldn't have been quite the opposite of what I intended. But there was love in my voice and in the deed. And, glad to say, she's appreciative of it in her later years. As a college student, Lydia herself made a life-altering pilgrimage to Palestine, with a Michigan Peace Team group that included her future life partner, Erinn Fahey.

The trip Jeanie, Lucy, and I made was during the first Intifada. Truth be told, we went sympathetic to the Palestinian struggle, but we spoke to people of every faction and stripe. That included an amazing set of nonviolent activists, both Palestinian and Israeli.

I could write at length of the trip and our assorted conversations (and have), but here I want to refocus on the Lucy kid. In the planning, we had intended for one of us to stay with her in safer territory while the rest went to Gaza. But she was traveling and coping so well once we were there that we were reconsidering and decided to put it to the group.

Lucy had long since made converts of even the strongest holdouts, and everyone was quite receptive. Even then, our plan was for one of us to stay with her in our hosting hostel during

the trip to the refugee camps, but both Jeanie and I wanted to
go. So in the end, Lucy took in absolutely everything.

At Jabaliya Camp, she was sociable and gregarious, a big hit
with the children who crowded around. Jabaliya was one of
the few refugee camps with an Israeli military installation at its
center rather than guarding an entrance. This made for a constant air of tension.

I heard a "backfire." Some of the *shebab*, or young people,
were throwing stones at the elevated guard house and then
dashing away in zigzags, dodging rubber-coated bullets. A tear
gas canister had been fired from the tower (illegally) into the
wide dirt perimeter.

I knew the taste of gas from other contexts and recognized
it immediately in the air. We had seen spent canisters up close,
stamped with "Made in Bethlehem, PA." Jeanie and I had
fretted about such a moment. Infants are more vulnerable to tear
gas. If shot into an enclosed space, it can even be lethal to them.

Quickly, I ducked Lucy into the van. The driver peeled out
in reverse, and we were out of there. We carried dampened rags
in our pack and brought them out, should we need to cover
Lucy's face as we circled back through the streets. In the market,
women were covering their mouths with scarves as the gas
wafted through, but we in the van were protected from its bite.

The amazing thing on that trip was how Lucy reversed the
normal dynamic of Westerners coming to see the people of the
camp. We were hardly gawkers, but I assume it could feel as
such. Instead, a little blonde-haired baby became the focus of
attention, and we ourselves, though oddities to be sure, seemed
less of an invasive one.

For her part, Lucy rose to the trip like an extrovert, squealing
and throwing out her arms, particularly to the kids. Drivers
and hosts, speakers and soldiers, were all equally charmed.
Palestinians jingled keys and handed over their prayer beads for
her to play with. At Marna House, where we stayed in Gaza, our
host Alya Shawa declared Lucy's need for a Palestinian name.

"Well," we said, "Lucia means 'light.'"

"*Nura* means 'light' in Arabic," she responded. "Welcome, Nura!"

I thought I'd lost Lucy once, too. Another Florida beach. Jeanie was not along on that trip, so I was single-parenting. Boy, did that responsibility come home to me. With Lydia and my folks, we were all hunched down in the surf panning for sharks' teeth at a place where the Gulf is notorious for pouring them in with the sand. I looked up and Lucy was gone. Here's a piece from a poem she requested one Christmas as a present:

once on a beach
where huge and ancient sharks
sunk their teeth in the tide
I lost you,
swallowed whole in a father's final fear.

scanning the desperate directions
at a dead run
I keened the air with your name
in high pitched panic
while rumors were shouted on the wind
and only finally resigned to look
toward the clamoring waves' great jaw,
all but collapsing in despair.

whereupon should you,
blithely back from the dead,
over bouldered breakwater
clamber from limits unconstrained.

no secret tether reined this toddler's step
(yours so lax in free elasticity).
No, what pulled you home
was just some new curiosity,
even if scented with a whiff of someone's fear.

when I scooped you and wept
you were surprised to join my sobs for being found.

Detroit Newspaper strike, 1996. Jeanie with daughters Lucy and Lydia, with Bishop Thomas Gumbleton. Credit: Rudy Simmons

A Common Intuition

A Witness unpredictable

When Lucy was little, Jeanie took her regularly to work, nursed her to sleep, and tucked her under the desk while she set to writing. Jeanie was then editor of *The Record*, the Episcopal diocesan paper. In those pages she readily featured the trips to Canterbury, Israel/Palestine, and Nicaragua, in a series of articles. She was really good at that part of the job, but less attentive to the churchy news that necessarily goes with such a position. Her successor has done better at covering both fronts and holding the two together.

In 1991, Jeanie became editor/publisher of *The Witness* magazine. I had a spiritual hand in that. One day, pulling out of the cathedral parking lot, pretty much out of the blue, I said to myself, "Jeanie Wylie really ought to be editor of *The Witness*."

Next afternoon, when I picked her up, she laughed as she recounted how Hugh White on the magazine's board had approached her about applying for the job, which was, in fact, just coming open. I hit the brake and pulled over. I told her about my bolt the day before, and the coincidence was so providentially weird that it made her sit up and think. She applied and swept the field.

Among other things, the board was looking for a more urban location for the magazine, so they were pleased she was willing to move the operation to Detroit, first into a downtown office and then into an abandoned pharmacy at the end of our block. (The move was really rockier than I'm letting on, but therein hangs a tale for another time.)

Jeanie was good for the progressive Episcopal publication, and did in fact signal a new era in its life. Her politics were definitely of the left, but not in a slavish or flatly ideological way. She made some breaks—opposition to abortion being one.

She understood abortion as a kind of violence and found the feminist issues more complex than a woman's right to choose—recasting the debate as something other than a matter of "rights." When she named that, it wasn't long before the editorial board made its own public statement—but still they affirmed her editorial freedom. Not everyone smiled, but Jeanie was good at presenting issues with a unique take that put things in a new light.

Unpredictable. She interviewed controversial social critic Michael Moore for an issue on "social trickstering." *The Witness* was one of the few places I've seen him talk publicly about faith—even Resurrection.

Once, Marianne Arbogast, a member of the staff, came into the office laughing about a dream she'd had the night before that they were going to do an issue on glamour. Jeanie thought it was brilliant. And so was the groundbreaking issue they did on the topic.

For the 75th anniversary of *The Witness*, a party was surely called for. I imagine the board pictured a wine-and-cheese love fest at some congenial location with the usual suspects. But Jeanie and the staff had another idea: How about taking *The Witness* roadshow into the bastion of conservative Anglican theology for conversation and dialogue?

To their credit, the board agreed, and to their surprise, Trinity Seminary in Pennsylvania said "bring it on." Let it be noted that, after the fact, a small cluster of students approached the dean, urging the re-consecration of the chapel because of its use by the *Witness* crew. But, after Jeanie's death, I received a lovely note from a former Trinity student who said the conference turned him into a *Witness* reader.

Let me share Jeanie's opening remarks for that occasion in her own voice:

> *This is a day I've been looking forward to, and been terrified of, for quite a while. There's another day that I look forward to with some of the same fear and delight, and that's the Day of Judgment: having an opportunity to have the sins that I know I carry stripped from me and then having the ones I didn't understand to be sin, or pretended to myself that I didn't understand to be sin, subsequently stripped from me. And then the moment of standing in the communion of saints and looking into the faces of people with whom I had deep disagreements, and being able to see how my sin had contributed to that and seeing how their sin had contributed to that, and laughing. I just anticipate a lot of laughter, and maybe some sadness at the way we hurt one another in the process.*
>
> *Today is perhaps a time to move toward that. And I caution us in that. Growing up I used to hear that before you spoke, you were supposed to ask yourself, "Is it good? Is it kind? Is it necessary?"*
>
> *I would ask everybody to dispense with that today. And instead of trying to exercise the Golden Rule in the way the church often does—which means not saying anything offensive—only say what's on your heart. If what's on your heart is angry, speak in anger. If what's on your hear is reconciling, speak that. But don't try to*

*be polite, and certainly don't take your anger and turn
to someone beside you whom you trust and have it be
a snide aside about what's happening.*

*If you have to testify, if you believe there is something
on your heart that the group needs to hear, find a way
to say it and be as aware as you can that all of us are
children of God in doing that. But I'd urge us not to
be afraid of anger and to see where that lands us at the
end of the day ...*

That is pure Jeanie Wylie.

Without sacrificing a stand, Jeanie brought that open, creative tension to the pages of *The Witness*. She also brought an
unexpected eye for art to the work. Photographs, illustrations,
and full-blown works suddenly graced the pages. It may have
been nothing more than the editorial freedom, but something
was happening in her.

She published the haunting and visceral art of Dierdre
Luzwick. Well, more, she developed a correspondence with
her. Dierdre is my favorite letter writer of all time—sardonic
and skewering, even of herself. Her detailed apocalyptic ironies
graced many an issue and not a few covers. I don't think they
ever met face to face, but she and Jeanie would have done a
book together eventually—though that was not to be.

Betty LaDuke (mother to American Indian activist Winona)
was another gift. Her stunning shamanistic paintings alone were
enough to convince Jeanie to press for four-color art in at least a
few issues each year. Jeanie didn't have an art director. If I'm not
mistaken, she did all of the searching and finding on her own.

Sweet editor mine

Jeanie was an amazingly fast writer. Magazine deadlines rolled
at her like waves, but she was never swamped. Everything she
needed was all in her head. She summoned the written pieces
and the art, crafting it all for the pages. Then, the night before,
or even the morning of, she'd sit down to the keyboard and pour

out an editorial introduction, gathering the quirky angles and the salient points. First draft, brilliant and done.

Me? I agonize and pace, reworking the first draft as I go and combing for nuance right up to the last minute. I remember the first time I gave Jeanie something of mine to read. It was an article about John Wesley. Somehow it escaped Jeanie that she was mainly supposed to tell me how good it was, perhaps pointing to certain passages of particularly poetic prose or underscoring deft turns of phrase.

Instead, she seemed to think she was my editor. The manuscript came back all marked up, like I was her staffer or some high school student getting a report back from my teacher. Journalistic curlicues were intended, presumably, to send certain words or phrases spiraling off the page entirely. Jeanie had crossed out entire sections and reorganized the paragraphs as though the middle really played better as the lead.

I wish that I could say I was devastated, but in fact I was only pissed. Our marriage survived it, but it was touch-and-go for a tense moment. No doubt we both learned a good bit in the aftermath. Though I had the more to learn.

Jeanie's writing was vocabulary-rich (even in the home stretch of her illness—when she could hardly finish sentences—she could kick our butts at Scrabble), but it was clean and straight-forward. Journalism had honed her precision and nourished a certain economy of language. (None of the parenthesized self-conscious embellishments or asides to which I'm so inclined.)

In fact, an aside here: She spoke as she wrote. I think Jeanie had the gift to be a TV reporter or perhaps a talk show host (thank God she never considered either)—or to have a ministry of public speaking, at the very least. Although she was mostly a print person, she was good on her feet and spoke off the cuff in complete, unbroken sentences.

I interviewed her about Stringfellow once for a documentary. The camera guy was amazed and remarked so. He'd never filmed a Q&A that was such a perfect first take. Jeanie was totally focused, and there wasn't a single response he wanted to reshoot. I'd be glad if some of her clarity of mind and page eventually rubbed off on me.

Our protest action at the SAC base, which Jeanie covered for Michael Moore's *Michigan Voice*, became the seed of a book I wrote about liturgical direct action called *Seasons of Faith and Conscience*. Though I had the seasonal meditations in hand, the theological and liturgical upfront work suggested by an editor was languishing. I paced before a blank screen, the cursor blinking in impatient annoyance.

Jeanie eventually had it with my writer's block. She made arrangements to borrow a cabin in the woods, packed up my computer, monitor, keyboard, and a tangle of cables, and drove me to Michigan's Upper Peninsula. She dropped me unceremoniously with the machine parts and food for a week, saying I wasn't to call 'til the first chapter was in hand.

I didn't. She successfully jumpstarted me, and I ought to have dedicated the whole dang thing to her. Who knew half the mentors I named on the dedication page would outlive her?

For several years, Jeanie actually was my editor, in the sense that I was officially the book review editor for *The Witness*. A great job, if you can get it. The books just roll in from publishers, who send lists with boxes to check off whatever strikes your fancy. You start to ask about the FedEx guy's family.

I served the magazine at least adequately, and with some imagination, and the books keep coming to this day. My study in the attic at home has become so laden with unread volumes that a crack runs across my bedroom ceiling. I worry that it will all come crashing through and crush me in some absurd and deserved death. Save me, Jeanie.

A mighty, mighty union?

One of the issues Jeanie and I produced together for *The Witness* covered organized labor, by way of a newspaper strike, then ongoing in Detroit. It's funny, I think of our active participation in that strike as epitomizing our marriage in certain ways. We moved together in it with such unreflective intuition.

Our political instincts and theological sensibilities simply ran the same way. Our gifts complemented and encouraged each other's. We were yoked in that struggle. Jeanie was always, to be sure, more organized and more of an organizer than I, but she pushed me in that regard, and I stepped up.

I remember the conversation in which we hatched a plan to pull together our own community group to play an active, even aggressive, role in the strike. It was over eggs and hash browns in a booth at Jordon's, a breakfast place across the street from what would become the *Witness* office. Our friends Deb Choly and John Zettner were in on it.

It was late winter of 1996, and the strike had been going since summer. We were all astonished at the timidity and ineptitude of the council of newspaper unions running the strike, and at the major boring uselessness of their community outreach efforts. In my own version of the history, Readers United, as yet unnamed, was conceived at that table.

It's only in writing this that it occurs to me how clearly we were moving in Jeanie's vocational turf: journalism and media, combined with a righteous fight. After all our years of struggling in campaigns such as anti-nuclear work—up against the entirety of empire and its military-industrial complex, clinging to the hope of simple faithfulness just to keep at it—this seemed like a local, winnable fight, for a change.

Boy, were we naïve. For one thing, "the company" was anything but local. The papers were owned by Gannett and Knight Ridder—chains, or media conglomerates really, with total profits approaching a billion dollars a year.

Since the last successful strike against the *Detroit Free Press*, it and *The Detroit News* had fused their business management in a "joint operating agreement," which pre-empted competition, reduced work force, presented a single bargaining front, and earned profits of a million dollars per week the year prior.

Unknown to the 2,600 workers who bet their mortgages and car notes on a successful strike, the chains were prepared to lose a quarter of a billion dollars as a one-time cost to break the union.

Great writers on serious city subjects let go of their newspaper careers by walking the picket line. And others virtually made careers—lucrative ones—slipping in as "replacement worker" columnists into other people's chairs.

Jeanie had sometimes written as a stringer for both papers, and had even applied once for a job on the city desk of *The Detroit News*. However, the day the editors were making their decision, she was an item on the front page of the paper, for her arrest at Immaculate Conception Church in the Poletown struggle. I suppose that clarified everything a little too much, and they decided not to hire her. As things turned out, best for us all in the long run.

The beginning of the strike in the fall of 1995 was pretty bloody, and virtually all of the blood belonged to the strikers. I'll come back to that. By November, *The New York Times* had essentially declared victory for the company. That winter was cold and bleak, with strikers clinging to picket signs in threadbare gloves.

So when Readers United announced itself in leaflets and stepped onto the streets, we were like a breath of spring air. The union council had so often looked over its shoulder, staying legal and tiptoeing around the National Labor Relations Act as if it were a pro-union document. But we were not bound by such fears or strictures. Straight to it: We organized nonviolent direct actions, blockades mostly, at the newspaper headquarters.

Readers United met in our living room and around our dining room table. It was essentially a letterhead of religious and civic leaders who were committed to the strike and trusted us publicly with their names. Their endorsement helped our organizing, and they stood behind it in the long run.

Picture some 300 arrests (all non-strikers), including county commissioners and state representatives, four City Council members, three bishops, veterans and teachers and retirees,

and lots of prominent pastors and lawyers. Our Detroit Peace
Community stepped up, and activists from other unions were
quick to help as well, with outreach, nonviolence training,
press work, and legal support—all cranked up again weekly.
Meanwhile, 800 clergy and members of religious orders signed
an appeal denouncing the hiring of so-called "permanent
replacement workers" and urging the community to boycott the
newspapers as morally unreadable. Subscriptions went down by
as much as half.

To be frank, in a black majority city, the unions were partly
up against their own history of racially guarding the gates and
apprenticeships. The company openly played on and accentu-
ated this by hiring replacement workers from the community
and advertising the racial shift. The boycott could have gone
even further.

For at least a year, Jeanie and I were consumed with it, but
in a life-giving way. A year or more along, the National Labor
Relations Board summoned us to testify. Coming at the instiga-
tion of the newspapers, it seemed partly a tactic of intimidation.
On the premise that we were simply fronting for the newspaper
unions, and with their direct assistance, they wanted to probe us
in sworn testimony. We showed up with a roomful of religious,
civic, and community leaders, all asserting our integrity and
independence. The letterhead host meant something.

Only once were Jeanie and I arrested together, and that
was impulsively spontaneous. Sweet, but a little reckless. I
have a dear photo of us—pensive, her arm in mine, just prior.
Otherwise, we took our turns. She brought the resources of *The
Witness* to bear on things, not only her time but also allowing
the office machine to spit out broadcast faxes about the actions.
She was often the press spokesperson, and I can see her now
talking to reporters or the cops, with Lucy on her hip.

The girls were thoroughly present to this. I remember them
climbing a pile of hardwood dumped for the winter drumfires
of a printing plant picket line. In fact, they sat atop that pile
to hear Charlie King, movement troubadour, sing yet again his

reviving medleys from labor history. I can hear a picket chant
working its way into their own repertoire of playsongs: "We are
the union, the mighty, mighty union ... " I see them peeking
from behind the flow of Jeanie's skirts as I'm taken away in the
police bus. And playing puzzles or reading books on the floor
through those endless meetings.

Among the folks at those dining room table sessions was
Grace Lee Boggs, dare I say one of the most notorious community activists of our time. Jeanie had known Grace for 15 years,
going back to Poletown days. I want to say Grace is an organic
intellectual—but, actually, she has a Ph.D. from Bryn Mawr,
though at street level she wears it well. Her husband, Jimmy,
an Alabama-born African American who came to work and
organize in the auto plants, was the true organic intellectual, the
real deal. He had just recently died, and Grace, then 80, was
pressing forward in the work without benefit of their amazing
partnership.

I'll spare you the history, but Grace had participated in virtually every transformative movement to emerge since the '30s.
For example, they put together the Grassroots Conference—as
in Malcolm X's "Message to the Grassroots"—and were among
the invisible organizers of Martin Luther King Jr.'s Detroit
march in the spring of 1964, which convinced him to undertake
the better-known March on Washington. I'm only hinting at the
scope and import of Grace's work.

Grace understood and helped us see that the absentee
conglomerates had long put profits not only before their
employees, but before their readers as well. The contempt they
demonstrated for their workers was one and the same with the
contempt they were showing for our community. Globalization
and the technological rush had not made them better papers by
any means. Marketing predominated, and real news shrank.

In fact, we could see the establishment news slant exposed
by strike coverage that, if not an outright lie, was crafted as
though by ad agency spin doctors. Reporters came and went in
the system without lives or roots in the city's life (or the union's,

for that matter). Crucial management decisions (such as those affecting the strike) were made by people who no longer lived among us, either. The company strategy was little more than a calculated assault on the political culture of a union town.

That was Grace's critical take, though the translation is entirely my own. She helped us understand that while globalization was uprooting the shop floor as the location for organizing, community-rooted unionism offered the possibility of reclaiming place-based organizing. Readers United attempted to reframe a labor struggle as a community struggle.

Were we inadvertently on the cutting edge of something? Perhaps.

One upshot had to do with the community's impact not just on the company, but on the unions. We suddenly felt a prerogative to hold their feet to the fire as well.

I mentioned that the strike was quite bloody. The company had brought in Vance Security, a paramilitary outfit that presents itself as a strike-breaking operation. They advertise in *Soldier of Fortune* and have big mercenary security contracts in Iraq.

One of their skills, as advertised, is the ability to provoke striker violence, capture it on video, and turn it into ads denouncing the union—or even employ it to secure injunctions. (The company did both, in this case.) Indeed, I was present when riot-equipped forces charged or postured to provoke a reaction, filmed from the roof above. Driving a truck into an angry, and then wounded, crowd drew sticks and rocks, equally photogenic. The company's ubiquitous commercials would "deplore striker violence" (in order to mask its own). Some of them even showed burning vehicles that I believe were actually set afire by their own security forces.

Not that the strikers were disciplined in their nonviolence, or even broadly committed to it. We're talking partly Detroit Teamsters here. So, Jeanie and Grace took Clementine Barfield to meet with the union council. Clem, the mother of a murder victim, founded an anti-violence movement in Detroit in 1987.

The city was suffering, on average, one murder every day. Clem's group, SOSAD (Save Our Sons and Daughters), was holding weekly vigils, running griefwork sessions for families of shooters and victims, mounting anti-gun campaigns, and running programs in the high schools.

Here was the pitch to the union leaders: Imagine a creative and actively nonviolent labor struggle that could be a gift, a learning moment for the city and its youth. Sadly, blank stares— they didn't get it. No light went on for them. No opportunity was seized. My own read in part is that they didn't get that community and labor meant a two-way street. They eagerly sought solidarity and support for the strike but couldn't feature how the strike could truly be shaped to serve the community.

The other example of that same blind spot was the matter of the boycott. Readers United supported it and even coined a phrase, calling the papers "morally unreadable." But boycotting the dailies and refusing to talk with scab reporters was entirely different from refusing to buy Gallo wines or eat Mt. Olive pickles.

A newspaper is not just a news commodity, it's a vehicle of public conversation. People who refused to talk with the papers, including the best of the politicians, had their public voices substantially silenced. Political discourse was weakened at a moment when major decisions about the city's future were being made.

Jeanie and I went to the union council, asking them to publish an alternative news source for the community. "No go," said the local Teamster president. "We did that in '68"—during the last successful strike—"and the members liked the alternative better than the company's and didn't want to ratify the labor agreement. We're not doing that again." Another version of not getting it.

A few weeks later, leafleting at the *Detroit Free Press*, Jeanie recognized the national president of the Newspaper Guild and flagged her down. Pure providence. Right there on the sidewalk, we had our meeting. She'd never heard tell of our request, but she thought it made total sense and promised to pursue it.

Within a month or two, the unions began publishing a weekly, the *Detroit Sunday Journal*. Grace began writing a column for them and until the day it ceased publication in 2014 I counted it the most important source of Detroit news available.

In the long run, the *Journal* was a disappointment. Great on strike reporting and union news, it never developed into the community-based investigative journalism source the moment required. Far better was the *Michigan Citizen*, another weekly. Focused on the black community and being the self-declared "most progressive paper in the country," it did step consciously into the gap. Grace began writing a column for them, and to this day it's the only Detroit paper I read with regularity.

Reading the building, seeing the powers

On a theological note, I'm struck even now how our biblical view of the "powers that be," Stringfellow's influential take on the principalities among us, figured into that struggle. Of a particular principality, we were in effect asking, what is the vocation of a newspaper? How is it called to serve human community? What is a paper for? These are radical questions which, in the biblical view of things, humans are authorized to ask.

One time, during a large picket around the newspaper headquarters, I noticed high above the street, nearly out of sight and mind, epithets etched in stone, ringing the façade above. I pointed them out to Jeanie, and we read as we circled. Later at the rally in front of the edifice, I took the microphone and asked, "Have you ever read the *Detroit News* building?"

It was a confusing moment for the strikers. Then I pointed aloft and began to utter the names, among them: Friend of Every Righteous Cause, Reflector of Every Human Interest, Mirror of the Public Mind, Dispeller of Ignorance and Prejudice, Bond of Civic Unity, Protector of Civic Rights, Troubler of Public Conscience, Scourge of Evil Doers, Exposer of Secret Iniquities, Unrelenting Foe of Privilege and Corruption, A Light Shining in All Dark Places.

Were these intentions a pretense from the beginning, a mere "facade" covering the machinery of power and profit—or did they publicly remember the true vocation, the calling of a community newspaper? In Jeanie's and my biblical reading, every structure of power with a life and integrity of its own, every "principality and power," is called by God to serve the human community in particular ways, notably in this case by being a servant of the truth, and even justice.

These phrases written in stone, romantic and pretentious as they were, actually suggested the very basis on which Detroit Newspapers Incorporated stands before the judgment of God.

As I read out each one at the rally, the strikers laughed. Their laughter identified the incongruity. It signaled their theological understanding of "the Fall."

The *News* was indeed a "troubler of the public conscience," but in a way exactly opposite of that intended. It had become the trouble, when it should instead be the conscience. I noted that Turner of Profit was not even mentioned in the auspicious list. Neither was Master of Marketing, Doctor of Spins, nor Twister of Truth—let alone Buster of Unions. This is to say that in the Fall, the vocation of a newspaper becomes distorted or even inverted. It gets turned upside down.

Instead of serving the community, it imagines the community exists to serve the interests of the newspaper. It puts profit before both readers and workers. It has contempt for both, actually assaulting the community. That is the reality of the Fall. The work of redemption in that moment had to do with exposing the lie, rebuking the distortion, and calling the papers back to their creaturely purposes. If you think about the work of Readers United from this standpoint, you'll notice that we were also exercising the same discernment with the unions, recognizing them as creaturely powers.

The New York Times may have been premature, but in the end it wasn't wrong. We did lose that strike. It slipped away in whimpers. That's a source of grief in our life. Certainly for the workers who lost cars and homes. Some fell off the 12-step wagon, and others saw marriages go belly-up from the strain.

But you also had to grieve for Detroit, a union town taking another hit, "Murder City" losing another of its lives. The dailies never fully recovered their circulation as they'd presumed. And, to be honest, two decades later, I still can't bring myself to buy one at a box, let alone subscribe.

Jeanie and the girls, Port Sanilac, 1998. Credit: Bill Wylie-Kellermann

5

No More and No Less than Herself

Though we didn't yet see it, the latter strike days coincided with Jeanie's early symptoms. She began to suffer migraines that could incapacitate her. And she became chemically hyper-sensitive. Cigarette smoke in a union hall drove her away. Perfumes in church could set off a headache, or worse. She began wearing buttons, a kind of personal campaign, for chemical-free space. We'd scope out seats in a darkened theater more by smell than sightline.

Jeanie Wylie was deeply intuitive. If she didn't consciously recognize the symptoms, she nevertheless began laying the groundwork for her illness in major ways. For one, she started circling the inner landscape, doing her inner work. In a certain sense that simply goes with turning 40 and facing middle age, but this work had consequences that you'd have to say were sage preparations. None of this was by conventional therapy.

One path was to join a "women's hoop," several years running. The hoop was led by Debbie Mast, a nurse-therapist who aspired to be something of a shaman, apprenticed in a tradition that drew on Native American wisdom. Jeanie was sensitive to the ambiguities, contradictions, and potential presumptions of such an appropriation, and I wonder if today she would refrain, but she found the practices very useful.

She was never attracted by the elaborate cosmology behind it, as far as I know. She simply loved the women and their honest struggles. Together they did sweats and fasts. Jeanie made effigies of herself from earth materials, designed and sewed a dress for dances, and went on a vision quest alone in the woods with no shelter but the sacred circle cast.

The Four Directions, which I've always found so useful for intercessions, functioned as a kind of psychic map for projecting and tending parts of her self. Jeanie made decisions. She moved toward earth, toward beauty. This fit as well with her Yellow Thunder experience and comported entirely with the ancestor work. "Ho," she would say in a sweat, "all my relations."

Something funny in this regard. One of the aspects who lit up in the psychic horizon was a "Pink Person." That's actually what Jeanie called her. Jeanie wore no makeup, and like me generally underdressed—another of our marital compatibilities. We always joked that you could tell when we were dressing up because we changed our shoes.

But the Pink Person, long suppressed I presume, wanted frills and parasols. One of the tenets of the hoop was the ritualization and enactment of self-discoveries. Jeanie bought a dress. Jeanie put on eye shadow. Jeanie painted her nails hot pink. Jeanie picked up her elder daughter at school and freaked her out big-time. Ah, what a woman will do for shamanism.

Her embrace of ritual helped me as well, when I faced having to give up my beloved sport, basketball. The pounding it gave my knees yielded several surgeries and attendant medical devices and cautions. The only record of Michael Jordan's that I've successfully broken is the number of times I've come out of retirement.

The "final retirement" was a big choice— between a few more years of the game or long walks with Jeanie in our old age. I chose the latter, firm and quick, but then muttered and moaned. "You need a grieving rite," Jeanie asserted.

Trusting her advice, I began a basketball poem. It had the smell of my junior-high jersey and the voice of soulful high school chants. It had linoleum jail courts and cracker-box church gyms. It included my musings on writing subliminally while moving through half-court games—stepping off the court having conceived an article or landed a chapter—and a history of friends who'd moved together to the rhythm of the ball's dance. The poem turned first epic and then essay-ish.

In the end, I convened my beloved local court mates, bought a round, read the poem, hoisted a glass, and brought it to a close. Then I copied the poem and mailed it off to every former teammate I could think of. A satisfying rite if ever there was one.

But then. A friend, Laura Markham, who owned a chain of cultural-political weeklies, including one in San Antonio, needed an article for an issue when the NCAA playoffs came to town. Says her politico athlete husband Danny Cantor, "What about Bill's?" Suddenly, with some minor edits, I'm on the cover for the weekend of the finals: "To the Hoop Dance: A Grieving Rite."

They even paid me handsomely. The cash bought a sturdy and official wheel-able basketball hoop for aspiring hoopster Lydia—a vast improvement over the homemade plywood back-board I had been mentally jerry-rigging to the roof of the garage. But, as it turned out over the course of time, Lucy was the one who actually learned the baseline dish.

Jeanie's inner work also led us to the writings of Tom Brown, a tracker who had taught himself to survive in the wilder-ness. We even did a weekend with friends, led by some of his protégés—building debris huts, firing up twigs from scratch, distilling water without fire or pot, weaving hemp twine, listen-ing in various ways to the woods—such as that.

One thing we learned was what he called "splatter vision"—though there has to be a better name for it. It's a kind of totally unfocused Zen way of seeing in the woods that catches not detail, but movement. I know it from juggling, when you focus on nothing so you can see everything.

Jeanie practiced it on land we owned up north by then, sitting in her favorite perch. She once spotted a lynx. To confirm her sighting, she collected scat and sent it off to the Department of Natural Resources for analysis—until they told her she didn't need to send any more.

In one particular cycle of the hoop, the women undertook a reflective exercise wherein they wrote eulogies for themselves. Jeanie's included this partial self-accounting:

> *Here lies Jeanie, who said she would not be political if it had not been for her Christian faith. Honoring the gospels, she read that God loves those who take risks: the prodigal, the one who invests her talent. What God does not like are the tepid, who are spewed from God's mouth. Jeanie believed in a God who wanted her to be no more and no less than herself.*
>
> *The second lesson she took from her faith was that justice generally requires turning the existing order on its head. In her magazine work, she tried to hold the powerful to account and took delight in lifting up the voices of those spurned or abused in society and in the church: women, the poor, people of color, the disabled, children, gay men and lesbians, creatures of the earth, and earth itself.*

Perhaps most decisive about her eulogy was its focus on having slowed down. Written in mock retrospect, as though a fact accomplished, it identified Jeanie's desires to unhook from obsessive busyness, to spend time as a mother with her children, to enjoy beauty as a contemplative, and to live a life rooted in the earth. Was it prescient or causative? Who would have known, far more completely than she even foresaw, what a thoroughgoing contemplative illness would render her?

But it did provoke job and family changes. And it certainly pushed her toward acquiring a piece of earth to love and enjoy.

A place for thin times

Which brings things to that land up north in "The Thumb." Michiganders, at least downstaters, have a way of identifying where we're from by pointing to a spot on our right hands. This place is about where your thumb knuckle is.

We had a long history of visitations up to that area, going back to the days of a Catholic Worker farm, which was linked in a land trust with our Detroit Worker. After its sad demise, we regularly spent weekends as a family in a cottage tucked in woods that belonged to friends—who eventually moved there permanently, closing that door as well.

We joked about placing an ad in the paper—"Willing to Inherit: Couple with two beautiful daughters looking for wooded acres with stream, walking distance from the lakeshore, with adequate dwelling." At some level, Jeanie was always on the hunt for a place to buy, but suddenly the search got serious.

One April 1st (I remember the date precisely), we were driving the back roads, tracking down listings and keeping an eye out. Jeanie, at the wheel, decided to turn around and pulled into a driveway. Because of a layer of clay just below the topsoil of The Thumb (once a lakebed, not many millennia back), the spring is mudluscious. The car sank, the wheels spun, and the fenders became splattered with rust-red clay.

I was useless, being on crutches from a basketball knee surgery. The tow truck we called was afraid to come near, lest he join us in the mire. So he winched us out sideways from down the road, tearing our poor neighbors-to-be a whole new entranceway.

We did eventually find the place of Jeanie's dreams (or more accurately, she found it with our friend Nancy Cannon): a two-room cabin on a cement slab with a crock well, a hand pump, and an outhouse, near Port Sanilac. The five acres were exactly as our imaginary ad had described, with one worrisome snag: It seemed to be a good bit of wetland.

Or was this just the result of the spring downpours? During our time of consideration, we kept referring to the place as "The

Cedar Swamp." Happily, the drainage issue turned out to be temporarily caused by an especially rainy season.

The other snag was me. I was leery of a mortgage. I had just taken a job so that Jeanie could cut back, but she offered to hang in full time at *The Witness* for another year and pay it off in one fell swoop. She argued that for her to stay in the city, she needed this place for respite and escape.

Of course, the swoop fell differently from the way we had imagined (a bank long held the note), but Jeanie was righter than we knew about her need. And I couldn't be happier that I yielded. Buying "Cedar Spirit" (she changed the name when we put the money down) proved to be part of her healing and survival, the intuitive groundwork for her illness.

And not just for her. I love this place so. I'm looking out the window upon it as I write. Earlier this morning, a hawk perched beneath the canopy of the beechnut in my view.

I've become a tender of trees. I watch them in the slow of time. I pull down vines that would overtake them and ache for their wounds. I confess that without much real knowledge, I encourage some and thin others to make a way. (Can you believe I discuss it first with those to be thinned?)

I prune them, at least in the course of tending the paths. I harvest their fruits, and they fuel our fire. They inhabit my dreams and utter messages. In a clump of cedar at the back, the girls and I built a two-story tree house that is an architectural wonder, if I do say.

Jeanie is buried in a stand of cathedral-like white pines, but she is everywhere here. Thank you, dear intuitive heart. These trees affect my healing and my grieving and my surviving.

Cedar Spirit connected us with the cycles of the year in a new way. It became part of our natural earth-based ritualizing. As a family we created a large, beautiful wooden sun, with stained-glass face and rays. It ordinarily hangs in a cabin window. For festivals, such as the solstices, we take it down and bring it into the clearing at night, hanging it before a torch to preside over the campfire and other doings.

In her explorations, Jeanie discovered the Celtic cycle, marking the year into four cross quarters. These "pagan" feast days, each set between a solstice and an equinox, fall on February 1, May 1, August 1, and November 1. They are actually beneath—some say covered over and suppressed by—certain Christian festivals, especially Catholic ones.

February 1 is *Imbolc* and now marks the feast of Brigid, whose life as a saint is full of stories right from an Irish goddess of similar name. May Day is *Beltane*, which Jeanie liked for its fertility rite of leaping over the bonfire. August 1 is *Lughnasah*, revived of late in cultural memory by the Brian Friel play/film about an Irish family of sisters in the 1930s, whose missionary priest uncle returns from Uganda. Now the ancient feast calls to him from the hills, because in Africa he had crossed over to indigenous paganism.

Chief among the feasts for us was *Samhain*, on November 1. Notice that our Christian anniversary, Feast of All Saints, coincides. It was always, even in deep memory, a "thin time." *Samhain* (pronounced "sow-hen") was another fire festival, in which everyone extinguished their hearth fires to end the old year and begin anew.

Festivities around the communal bonfire concluded with each household carrying back a coal from the big common flame, to reignite their hearths. They carried the embers in hollowed-out turnips. What do you suppose that became? Need I say jack-o-lanterns?

Just a further footnote: When All Saints Day came to the Western Hemisphere, it merged with a new crop of indigenous folkways. On *El Día de los Muertos*—the Day of the Dead—Latin American peoples go to cemeteries and set up altars on the graves of their beloved ones. They remain for the thin-time day, eating, drinking, and talking with one another and the shadows of memory. Others do the same by constructing *ofrendas* at home or in public places—elaborate offering altars where those who have passed in the last year are honored.

Intuition and a working readiness

I need to come back to the job thing. Both hers and mine. For most of our life together, Jeanie had been the primary breadwinner. Initially, this stemmed from my history of war-tax resistance. Refusing to pay for war-making, I had lived largely below taxable income and continued to do so in the early years of our marriage. I was a househusband who pastored part-time and taught adjunct, wrote, and went to jail periodically.

Our life was great, but I did have the better part of the deal. In the year before her illness, Jeanie discerned that it was time to switch. This came clear from the hoop conversations. She was ready to slow her life down. To get out of the path of the dead-lines. She was looking to spend more time with her daughters, to savor beauty.

I could hardly argue. So I jumped when a job in Chicago found me. When Dave Frenchak, now of blessed memory, the president of SCUPE (Seminary Consortium for Urban Pastoral Education), called to offer me the M.Div. program director position, he prefaced, "I know you won't move to Chicago, but would you consider …"

Ironically, working in Chicago from Detroit meant I was able to do most of the administrative and prep work from our dining room table, and over the long haul, to give myself to Jeanie's care. I couldn't have had an employer more gracious when the demands of serial crises hit. Jeanie can't take credit for the intuition on this one, but she sure was wise to set it in motion.

As to her own work, certain key arrangements were made. In the effort of her inner work, Jeanie had also discovered the Enneagram, as already mentioned, and introduced me to it as well. Much of our exploration came from reading, but Jeanie also organized a couple of retreats for the full staff of *The Witness*.

Everyone came to self-identify with a personality type, and on that basis Jeanie altered job descriptions. She played to the staff's passions, built on their strengths and covered their weaknesses. The operation got reorganized to a degree.

Certainly the most significant change was turning Julie Wortman, the magazine's managing editor, into a co-editor and co-publisher. This move both suited her gifts and opened space for Jeanie to cut back. The board was wary, but acceded. By the time Jeanie collapsed on Labor Day weekend 1998, Julie was trained, set to go, and had her own future magazine issues slated. The place never paused a beat. Everything was in readiness.

Everything was in readiness when we were completely blindsided.

Before the mirror

Jeanie had been invited to a women's retreat in honor of a friend's 40th birthday. She'd waffled a bit on her commitment, and I now wonder if she wasn't, even then, having trouble making decisions. Over the summer, there had been times when she was sitting at her computer, trying to edit an issue, when she turned and said to me, "Oh Billy! I can't think!"

But in the end, she decided to go. When Lydia and I headed north to the cabin for a weekend with the Kellermann clan (Lucy was off elsewhere with friends), Jeanie was expecting to be picked up shortly by our friend Julie, so they could ride together. By the time the knock came at the door, Jeanie was already incapacitated, and Julie—aware of the earlier indecision—presumed she'd changed her mind or gone another way.

A strange confluence of factors was at work. Because Lydia and I assumed Jeanie was on the retreat, it never occurred to us to check in or inquire after her. The women on retreat wondered, and did try more than once to call, but without answer until late the next afternoon.

What happened with Jeanie, according to her memory, breaks my heart to think on. After Lydia and I departed, she was looking in the bathroom mirror when her right arm began to dance before her of its own accord, her thumb and first finger tight together in a pinch. She was having the first in a series of seizures.

The phone rang, but she couldn't get herself to answer it. She ended up on her hands and knees down on the floor. (We never saw bruises, so I take it this was by squat rather than crash.) There, she vomited and lay down.

When she woke, she crawled into the bedroom, got up into bed in the dark, laid down and threw up again on herself. The phone rang, and she could hear the voice of her best friend, Deb, on the machine. But again, she couldn't make the necessary decision to get her body there.

Next morning, she got up and went to the kitchen table. There she sat for hours, reading over and over and over a letter from Lucy's new teacher, and then fell asleep. It wasn't until she woke again to the voice on the phone machine that by an enormous act of will she was able to get herself there and pick up.

Her speech was slurred and her responses slightly incoherent. Deb offered reassurances, hung up, and promptly called Herb and Joan, neighbors with a key, who got to her straightaway. As they cleaned her up for the run to the hospital, they called us at the cabin.

With the ring of that phone, my life changed.

I'm going to suggest that it changed even more for Lydia. When she tells her spiritual journey, that call marks the beginning of her life, self-aware, in God. For that reason, I think I should let her tell it. In her own words. This account is from a "spiritual life talk" she gave in high school at a retreat.

In an instant seeing everything

> It was not until I was twelve years old that I finally woke up. It hit me so fast, I did not even see it coming. It put me into this space where suddenly I could see everything. I could see the past, I could see where I was, and I was terrified of the future. This was the moment when I finally made a decision to learn who I was, love who I was, and be who I was ...

September 1, 1998, my world changed forever. It was a beautiful, sunny day. It was Labor Day weekend, I was twelve years old. My eight-year-old sister had been invited to go to Cleveland with her best friend's family. My mother was going on a spiritual women's retreat.

So my dad and I went up north to our cabin. This cabin was a dream-come-true for my mother. We live in southwest Detroit, in a poor, rundown, busy little neighborhood. My mom longed for peace, quiet, neutrality, and earth. She would have loved for our family to move up there.

My cousins, uncles, aunts, and grandma came up to spend the weekend with us. I woke up that Saturday morning to a gorgeous day. It couldn't have been more beautiful. The sun was shining; it was warm with a nice breeze. Warm enough to go swimming in Lake Huron. We packed food, drinks, beach toys, towels, and headed down for a day at the beach. I swam in the waves all day. I conquered those waves with a giant smile on my face. I had no clue that my life was changing with every passing wave.

Mid-afternoon we packed up and went back to our cabin. My cousin and I decided that we wanted to go build a fort down by the stream, so I rushed to my room and began to change out of my bathing suit. The phone rang.

That moment is forever in my mind. I was half out of my bathing suit. There was laughing downstairs. Everyone was cracking up about something. My dad picked up the phone and said hello while trying to hide his laughter. My heart sank. Something was wrong. The conversation was short. I didn't get much information from listening. My dad said he was coming and he hung up the phone.

I ran downstairs half naked. My dad told my family that my mom had been taken to the hospital. They did not know why or what was wrong, but a neighbor found her and she could tell something was wrong, my mom was slurring her words. Slurring her words, slurring her words. That phrase must have gone through my head fifty times that day. My dad said that was all he knew.

He was in the process of packing. I told him I was coming too. My dad said no, I should stay here with his family and he'd call when he had any information. I started crying. My grandma tried to comfort me and told my dad I would be fine.

Our house was only an hour and a half away. But suddenly that distance seemed like it could not have been farther. I wouldn't be separated from my family and be left with my extended family, which suddenly felt so distant from me. I needed to be with my dad. I screamed at my dad. I said, "I am coming with you!"

My dad looked at me. We stared at each other for a few seconds. I'll never forget the look in his eyes that day. There was so much in those eyes. He was frustrated with me for being difficult. But there was more; deep within, there was fear of the unknown, the fear of the endless possibilities.

This would not be the last time that I would see this look, but rather the first. I think we knew that we needed each other at that moment. We needed each other's company for that short trip home, which seemed to last an eternity.

The whole way home we sat in silence, except when I would voice a question. A question that we were both thinking but I said out loud. I asked him questions over and over, as if I thought he knew the answers. He knew as little as I did.

I remember at one point I said, "I know this would be the worst, but do you think she could die?"

"I don't know, sweetie, I don't know."

After what seemed an eternity, we reached the hospital. We parked and both sprinted inside. Right outside the door were the two neighbors. They pointed the way to my mom.

My dad said, "Lydia, stay with them." I knew this time I couldn't argue. My dad ran so fast inside the electronic doors. I watched him disappear.

This began a period of waiting. We waited and waited and waited. After hours of sitting in the hall and making chitchat to hide our fears and the questions behind them, my dad came out. "She has a brain tumor. It may be cancerous."

That was it? It was not possible. I saw my mom the day before and she was perfectly fine. I began asking more questions. What's a tumor? What's cancer? I had heard these words in science class a couple times, but I had no idea what they meant.

My dad was tired; he didn't know what it all really meant, either. From that day on, I've learned more medical terms than I ever wanted to know. That day my world was turned upside down forever.

My mom went into surgery within two weeks. The doctors removed a tumor from her brain the size of an orange. And it was indeed cancerous, one of the most deadly kind. The doctors told us that at best we could expect six months for my mom to live.

In D.C. for an anti-war demonstration, Jeanie considers the
Potomac and the Pentagon. Credit: Family collection

6

Beyond Death's Grip

A Sacrament of Dying Well

Among my treasures, more precious now than ever, is a liturgical stole that Jeanie made and gave me as a present. A stole is an emblem of sacramental authority, a drape of cloth worn by one who presides in worship. This one is made of coarse, bleached linen and has seven square panels sewn to it, representing each of the seven sacraments.

There's almost a subtle joke of Catholic Episcopalianism at work—the faintest of smiles, or maybe a loving wink of ecclesial summons. You see, I am a Methodist pastor, and by tradition we celebrate only two sacraments: baptism and communion. Jeanie was an Episcopalian, and they do all seven, so she designed and embroidered an image for each.

Confession, or reconciliation, a hard one to convey, is represented by a cross entwined with a vine of lilies. Marriage (which, by the way, is the only sacrament that lay people do themselves) is shown by two candles lighting a single central marriage candle. Confirmation is portrayed by a fire, presumably Pentecost flames.

Ordination is demonstrated by a figure on whom hands are being laid—with a smaller flame burning above. Eucharist, or Holy Communion, is symbolized with a chalice and a broken host of bread above it. And baptism Jeanie portrayed with a scalloped seashell half submerged beneath a wave of waterline.

In the middle, at the place that sits right behind my neck— the place that a priest might kiss before putting on the stole—is extreme unction, or last rites. This, Jeanie represented with a face, eyes closed, with the sign of the cross upon the forehead. I want to say it looks like her in the end, with short cropped hair, but there is a line above the lips which might, in fact, be a mustache—my own?

Before going back to the keyboard just now, I kiss that sign of the cross and think of her own sweet brow. I put on the stole. Add me a sacramental eighth: call it "writing in tears."

On the face of it, last rites signals the church's commit- ment to dying well as a practice of faith. Plainly put, dying is embraced as a sacramental act within the faith community. No surprise that a tradition founded upon the death and life of Jesus should think as much. The shock is that we could so readily forget, that the echo should become so faint.

Jesus' execution was not pretty. It was brutal. But his death was free. No one took his life; he laid it down for his friends. He expected those who would be his disciples to take up that same freedom, not being bound by the power of death, or the fear of death—which is also to say, not bound by "the powers that be." That freedom is the secret of the resurrection.

In the Apostle Paul's version of this same thing, our radical freedom is predicated on the fact that we "already done died." In water and Spirit. We are baptized into the death of Jesus, and so into his life as well. Extreme unction for Christians, I suppose, is little more than another confirmation of our baptismal dying.

If this seems theologically opaque, think back and read on. See if Jeanie Wylie's saga in missives and the way of her death, never mind her life, don't slowly unpack this confession of faith.

Feel free to come back to it in the end and check. You may want to dog-ear this page.

To die well, to die sacramentally, in this culture virtually requires an act of resistance. Death is everywhere—not just in our hyped fear of random terror death or in our military projections around the planet, but in our streets and cul-de-sacs. Given the realities of global land-grabs, wars over oil, and polluting profit-driven corporations, it's also in the food we eat, the cars we drive, and the air we breathe. Death is everywhere—and so everywhere aggressively denied.

You think that doesn't affect the way we die? A good death is thoroughly preempted by American culture's deep anxiety about death, expressed as fear and denial. Put conversely, a truly good death subverts the culture at its worst.

Jeanie's story of healing finally turned into a story of dying. To understand the graces of both that healing and that dying, it would help to understand the community in which those graces (truly one, single, undivided grace) have been nurtured for us. The mentors who formed our family and community, who helped us to live well, also tutored us in dying well. Jeanie died so well, I want to think, because she was part of a community that tried its best to unmask the power of death, refusing both fear and denial.

Which cannot separate us

My own earliest connection to this community came by way of Peter Weber, who, along with Tom Lumpkin, Elaine Pero, and Mary West (all still connected to our community in one manner or another) had started a new Catholic Worker house in the same Detroit neighborhood after an earlier incarnation had passed from the scene. These four had traveled the country together, recipients the whole way of Worker hospitality, gathering in the stories and spirit of the movement. With this running start, they leapt on faith, committing to one another and to the works of mercy.

When I moved back to western Michigan with friends after seminary in 1975, we expected to be solitary voices crying out in a political wasteland—only to find a rich and simultaneous arising of nonviolent community across the state. Day House, whose name was a minor scandal to a few in the Worker movement—premature, as it were, since Dorothy Day yet lived—was the new Detroit hospitality house, and part of that arising. A few years later, when my community collapsed, I came to Detroit for solace and, yes, hospitality. I lived for several periods with Peter.

Hence, I was privy when he began with a circle of friends to discern a liturgical direct action to be done at the nuclear weapons facility in Rocky Flats, Colorado. It was first pulled together at a kitchen table by Ladon Sheats, a political mendicant who had heard the call to radical discipleship, quit his rising-star position at IBM, sold all he had, and gave it to the poor. Ladon was just beginning a life that would have a cyclical rhythm of travel, speaking, public action (generally praying in a place forbidden), a stretch of imprisonment, then contemplative life in a desert monastery, wherefrom to begin it all again.

Peter and friends signed on. Together they walked through the desert with Ladon into the weapons plant at daybreak. It's always hard to assess what success or effectiveness would mean with such an action of public prayer. It's like asking, was that an effective Eucharist? Efficacy is simply the wrong question to put.

Their prayer action certainly moved and encouraged us in Detroit as a budding community. And it helped to put Rocky Flats on the political map of nonviolent anti-nuclear protest, seeding an ongoing campaign of presence and action.

Peter did 30 days in jail, which he found difficult, even depressing, and returned home to the soup kitchen. He met Barbara, a teacher and musician who had just moved to Detroit, tender and quick to laugh, and he drew her immediately into our community orbit. They fell in love. They got engaged.

Two weeks later, suffering from pain in his shoulder, Peter was diagnosed with cancer—an aggressive fibrosarcoma that came with a prognosis of less than two years to live. He underwent surgery, declined the conventional regimens of radiation and chemotherapy, and pursued a series of alternative treatments and a macrobiotic diet. He enjoyed a two-year remission, but eventually the cancer returned, and before the end, his arm was amputated.

There were a few hushed wonderments about the cause of the tumor in the community. It was an oddly focused malignancy. Walking toward concentrated plutonium in the desert surely had its dangers, and these had been taken into account.

My own imaginings tended toward the more suspicious. Anti-nuclear activist Karen Silkwood had recently died in a mysterious car accident while organizing for safety standards at a plutonium processing plant in Oklahoma. An investigation revealed her home to be radioactively contaminated (things in the refrigerator and medicine cabinet being found quite "hot"). But I did not indulge in or circulate these fantasies.

Peter and Barbara married, mindful of the shadow upon him. I preached their wedding homily on the Beatitudes. For their vows, they adapted this text from Paul's Letter to the Romans: "For I am convinced that neither death, nor life, nor angels, nor rulers, nor things present, nor things to come, nor powers, nor height, nor depth, nor anything else in all creation, will be able to separate us from the love of God in Christ Jesus our Lord" (8:38).

It is a passage read aloud more frequently in the hospital or the funeral home than at a festive wedding. These two said more than "'Til death do us part." They claimed that neither death nor its minions could separate them. A bold and nervy faith.

Bolder still, when the remission came, they determined to get on with their ordinary lives and decided to have a child. David was a claim on the future and a reason to defend it. He was, in all likelihood, also an embodied faith intent about sticking around for the long haul. One thinks of the practice of the Hebrew prophets, naming their children as walking signs or messages. David might well have been called: There Is a Future.

When the cancer actively returned, Peter laid down a different provision for the future: He made videotapes for his son. One of their family, the three of them together. Another just of him and David, playing, holding, loving. And finally, one addressing David directly. All of these proved gifts immeasurable.

During the remission time, Peter was trained as a spiritual director. I think of this as an outgrowth of his earlier work as a draft counselor, when he helped young people come to the truth of their own consciences. He tutored them in the legalities and regulations of the system, in order to provide them not just options, but real freedom, in the face of military registration, with the attendant issues of death and its power. Spiritual direction was simply a broader and deeper version of that conversation: helping people find their center and spiritual footing.

No doubt it necessarily offered a formal framework for his personal inner work as well. (You can't properly encourage others to face their own heart and guts with God if you aren't at the same time navigating your own.) But beyond that, it opened the door to chaplaincy work at a local hospital, where he learned to tend the sick and dying. When the tumor reasserted itself, his ministry only deepened. Imagine pastoral care from someone at bedside, himself unabashedly ill and even looking death in the eye with resurrection freedom. This, in turn, blossomed into a speaking ministry for which he was well-positioned, giving talks on prayer and dying. He spoke until he could no more.

When the tumor returned, a handful of folks from our sister community, Church of the Messiah, began a weekly presence of prayer with him. Messiah was a fascinating Episcopal congregation on the east side of Detroit. It had gone through charismatic renewal, drawing a host of young white evangelicals into a mostly black and distressed neighborhood. In my own period of deep brokenness, I nearly cast my lot with them. I certainly wept in their midst and was washed in the sweet and healing tongues of their worship.

They lived with a community discipline of common income and property, and were drawn to the anarchist social commitments of the Catholic Worker community. Any naïveté or privilege they suffered was tempered by the long-haul presence demanded in rebuilding a neighborhood from the ground up, and also by the brutal and unsolved murder of member Michelle Rougeau, which their rector, Ron Spann, had fittingly termed an urban martyrdom.

Michael Lauchlan, then a builder and poet who was also Peter's best friend, gathered it up like this:

Elegy in April
For Michelle Rougeau (1952-1988)
And the St. Paul Housing Coop

> In our hunger for you we turn a corner
> full of guys wearing troop coats over .38s
> onto a street where remnant buildings
> gleam like the bared teeth of a dog,
> where you and yours bought shells of bricks,
> made homes together, made us
> love a geography we never wanted.
> In our hunger for you we enter a bloody room
> as a neighbor's child has before us,
> pushing open a familiar door to find you
> as the killer left you,
> your nurse's hands, theology,
> and delicate features—useless weapons—
> lying now in a new red pool.
>
> After the words and songs, the vacant
> smack, smack of hammers again echoes
> between houses as we walk heavily
> where you had lightly; and work starts up.
> What choice have we got, in our hunger,
> having bet our mortgages

on this piece of thirsty earth.
Honking begins among geese and trucks.
Sun rises. Elms, willows brighten.
A small boy in a red sweatshirt
carries a fishing pole to the river.
We peer into a corner of the sky
as though it is your face
hovering over the boulevard.
We peer into a corner of the sky
as though it is your face
hovering above the boulevard.

I report this to suggest that the weekly intercessors had not only the fervent spiritual exuberance of charismatics, but the chastened wisdom of those who know death as a lurking presence in the streets of history. I don't know if, with Peter, they shifted away easily from the doggedly steadfast expectation of the miraculous. But in the end, their beseeching yielded to bearing. If they could not prevent his crossing over, they would at least walk him to the very banks of the river.

Peter insisted on dying at home, and so was an early participant in the hospice movement. Tom stayed close, anointing him with last rites. Michael, and Peter's soup kitchen partner, Deborah McEvoy, who was an oncology nurse, stood by him and Barbara for the final weeks.

Here, I need to reinsert myself into the narrative with a confession. I wasn't as present as I now wish. I had stayed close in the first hospitalization, even facilitating some ameliorative escapades I forebear to mention. But in the end, I don't recall being fully there. Was it weak-heartedness? Or things between us? Or the sway of the culture and its ready deniability? I got the reports from Deb and Michael. I said my goodbyes and prayers, but I didn't hunker down and vigil. May I be forgiven it.

Deeper accompaniments did not fail him, however. As the pain increased in the final weeks, Peter, having taken recourse to morphine, was mostly mentally absent. Yet, Barbara reports being woken by him to two stunning moments of sudden lucidity.

In the first, he shook her awake, lest she miss the sight: "Do you see them? Do you see them? All around us, the angels and saints?" The other, equally abrupt in the wee hours, informed her, "I spoke with Kit [Concannon], and it's going to be the 9th." Barbara still wonders what heavenly event they arranged. Peter died on the 7th of May, 1987.

His funeral was in the same Church as their wedding, with in essence the same crowd that had pulled back the chairs and danced. The Romans text had a more familiar reading place, but it bore the vows along in trail. Michael exercised yet again his poet's vocation among us and preached.

We were a young community, already disabused of our own naïveté. Already looking death in the face. We were getting it early that acting in freedom from the powers of death and the freedom to die on the deathbed day were really one and the same.

The blood of the martyrs is the seed of the church, it is sometimes said. "Unless a seed fall to the ground and die ..." Something like that was now sown among us.

In a voice the richer for it

Another such planting was done by Julie Beutel. She is a teacher and musician with a sultry contralto voice that would have lent itself to a professional folk-singing career. She performs in local cafes and does concerts, but more often she sings for political demonstrations and community or liturgical events.

In 1984, she took her guitar and went to live and work for a time in Nicaragua with Witness for Peace. She was a long-term volunteer, establishing a presence in a little village called San Juan de Limay, laying the groundwork to welcome short-term delegations, and above all documenting human rights abuses by the Contras in detail. Jeanie and I saw her briefly on our trip as part of a short-term delegation to a different part of the country.

Julie's letters home made the situation in Nicaragua immediately personal. We learned to love people we had never met, including the children who flocked to her guitar, eagerly learning her songs (and vice versa). Most vivid in my memory was Tranquilino, with one son murdered and two others kidnapped by the Contras. He would stand on the road awaiting their return, then retire to his bed in tears.

Julie was constantly narrating funerals, exposing the deaths and teaching us how a community copes, or at least survives, in extremis. This from Christmas 1984:

> I've never seen so much death as I have the past three weeks ... Funerals all over town ... When people are killed so suddenly, there isn't time to get coffins. The bodies get wrapped in sheets and lie there while people sit around looking at them or saying the rosary or crying or spacing out or thinking. By 11:00 or 12:00 the bodies begin to stink. There's nothing they can do. The bodies decapitated start to smell sooner, of course ...

Jeanie recognized the value of the letters and knew instinctively they needed a wider circulation. With several people in the community, she set to work transcribing and laying them out for printing in a little booklet, with an artfully hand-drawn cover of Julie and her guitar. On certain occasions, Jeanie would draft a press release, handing reporters a deft lead and then providing a letter as raw material for a story.

One such occasion was just after the 1984 election, when President Ronald Reagan threatened air strikes against a Soviet ship docked off the Nicaragua coast, claiming that it contained MiG fighter planes. (It was loaded with tractors.) Witness for Peace members set up camp at Corinto Harbor, notifying Washington of American lives in the target zone. Julie was among the North Americans and journalists who boarded a boat to go out and meet the U.S. warship sending its threats just offshore of the harbor.

Another such moment was when Julie was kidnapped by the Contras in the summer of 1985. Another boat. This time taking a delegation up the Rio San Juan along the border with Costa Rica, territory rife with Contra violence.

There was reason to go, and reason to go with some trepidation: Eden Pastora, leader of the ARDE Contra faction active in the region, had announced that his soldiers would shoot to kill. Herb Gunn, another long-term Witness for Peace volunteer, gifted photographer, and Julie's husband-to-be, was monitoring the shortwave radio in Managua. The delegation called in to report being fired upon, ordered to beach and disembark.

The radio was left on, and the channel open to pick up subsequent events, which included angry commands followed by a burst that sounded like automatic weapons fire. Then silence. We feared that Julie and the others with her were dead. That silence went deep in us, another seed. Find the cost of freedom, buried in the ground.

The burst, thankfully it turned out, was probably radio static. The delegation was marched into the jungle at gunpoint by the Contra group. Their lives may have been saved by the headlines quickly generated in the United States. Network media helicopters filmed their release 24 hours later. One could only wish as much for Tranquilino and his sons.

One naïveté we suffered was failing to imagine the spiritual toll of such traumatic stress upon folks like Julie. We certainly understood it, such as we could, for the villagers of San Juan de Limay, but we underestimated it entirely for witnesses living with them and documenting atrocities. Julie lived amidst terrorism, not on the scale of the crashing towers of 9/11which have become its icon, but terrorism of a greater frequency and much higher odds. Constant and immediate.

In January 1985, Julie reported finding the body of Freddy, seventeen-year-old son of Tancho and Panchito, and brother to Pedro, who had been disappeared several days earlier, taken from a truck. Freddy's fingers and toes had all been fractured and his heels were worn, as if running on them with the toes broken.

Acid had been poured on his head, burning off his hair. His face was smashed, and other parts of his body showed marks of being beaten with the butt of a gun or similar object. Two bullets to the forehead had finally killed him. At his funeral, Julie cried hard—for the first time in Nicaragua.

First tears in a year! How many more blinked back or stilled at their source? When Julie and Herb returned to the States and married, the culture was almost too much to bear. They knew its price firsthand and the death it masked. The war zone had intensified their romance, but even more exacted its toll on their lives.

The marriage failed. Julie has consciously attended to her inner work, but to this day she has chronic ailments that I associate with her trauma. Her voice is perhaps more beautiful than ever, bearing the resonance of those backed-up tears.

From the impulse to forgive

Another death profoundly affected our community. Susie Jaeger, just seven years old, was kidnapped from her family's camping tent in Montana in 1973 and in the next few weeks brutally murdered—though the latter was not known for more than a year. Susie was youngest of a large Catholic family from Detroit.

Her mother, Marietta Jaeger, was devout, and through the rages of the ensuing year wrestled with God in her devastation. Though she could have (and given opportunity, would have) killed her daughter's murderer with her bare hands, she somehow knew the Gospel laid a contradiction upon her. If she took the Scriptures seriously, was she called in any sense to love this enemy? Even to forgive him? She began to pray for the kidnapper. And her heart began to open.

As the one-year anniversary of the abduction approached, she let it be known in a newspaper interview that she wished she could speak with him about what he had done. On the day precise, he called—to taunt her. But she disarmed him utterly by

asking how he was feeling, knowing his act must have placed a
heavy burden on his soul.

Taken aback, he cried. They talked for an hour, and later
again, in the course of which he revealed, in hints and clues,
enough information for the FBI to piece together his identity
and location. Marietta never did get to meet the man face to
face (he hanged himself in his cell shortly after arrest), but she
was indeed able to forgive him, freeing her own soul from the
grip of vengeance. And who knows? Even perhaps his own.

It was a forgiveness that would touch our community and
circles far wider. Marietta began giving talks around Detroit.
Repeating her story over and over was certainly part of her
grieving and healing. But it also functioned for others as a parable of the Gospel, which set moving all sorts of reverberations,
personal and communal.

I think among us Peter Weber had first heard tell of her. It
wasn't long before she was recounting her spiritual journey to
us in a packed session at the Catholic Worker house. This was
when we were thick in the liturgical direct action campaign at
the suburban cruise missile engine plant.

It was a leap for Marietta to connect personal forgiveness
with active public nonviolence. She pushed us to think more
deeply about the personal power of forgiving love, and we
pushed her to think more broadly about its political significance.
She wrote a poignant 1983 memoir titled *The Lost Child*, and
more recently she reflected:

> *If I have to forgive the kidnapper of my little girl, then
> it is not right for me to bomb an enemy nation. The
> same principles that apply to us on a personal level are
> also operative on a larger, global scale. I talk about the
> entire spectrum to help understand forgiveness from
> a different perspective: of the ways of the world, the
> way of our own flesh, and the way of the powers and
> principalities that so often hold sway in our spirits.*

At some point, Marietta and Jeanie ended up together in jail, where their friendship was forged. Marietta moved into the neighborhood and established a lively street and community ministry all her own. She quickly gained a reputation among us as a powerful and Spirit-tuned intercessor, someone you'd want in your prayer corner come spiritual crisis. More than once, Jeanie and I sat with her over life discernments and her help availed.

Meanwhile, Jeanie hired her part-time at *The Record* to manage circulation, and eventually took her along for the same task when *The Witness* door opened, so they became daily co-workers over several years. Wherein a further providence. Just down the hall from *The Record* at diocesan headquarters was the office of the Michigan Coalition for Human Rights. Lucy's godfather and one of the best organizers in the city, Tom Fentin, was its director.

At the time, a rightwing prosecutor was launching a campaign to put the death penalty on the ballot of a state referendum. Ironically, Michigan was the first state in the nation to constitutionally abolish the death penalty in the first official act of its legislature in 1846. A notorious hanging several years earlier in Detroit, which had been treated as a festival event, with invitations and bleachers, vendors and brass bands, figured into the political wisdom of that decision.

Standing on the gallows, the condemned man was offered the opportunity of last words. In a baritone voice, he hushed the crowd by singing a plaintive hymn beseeching forgiveness: "My crimes are great, but can't surpass/The power and glory of Thy grace./Great God, Thy nature hath no bound,/So, let Thy pardoning love be found." Whereupon, the trap beneath abruptly opened, and his neck was snapped. The crowd, eyes suddenly opened, turned away in shame and self-disgust, but the event lived in a legislature's memory.

Marietta began to tell this story frequently and in considerable detail. She worked part-time with Jeanie and then walked up the hall to work her other part-time job with Tom, as the campaign was cranked up to stop the referendum. Even more to the point, for the first time in her life, she told her own story publicly, not just as a spiritual journey of God's reconciling love, but openly, even politically, on behalf of those convicted.

The referendum never made the ballot, and Marietta's spiritual journey took a turn into a honing of her vocation. She became an articulate and, given her experience, almost irresistible advocate for those on death row. In the coming years, as part of a national movement, she would co-found Murder Victim Families for Human Rights and it offspring, a traveling campaign called Journey of Hope from Violence to Healing. She entered the Amnesty International orbit and has been flown halfway round the planet to tell again, through translation, Susie's story and her own.

Dying well means naming death, and facing death, in freedom and grace. There will be other names for it, but I call it the freedom of the Gospel. Check the dog-eared page: Jesus calls disciples to take up his freedom, not being bound by the power of death, or the fear of death, which is also to say, not bound by "the powers that be."

At the very least, that means not suffering the constant state of denial that the culture foists upon us, the perpetual flight from death that really ends up giving it pride of place in everything. Peter and Julie and Marietta helped us as a community to recognize that freedom in diverse and multiple ways—even in our failings, our gropings in the dark. And they prepared us to face what lay ahead.

On Block Island with Stringfellow scholar Uncas McTenia, summer 1995.

7

Mentors in Resurrection

Daniel Berrigan: Should guardian angels peel away

I believe I first came across the notion of "dying well" in a book by Dan Berrigan called *We Die Before We Live*—the order of things being important to him. It's fair to say, though this would be fair for many, that Berrigan was also a mentor to our community.

He had taught a course in the late 1970s at the University of Detroit, which Peter and Mary had more or less officially taken, and he effectively nudged the Day House journey onto the road. He also periodically passed through among us, giving talks or leading Bible study, often as not in connection with the underground seminary doings.

In that same period, he was volunteering at St. Rose's hospice for the dying in Manhattan—specifically, the dying poor with cancer. Of course, he made the contextual political links—they were built whole cloth into the fabric of his life. He recognized Hiroshima as the emblem of unleashed fallout in culture, history, planet. Genes corrupted by the poisoning of water and air was simply to be seen as the ailment of this world. Cancer? They declare war on that, too.

The targeting of civilians in the atomic bombing flowed from the longtime casting off and casting out of the poor. All one in the poison plutonium of the war god, Mars. And in response, like Camus' doctor in *The Plague*, Dan simply set out to do what humanity, plain and simple, required: tend the victims as a way of saying no to the executioners.

Berrigan also told their stories. *We Die ...* reads partly like a journal, feeling his way forward in the hospice halls. Learning the clumsy arts of touch or silence or a word, even prayer. But largely the book collects vignettes, accounts of the dying, their ways and faces.

Dan had been led to St. Rose's by a young Catholic Worker serving there as an orderly. I venture to imagine the influence of the Worker here in a further way. Going back to the days of Dorothy, the New York Worker paper had a practice, picked up by others around the country, of eulogizing guests who would ordinarily cross over in blank and nameless obscurity. Often as not, sizing up characters fit for a Dickens novel, these descriptions could be funny and heroic and quirky, but above all, honest and loving. I always read them. And I know the style crept into my own approach to doing funeral liturgies.

I've concluded that if you find the Gospel in someone's story only by smoothing the facts, then it's really less than the Gospel and actually less than truly human as well. Consider how much of conventional burial liturgy is taken up with smoothing and fluffing as denial. Or saying, in effect, nothing at all. Face-painting a corpse. Anyway, I think the humor, poignancy, and refusal to look away, evinced by these tales in Dan's book of the dying, owe something to that Worker literary genre.

Jeanie once prevailed on him to recount a coastal Irish burial to which he'd been present for an issue of *The Witness* on "grieving rituals," no less. It was at the Block Island cottage over broiled swordfish, as I recall (Dan is a wonderful cook and gracious host). I'm afraid it really was a bit of prevailing.

I had previously recorded interviews with him for projects on Stringfellow. Just that morning, I had overcome his reticence to be filmed and got him to tell the tale, on the hill where it happened, about the FBI's stakeout of Bill's home and the arrival of agents disguised as birdwatchers to arrest Dan there at the end of his notorious underground journey in 1969.

Anyway, I must have cashed in a few friendship chips and even said something like, "I'll never ask you to do one of these again." Because when Jeanie pulled out the tape recorder and made her request, he quipped, "When does never begin?"

Berrigan and I once talked of our own deaths. That was also at the cottage on Block Island. Under doctor's orders, he had switched from scotch to vodka, so I was being introduced to Manhattans, dry.

Beneath my questions, I suppose, was my longstanding presumption that his potent truth-telling put him at risk from crazies and the powers behind them. But then, can you believe he lived to be nearly 95, watching so many dear ones falling around him. In some sense, it's amazing to me that he's survived the times to such an age.

I brought up the absurdity of Albert Camus' death by car crash and confessed my own presumptuous desire for "a meaningful death." To my embarrassment and greater pleasure, he later summed up the exchange in a poem:

> Drinking one night, Kellermann and I
> talked the moon down, 'Think of mad racers
> we're at the mercy of
> And stuttering engines of air craft
> so high the guardian angels peel away—
> Then street knifings. And bloody so on.
> It's certain we exist
> courtesy of bellicose junkers, by merest
> suffrance.'
> Significant death?
> Gold leaf of history, cosmetic
> on a split skull.

That appears in a little-known book of his called *Block Island Poems*. Its writing was part and parcel of his own griefwork over Stringfellow's death. I suppose I take some cues from that in my own writing here on Jeanie's.

The keeper's mantle

Jeanie and I were with Dan when Stringfellow died in March of 1985. It was I who conveyed the word. I recall receiving it over the pay phone at an Episcopal camp in Michigan and going straight to his room with the news. My voice cracked in the telling, but apart from that spare emotional display, we simply sat in silence for a while. Neither of us was shocked, as in a sudden surprise, but you know the shock one's spiritual system takes in any event.

Each of us, on different occasions, had been to his bedside in the weeks prior. I had dropped everything and hopped a plane when news of his dire straits arrived, sparing no expense in the haste and flying to the coast from the Providence airport by prop plane. He was in an ICU all intubated and plugged in, but conscious. Only his eyes were available for conversation.

I declared my thanks and love in the plainest terms and sat down on a stool to read him some psalms. Accidently, from the *Book of Common Prayer*, I suddenly found myself intoning, "Precious in the sight of the Lord is the death of his saints." (Ps 116:15) He stiffened, his eyes fired, and he shook his head *no*. His hour, apparently, had not come and his fight was not yet exhausted.

I was struck deeply by this. There is no theological interpreter, in word or life, more articulate than William Stringfellow about the Christian freedom to die. That, for him, was synonymous with the fact of resurrected life. And yet, that freedom is one with not giving up, with the freedom to fight for life.

Bill is my mentor in these, as in other matters of faith. I feel free to lean heavily on him here, because he was as well for our community. It would be unfair to say that everyone read him. He can be—and some do not hesitate to point this out—a daunting read. But a number of us were studying him, and like Dan, he had passed through on occasion, opening our minds to the Scriptures. In any given Sunday evening homily at the Worker, I'm as likely to bring his theological voice to bear as Martin Luther King Jr.'s or Dorothy Day's.

I suppose that look in his eye figured into a subsequent decision we made to move him to the big university hospital in Providence. Jim Wallis had since arrived. Along with Dan Wetmore, another young friend of Bill's, we collaborated in arranging the move, chasing behind the ambulance in the night and talking our way in behind him at the hospital by claiming to be his sons, a deception we thought not all that far from the truth.

By the time I left, he was out of intensive care and into a regular room decorated with his beloved circus posters. Dan's last visit was some weeks later in the same room. He bore along a forbidden substance: ice cream. Bill's last dish from a cardboard cup.

Upon news of his death, I made straight for the Island to assist in funeral preparations. Dan returned home to New York City and came a few days later. Jeanie arrived just in time for the service.

Because of Stringfellow's notoriety, the funeral was the sort of event covered by the *Providence Journal*, with photos and quotes from attendees. His Bible, held together with layers of red MyStik tape, was brought forward to the altar with the gifts. I read the Gospel from Luke 24, the resurrection account of the two disciples on the road to Emmaus. I was doing fine 'til I got to the line about how as they walked, he opened their minds to the Scriptures.

Berrigan's homily was, quite simply, one of Berrigan's homilies: trenchant, poignant, inspired. He gathered up Stringfellow's role in East Harlem, and on the Island, and even in their friendship, as one of being faithful, of being a non-betrayer. This latter transformed into a refrain: He was a "keeper of his word." A keeper of The Word. The service concluded with what for

Stringfellow would have been a signal of resurrection, or at least of eschatological hope: calliope music.

Jeanie, let it be said, was not entirely at ease. Our honeymoon, less than a year prior, offered her the chance to know and dearly love Bill, but also, recall, to surmise the male ethos. All that reprised for her again at the funeral, where his "sons" seemed so intent on inheriting the mantle. Things in her view, as she wrote in a long postmortem letter, were "overly certain of right choices, overly mentor/junior successor." She probably named it right.

Flags at half-staff

Block Island was, at least in the off-season, a relatively small community—about 400 people. Stringfellow was a participant in any number of Island funerals. He and Anthony attended them eagerly as vehicles for the recounting of Island lore.

If he was himself speaking in such connection, he was an advocate of complete honesty in the face of death. I recall he preached at Norma's funeral. She was a classic Block Island character: a client of his in minor legal matters, but truly a friend; an Islander of the old credentials; owner of a farm up Corn Neck Road; and when I knew her, a taxi driver ferrying tourists around in a big unwieldy Cadillac. She was also an alcoholic. And Bill said so out loud at the Baptist Church funeral.

His naming it was truly a service in a variety of ways. Alcoholism is the classic disease of denial. People are prepared to be quiet enablers right through the memorial. A shared and comfy silence reigns to the end. Bill broke that by uttering simple truth. He also named it aright as an Island ailment, unduly common in the lonely places of a Block Island winter.

Bill and Anthony used to read the obituaries in *The New York Times*. They were also flag aficionados. They had in their possession a rather thorough collection of Revolutionary and pre-Revolutionary flags, which they flew from a pole on their front lawn, the highest point on the Island. One could go so far as to say that they regarded raising a flag as akin to daily intercession.

Funny story there. Down the hill and next door to them, "The Commodore," whose politics were entirely at cross purposes to their own, regarded their flags as subversive. It was The Commodore who had allowed the FBI agents to place directional surveillance microphones on his property, monitoring Stringfellow's dining room window during the underground search for Dan Berrigan. His place was made available to them on the premise that they were the FBI and could do anything they damn well pleased.

He saw these odd flags, "Don't Tread on Me" and the like, as being Viet Cong emblems, or worse. His nephew, however, looked close and opened up some books to demonstrate that they were nothing less than historic American flags. Whereupon The Commodore became convinced that Bill and Anthony were really, after all, flag experts.

So when Margaret Rutherford, the great British actress, turned up one morning over a breakfast reading of the obituaries, Bill ventured that they ought to fly the flag at half-staff for the day. When Anthony returned to the table having accomplished the honor (or intercession, as it were), they observed The Commodore come out and lower his own flag to half-staff as well.

Beneath the bleed of water marks

Stringfellow's obituary in *The New York Times* was concise and accurate, after the manner of *The Times*. He had secretly fretted about it. He and Anthony had bought their house when the Island was yet undiscovered by New Yorkers and property still went quite reasonably. Over the years, however, the overdevelopment that he was unable to forestall had rendered property values irrational.

Bill was forced to sell off portions of the land just to pay certain taxes, and the assessed value kept rising. He lived hand to mouth, was in debt all his life—in the end still paying on a

30-year mortgage. But he was fearful that beyond any scope of his own control, *The Times* would end up reporting that poverty lawyer William Stringfellow had died a millionaire. Thankfully, not so.

A year later, the burial of his ashes convened a gathering of friends on the Island. A party was had. Berrigan cooked a great and glorious meal. The ashes were interred on the cottage lands by the cliff. The event also occasioned the moving of Anthony's ashes from the foot of the flag pole on the main property, which had, in the meantime, been sold. The "cremains" of both were set side by side next to the stone wall. Wallis and I dug.

For many years, a small sculpture, now overgrown with a gnarled pine, marked the spot. But inside the cottage was a plaque that reads: "Near this house the remains of William Stringfellow and Anthony Towne await the Resurrection. Alleluia." Indeed.

Stringfellow left me his Bible as my inheritance in his will—a cherished gift. I also have in my possession a little booklet that belonged to him, entitled *Exorcism: The Report of a Commission Convened by the Bishop of Exeter*. It introduced and published an ancient rite that he had acquired and first utilized to publicly exorcise President Nixon on the eve of his second inauguration. (Stringfellow was later not surprised when Nixon's administration began unraveling at the seams.)

Perhaps more to the point, Bill employed it again with a small circle of friends to banish from the place of his household the presence of death after Anthony passed in 1980. (It later figured into a service of healing and passage for sweet Jeanie herself.) Stringfellow considered these liturgical events neither spooky nor weird, but in fact enjoyed regarding them with deadly seriousness as inherently political, while in practice having specifically to do with pastoral care and healing.

Where the prayers in the booklet name "the devil" or "the enemy," his own hand had consistently altered the text, substituting "death" or "the power of death" (which he accounted a "living moral reality"). These are synonyms he would also likewise transpose back into his own baptismal vows—or any-one's, for that matter.

Baptism specifically has about it elements of exorcism. In his reading, that would be, "Do you renounce the power of death and all its works?" For William Stringfellow, this foundational rite of redemption and ministry celebrated freedom from the power of death—indeed from the principalities and powers of this world.

As it happened, during the exorcism of the house, a brewing storm blew in. Stringfellow noted the portent, but read on undeterred. As Berrigan put it, "The demons were all warm and cozy by the fire inside, and there we were stranded in the down-pour." Where Bill had made the changes in the booklet, the bleeding water marks of the rain still testify to this day.

A book of griefs

An account of that event, and I believe the Nixon exorcism as well, is told in *A Simplicity of Faith: My Experience in Mourning*. I'd be hard-pressed to name Stringfellow's most important book, but not his most beautifully written. That would be *Simplicity*, hands down. Personal and poetic.

I was on the Island for a bit the summer he was writing it. He read me sections. They received my unqualified endorsement. My signal contribution, modest in the extreme, was in the part on prayer. He was sitting at a picnic table on Harbor Beach and was trying to generate a list of things that prayer is *not* and turned to me for my qualified assistance. It's one of the few topics on which I feel adequate to hold forth.

In another wonderment of irony and providence, that book is dedicated to me. It's hard to say just what a gift that is. And it strikes me this moment how much of its spirit and style may be subconsciously inspiring my writing here, the shape of this very book. It too is partly pieced together from assorted texts: poetry, talks, letters. It is autobiography and spiritual memoir. It takes the form of narrative theology and political critique. It is a reflection on death and dying, personal and political.

The first book of Stringfellow's that I read, in high school, was also about death—theologically and in the culture. It was called *Instead of Death*, and he had to fight for the title. The publisher was convinced that from a marketing perspective, it would be a downer, dead in the water. But Bill was not about to let death go unnamed. Or permit cultural denial to banish the true topic from the cover page. Happily, he prevailed.

Simplicity is also a book about a place: Block Island, its landscape, its character and characters. As I think about it, the book also, at least in premonition and foresight, concerns the dying of a place, under the assault of economic and commercial powers.

Lydia and Lucy still love to go there, and we took our last family vacation on the Island—bit of a risk, given Jeanie's dicey medical straits at the time. Hmmm ... from first summer to last, from honeymoon to final hurrah, the place framed our marriage. But even in that time, it has become but a shade of itself. Cedarshake sepulchers.

Simplicity is a book about Anthony Towne, and about their life together, which Bill regarded as monastic in temperament and vocation. In point of fact, they were partners in every respect, including culinary, literary, theological, liturgical, political, and romantic. The closest he comes to saying the latter outright is to call Tony his "sweet companion for seventeen years."

When Anthony died, Bill inherited by will his half of the property ownership. This was slightly ironic, since Anthony never really had any resources or income to speak of, Bill being the breadwinner of the two. The irony turned bitter, since Bill had to pay inheritance tax. It was this tax bill that forced the sale of the meadow, now developed.

"This wouldn't have happened if we were married," said Bill. He was right. And that is only one of the indignities such partners regularly face upon the death of one.

Because of his complicated ailments, everyone, including the two of them, assumed that Bill would go first and that Anthony would be a caregiver in the long haul home. Instead, Anthony went quite suddenly, though not without premonition. He left an obituary, written with a light touch in the parodied style of *The Times*. And he also undertook a short autobiographical piece in the months just prior. I recall a one-liner from the bio: "Life is a series of catastrophes, only the last of which is fatal."

His most notorious piece was another obituary, written after the fashion of *The Times*, this one for God. He'd been reading the Death of God literature, then current, and had found it worthy of satire. The scathing tongue-in-cheek piece was his response. The theologians were all attending physicians, duly quoted, pronouncing God dead of "an over-enlarged *omnipotens*."

In the end, however, *A Simplicity of Faith* is less about dying well than it is about an experience of mourning. Stringfellow made a distinction between grief and mourning. I'll take the liberty to quote him at length:

> *I understand grief to be the total experience of loss, anger, outrage, fear, regret, melancholy, abandonment, temptation, bereftness, helplessness suffered privately, within one's self, in response to the happening of death. By distinction and contrast, I comprehend mourning as the liturgies of recollection, memorial, affection, honor, gratitude, confession, empathy, intercession, meditation, anticipation for the life of the one who is dead.*
>
> *Empirically, in the reality of someone's death, and in the aftermath of it, grief and mourning are, of course, jumbled. It is, I think, part of the healing of mourning to sort out and identify the one from the other.*
>
> *In any case, of all those I have known and loved and grieved and mourned, Anthony's life was the closest to my own, and the most complementary, so his death is my most intimate experience in grief and mourning. From that experience—so far—what I have to say is:*

grieving is about weeping and wailing and gnashing of teeth; mourning is about rejoicing—rejoicing in the Lord. From that standpoint, I confess I have found mourning Anthony an exquisite, bittersweet experience. I enjoy mourning Anthony. (p. 22)

Need I say that, in this light, in this book, I enjoy mourning Jeanie?

Nelson and Joyce Johnson: Of the Word and in the World

I've already mentioned the collaboration of Dan Berrigan and William Stringfellow on the underground seminary that formed my vocation in so many ways and into which Jeanie was late drawn. For years after its demise, various ones of us, at this gathering or that, would intone a desire to resurrect this school of discipleship. The yearning was repeated so often that it was in danger of becoming a joke. In January 2001, a retreat was convened in Detroit to consider the prospect. Jeanie was there, already walking wounded.

What a wondrous and odd-lot collection of folk we were: Catholic Workers, hip-hop poets, retreat center directors, youth and community organizers, mendicant movement scholars, street actors and preachers, magazine editors and freelance writers, seminarians and professors with a foot on the margin, theologians, spiritual directors, jazz and gospel singers, movement veterans, convicted felons, and urban pastors.

Among them were Joyce and Nelson Johnson of the Beloved Community Center in Greensboro, North Carolina. I should say a bit about them. They had been organizers in the freedom struggle and become increasingly Marxist in their analysis and practice. In the late '70s, they were part of a cadre that was organizing workers across racial lines in the textile mills. That meant being up against the Klan and its threats, hidden and open. When they organized a "permitted" labor march in November 1979 from the housing projects to the university, a caravan of

Nazi and Klansmen, including a police informant/collaborator, drove in with trunks full of weapons and opened fire, killing five of their dearest friends and closest allies. Nelson was wounded and held one of his friends as the life went out of him.

Though the marchers were unarmed, the official narrative portrayed this as a shoot-out between outside groups and Nelson, in particular, was vilified and attacked. His only welcome was in certain black churches and that prompted, in effect, a gradual conversion. He rediscovered Jesus as he told Elaine Enns. "I saw dimensions of Jesus I hadn't noticed before: how he confronted people and challenged systems of oppression. Because church-talk about crucifixion is overly theologized, I had never realized that the cross was a consequence of Jesus' political resistance. I wanted to know what sustained Jesus in his ministry, and how his sense of reality transcended the status quo. He had a certain unshakeable confidence that while things of our world may come and go, there is a greater force at work, and even death cannot bring it to an end. I was comforted by that and felt called into this way of being."

Nelson went to seminary and developed into one powerful preacher. I never hear him without coming to tears. He can make me weep preaching on "the name of Jesus." With Joyce he founded Faith Community Church and the Beloved Community Center. Their work ongoing, often involving faith and labor, is among the most consistently non-violent work I know.

All this is to say, that while I might tell the underground seminary pre-history of the Bonhoeffer-Berrigan-Stringfellow thread of resistance, he and Joyce would trace a movement stream through the freedom and citizenship and labor schools of direct action. Yet others came to the circle having been awakened by the fierce and whimsical pedagogies of Christian feminism, including the struggles for womenchurch and for ecclesial inclusion of sexual minorities. And still others arrived among us, walking the path of liberation theology, tutored and tested in the base community movement, in which the language of preference is Spanish and the pedagogy entails a risky cycle of action and reflection.

These were not tidy, but overlapping and echoing stories—ones that resonated, each in its own way, with the biblical narrative that we held in common esteem. So for that very reason we spent time doing Bible study together. One evening, an astonishing session, was prompted by an obscure and appended passage from 2 Samuel (I swear I'd never read it before) about the grief of Rizpah for her sons publicly impaled and tortured.

We found ourselves hearing from one another accounts of grief and death: think of the comrades bloodied by Klan bullets dying in one's arms, and then add death row inmates, befriended in constant visitation, executed by the state before our very eyes; others more distant, disappeared and tortured out of sight by death squads, or by gang violence in streets close by; and yet other friends (count Jeanie in this number) suffering the slower but relentless assaults of cancer. We were suddenly and abruptly a community of grief and solace, a community that had felt the shadow, one that was beset by death and yet lived. A wide community knowing crucifixion and practicing resurrection.

In retrospect, even writing this, I see how important that was for seeding the "schools" we organized. We determined to do weeklong village institutes, in different locations around the country, one for each of the movement streams I've just hinted above. The idea was to connect those movements, while at the same time connecting three things so often separated: the seminary, the sanctuary, and the streets.

As it happened, the first school, focused on the civil rights struggle, was in Greensboro, in April 2002. The Beloved Community Center hosted. To plan it, we gathered in Greensboro on November 2, the very anniversary of the massacre.

We were joined by Vincent and Rosemarie Harding, genuine elders in the freedom struggle. Vincent, an eminent movement historian, was a close colleague of Dr. King. Rosemary was a teacher—what people call an "old soul," deep in wisdom, with an instinct for the ancient ways. Both have since crossed over to God. When we gathered at the gravestone of the five murdered activists, not far from where they were gunned down, Rosemary poured a libation of water upon the earth, in what I regard as the true founding moment of "Word and World." Ase.

At Vincent's urging, we formed the itinerant schools as national/local collaborations in which local movement history was central to the week's Bible study and social analysis. So at Greensboro, participants in the first student sit-in for desegregation in 1960, pastors like Nelson who participated in a more recent Kmart labor struggle (a successful community-based version of what we tried with the newspapers in Detroit), and above all, those present to the 1979 massacre were front and center to our listenings. At the very least, we honored the stories, so as not to lose them for future generations.

However, the school coincided with and effectively furthered the beginning of a Community Truth and Reconciliation process, examining the Greensboro massacre in detail and producing a report. That effort, initiated and shepherded substantially by Nelson and Joyce, has been momentous in so many ways. It offered the city an opportunity to heal from a twisting wound that goes far deeper than 1979. It was the first such process in the United States, which means that it was being watched and supported not only across the world, but in many places in this country that were then beginning to imagine how a Truth and Reconciliation process might look on their own history in their own locale.

In the course of Jeanie's illness, we managed to pull off Word and World schools in all four movement-theological traditions—in Greensboro, Tucson, Philadelphia, and Rochester—as well as a weekend "mini-school" in Minneapolis focused on William Stringfellow—Jeanie's last. I mention these because you'll see them reflected in the letters to come.

Also reflected are various members of the founding board of Word and World. Among them, Nelson and Joyce, Kazi Joshua,

Rosemary Berger, Joyce Hollyday, Ched Myers and Elaine Enns. Since this circle and history coincided precisely with the course of Jeanie's illness, the regular meetings and the schools marked a wider community of accompaniment. And more than that, the spiritual and political agenda of my own ministry was set and discerned in those gatherings.

Jeanie was present at most all of them, which was absolutely wonderful and bitterly excruciating, almost in equal parts. Her presence generally meant that I had my hands full, not only with teaching or leading, but with the unique logistical details that her care entailed.

But more to the point, in an earlier time she herself could have been teaching, planning, and administering those events with a Jeanie Wylie flair of imagination. I am mindful of all the conversations at the edge of which she sat, but never fully entered into. Yet, even so, she loved being there and was thoroughly loved in return. Her presence was highly valued, not merely for her love and grace, but for her truth-telling. Her illness was license for breaking the bonds of politeness—though she hardly needed cover for that.

I've had several people recall to me a dinnertime when a participant who was a good singer, but featured herself a self-appointed music leader for the school, began a singing table grace. Word and World's village sense of personal responsibility encourages this very sort of thing, but our friend had chosen one of those zipper tunes in which one word can be changed in each verse to make the song continue, theoretically, almost forever—and this one was threatening so. No one seemed prepared to challenge this relentless musical self-absorption. Finally, between verses, Jeanie cried out, "Someone make it stop!" And it did. In a sigh, everyone breathed thanks, smiled amen, and ate.

Since Jeanie's death, we've also convened a school in Tarheel, North Carolina, in support of striking Smithfield plant workers, at which Rev. William Barber, since of the Moral Mondays Movement and the New Poor Peoples Campaign, joined us. The local historical grist for our spiritual and pedagogical mill in the

latter was the sanitation workers' strike in 1968, which Martin
Luther King Jr. had gone to Memphis to carry forward. Both of
these schools were strategic support for a Southern Faith, Labor,
and Community and Coalition which Nelson effectively conceived and organized.

In Memphis, we heard testimonies from participants in the
historic strike and joined workers at the gates of local plants. We
walked through the National Civil Rights Museum there, where
(please do go sometime) you trace the rich history through
panels of photos, through lunch counters and the burned hulks
of buses. Finally, it leads to a sanitation truck and details of the
workers' struggle.

With the sound of Dr. King's Mason Temple mountaintop
speech in your ears—that sermon about his freedom to die—
you turn a corner, and there you are literally in a room of the
Lorraine Motel. You walk to the window and look upon the
balcony spot where he requested "Precious Lord" at the evening
service and turned to take the bullet. By then I suspect your
heart will be pounding and you'll begin to weep.

After our visit, outside the museum, a savvy friend of mine
said, "Walking through this place always seems too much like a
funeral." Perhaps. But fact is: We didn't go to Memphis for no
funeral. We went looking for resurrection.

That school marked the time, once again at Nelson and
Joyce's behest, that we'd connected our study and analysis to
a concrete plan of action, to a partnership with faith, labor,
and community. To an alliance that was a strategy for move-
ment-building in the South. Nelson brought us right to the
point: "What if the history of suffering and death were seen as
a treasure to be unlocked and released on behalf of the nation?"
Release it indeed.

John Wesley: Justification and the morbid fear

This will seem to some a strange connection, so bear with me.
Another movement personage and voice I want to invoke is John
Wesley. The 18th-century founder of the Methodist movement

which became my church, is decidedly not a mentor of our
community as such—though he could be if Catholics knew him
better. Jeanie liked Wesley. To his death, he was an Anglican
priest and so a kind of ecclesial bridge between our traditions.
As the founder of a renewal movement in England, he even has
a feast day in the *Book of Common Prayer*. And I should remind
you it was an article on Wesley to which she plied her editorial
rigors, prompting that emotional tussle during our engagement.

I am myself an "adopted" child of Wesley. I was raised EUB
(Evangelical United Brethren—a branch of German pietism),
but they merged with the Methodists in the '60s and I was led
to discover Wesley in seminary. Certain things I love about him
are personal and trivial: his large parsonage family and special
closeness with his brother Charles, or the botched and bungled
romantic episodes. Some affections are more substantial: his
struggle with ordination (he regarded Anglicanism being a
national church, and of course eventually an imperial one, as
patently unbiblical), his building a movement among the urban
poor who had been abandoned by that very church, the gutsy
field and street preaching, all his practical theology written on
the move (generally by horseback) and set down in plainfolk's
language, the strident polemical leaflets and pamphlets—notoriously plagiarized, improved, and circulated hand to hand, his
genius, of course, for organizing (from which methods the
budding labor movement partly learned), and his willingness
to bring his church movement into the service of abolitionism.
Here is, in fact, what he says to the investors in the slave trade:

> *Now, it is your money that pays the merchant, and
> through him the captain and the African butchers.
> You therefore are guilty, yea, principally guilty, of
> all these frauds, robberies, and murders. You are the
> spring that puts all the rest in motion; they would not
> stir a step without you; therefore, the blood of all these
> wretches who die before their time, whether in their
> country or elsewhere, lies upon your head. "The blood*

*of thy brother" (for, whether thou wilt believe it or
no, such he is in the sight of Him that made him)
"crieth against thee from the earth," from the ship, and
from the waters. O, whatever it costs, put a stop to its
cry before it be too late: Instantly, at any price, were
it the half of your goods, deliver thyself from blood-
guiltiness! Thy hands, thy bed, thy furniture, thy house,
thy lands, are at present stained with blood.*

Do I need to say that he's naming "death" in the foundations
of wealth? Many of his churchly progeny would make him out
to sound like Billy Graham, but here his voice rings more like
a Jeremiah to me. Our hearts be one. (Just a footnote: at the
founding of the Methodist Church in the new United States, it
too was committed by discipline to abolitionism, but within a
few short years yielded to confusion, equivocation, and complicity with the intolerable.)

The Methodist revival first took off in Bristol. John Wesley
had been invited to come up from London and preach to the
colliers. Bristol was a coal mining center, a dirty town fueling
the furnaces of the industrial revolution. It was a big port city,
a mercantile center for colonialism, and a pivot in the slave
triangle—certain ships traded slaves for sugar for rum for slaves.
The poor had multiplied and so had the ale houses. Unrest was
afoot: the new class of urban workers who were just not making
it, erupted in food riots. Repression came down; the prisons
filled up. This preaching invite followed, by only two months,
an uprising in the region that had been suppressed by soldiers
and the jailing of the leadership.

Wesley feared to go. His brother Charles and many others
of their London circle tried to dissuade him. Together they
exercised bibliomancy—a random consultation of Scripture for
directed advice and discernment (a practice I do not generally
commend)— and it turned up ominous verses warning vaguely
of martyrdom. They cast lots and prayed together. Then he
packed his saddlebags and went.

Here the import. John Wesley preached the first sermon of the Methodist revival prepared to die. Not a bad way to enter any pulpit, even if, in this case, it was a hilltop on the outskirts of Bristol. This readiness was no small thing, especially because his journals reflect a recurrent, morbid fear of death which began in childhood after a narrow escape from a house fire. It comes up repeatedly, but he suffered it pointedly at sea in the midst of a storm, where he clung for his life to the ship, while a circle of Moravians (another branch of German pietism) sat calmly in prayer. Wesley wanted what they had. He wanted their freedom. In a certain sense his lifelong yearning for the "assurance of faith," was driven by the underlying human terror. That assurance had come to him precisely a year prior to the preaching invitation, in Aldersgate chapel, while listening to a reflection on the Book of Romans. His heart, you may know the phrase, "was strangely warmed," and he knew thereafter the freedom to die which put all his life at the pleasure and disposal of God. That freedom, of course, is the plain meaning of "justification by faith." It is the freedom, the gift of grace, to stand at any moment's notice before the judgment and mercy of God.

I'd like to say we learned that freedom of the resurrection from Wesley, or from Nelson and Joyce, or from Bill and Dan, but in fact, with them and through them and in them, we learned it from the Gospel of Jesus Christ.

8

'All Things Work Together ...'

A presence invisible

Death struck my own family early. I had an older brother, David, who died as an infant. He was born with hydrocephalus and, despite medical interventions, lived only two weeks. My parents, younger brothers, and I used to visit his grave at the family plot on Memorial Day.

While I was growing up, a verse from the Book of Romans echoed around me: "All things work together for good for those who love God" (8:28). Since I generally heard my dad preach at least twice a week, I'm certain I must have heard sermons on it, including illustrations from our family's life. But I remember it more around the dinner table.

This verse was one of the ways my folks dealt with their heartbreaking grief over the loss of David. It would come up particularly around funerals in the congregation or pastoral care in extreme hospital situations. My parents would intone that the tragedy made my father a better pastor, more able to empathize with the suffering of others, and so be present with them. And I'm sure it was true.

It's only since Jeanie's illness that I've figured out what a huge impact David's death, two years before I was born, had on my life. One day I was describing my Enneagram number to my younger brothers, explaining how Nines are negotiating peace-makers because they are rooted in a pacified and covered-over rage, which is basically anger at growing up overlooked ...

Whoa, Whoa, Whoa, they say. Overlooked? Captain of the basketball team, all-city football, class president, valedictorian, full-ride college scholarship, darling of Mom and Dad ... over-looked? We beg your pardon? For their personality struggles, I was the shadow they felt like they had to grow up under. Hmmm, I think. Right. Weirdness. So I stopped talking about it.

Some time later, I was doing a little more work on Nines—including stuff on birth order. Nines are not usually oldest children—the overlooked usually come later in the sequence. Except sometimes, I read, an older sibling has died. Now I say, Whoa!

I suddenly behold David's continuing invisible presence in our household. Was I striving mightily to be everything he couldn't be? Was I subconsciously laboring to fulfill all my par-ents' hopes for who he might have been? Struggling even to *be* him? And meanwhile, being overlooked for who I actually was? In the long run, something like that could make you mad.

I never talked to my parents about it. Don't think I even figured it out until after they were gone. But this year, cleaning David's gravestone on Memorial Day with my brother Jimmy, I think I was able to love him more fully as a lost brother, a real presence, and even to actually feel my mom and dad's grief. All things working together, finally, for good.

With my dad in two graveyards

My parents' deaths helped prepare me for Jeanie's. I learned from a failing at my father's, for sure.

Up in my attic study, I have rolled-up gravestone rubbings from another family plot, this one several generations back,

in Ontario. Our entire extended family, including nephews
and nieces, had gone there for a weekend on my parents' 50th
wedding anniversary. I can still see my dad leading us around to
the stones and telling the stories.

One concerned my great-grandfather, Leonard Kellermann,
who had migrated across Lake Huron into Michigan's thumb
area, I believe in connection with some sort of rebellion in
Canada. Jeanie would know. Folks in The Thumb remain
fiercely independent. Leonard acquired a good bit of property:
houses, stores, and lands—not exactly a real estate wheeler
dealer, but pretty close. Shrewd in business.

In his will, he parceled out the inheritables to his five sons,
including my grandfather, Garfield. Trouble was that after he
made the will, he continued to wheel and deal, rendering the
document incoherent. Certain properties designated were no
longer held, while others unnamed were there to be passed on. I
half wonder if he saw this coming.

After his funeral, the five brothers sat down at the kitchen
table to sort things out and began to argue. My grandpa
Kellermann (the preacher among them) reportedly reached his
limit, pushed back from the table, and walked away, saying he
didn't want any of it. And he never got any—at least that was
my dad's version of the story. And to be honest, I kind of like
it—for what it says about the Kellermann line. "All things work
together for good …"

My dad had been ill for years, though he lived a vital exis-
tence through it all. He had diabetes, and some of the chronic
degenerative things that go with it, plus cancer. Finally, in
August 1987, he suffered a heart attack—actually a recurrence
of heart trouble for which previous surgeries had intervened. He
was hospitalized and seemed to know this was the end.

He was in some pain, but entirely alert and present, orchestrating a series of visits and conversations with us all. He was
taking care of business. All the grandchildren made their way to
the bedside for hugs and goodbyes. Careful and loving.

We prayed for him and, at his insistence, for his roommate and all in the hospital as well. I kissed him and wept, even though I thought we yet had time. And then overnight, according to his expectation and willingness, he died. And well.

For all the times I'd counseled parishioners about medical decision-making, it never occurred to us, and nobody asked directly, to put a "do not resuscitate" (DNR) order on his chart. So in our absence, as they surely would have done even had we been gathered round the bedside, the alarms went off, the teams rushed to his room, his heart was shocked again into beating, and he was gurneyed off apace to Intensive Care, where all the tubes and lines and monitors were inserted.

When we arrived, he was tied down and struggling. He'd repeatedly attempted to remove the "life-sustaining devices." With the breathing tube clogging his voice, he couldn't speak, but I could see in his eyes that he was pissed. I was afraid he was pissed at me.

My brothers were around and experienced it more or less the same, but I was the oldest and bore it personally. I vigiled with him through one long night, and I tried to talk to him. To reassure and even apologize. He only struggled against the ties.

As he stabilized, some of the tubes came out. He could talk again, but was groggy. "Oh, Bill, just pay the bill, take out these things, and let's go home. This is an old Indian trick." The latter phrase was some racial slur buried in his past that I'd never heard, but which the drugs had released. I winced, but I got that the trick was the medical captivity. I later saw the insurance bill for this unwanted treatment and winced again. We certainly couldn't have paid it to go home.

Several sweet and stunning gifts emerged in these days. One Jeanie initiated: singing hymns to him at bedside. She brought her 1940 Episcopal hymnal and sat working her way through her favorites, and his that she knew: "Breathe on Me, Breath of God," "Let All Mortal Flesh Keep Silence," "Zion, City of Our God." Others of us, my sisters-in-law especially, picked up and joined. I suspect it's an uncommon sound in ICU—though perhaps not.

On Saturday, as he improved, the staff was eager to get him sitting upright and so brought in an impressive bed that folded itself and tilted into a chair. My mom and brother Paul wheeled him over to the window, where an interesting view was to be had. The day was gorgeous, clear sky and August sun.

It was the day of the "Woodward Cruise," an endless parade of classic and fancy cars to be ogled and toasted with beer aplenteous by admiring crowds. It is a unique Motor City spectacle, appropriately enacted in the northern suburbs. The hospital entrance served as a convenient turnaround for some, so an interesting procession of vehicles to take in presented itself.

But my dad wasn't seeing it. He seemed to be looking right past or through it. My mom asked if he was in pain. "Yes, but it's a happy pain." His countenance was a glowing and beatific calm. What he saw was his own, but it swept Paul and Mom along in the presence of a mystical experience.

The doctors, as often in such cases, were mixed. One heart specialist couldn't believe we wouldn't authorize a heart surgery! Didn't we want Dad back the way he was, say, six months ago? We had to explain to the surgeon's compartmentalized brain about the cancer and all, even bringing in my dad's actual desires. I thought us unduly gracious with him.

The ICU doc with a Central American accent, however, was completely tuned in. He understood our wishes and fixed the chart with the DNR order. He arranged a conversation with the local hospice team, for which we were most grateful. My mom was completely on board with the hospice move, since she knew we'd all be round even more to help. But we never made it to hospice care.

On Sunday morning, we gathered for the hospice consultation, all except my brother Jimmy, who was preaching at his church. Even as we began the conversation, the ICU nurse came in the room and said, "It's time. You should come, and quickly."

Dad was laboring hard, his breathing almost wracked. We gathered round the bed and laid hands on him as he heaved. We were sobbing, and the sobs seemed in rhythm with his own. We were praying. I was praying aloud, on behalf of us all, in thanksgiving and for his crossing. Those prayers seemed to conform in rhythm with him as well. He stilled and breathed his last.

A footnote on my own heart: just over a year later, I made another visit to the Abbey of Gethsemani, a stopover place on a seminary recruiting trip I was making through the South. I pulled into the guest house parking lot, opened the car door, stepped to the ground, and out of nowhere began to cry over my father's death. It's the place where my dreams release, why not my tears as well? They must have been backed up. I laid down on the cemetery grass at the gate and let them run free.

Another alleluia

When my dad passed, my mom remained for a time at their home in a suburb of Detroit, close to their church. She kept their winter cycle, taking up residence for some months in a rented Florida condominium with a train of family guests—she was nothing if not famous for the hospitality of her table, and especially for convening us as a clan.

In one sense, she got a second wind and blossomed in her own right. She had been an amazing wife and mother, but she was also constrained by those roles. I recall in the '70s when she served on a national board of the Methodist Church, which took her regularly to New York City and elsewhere. She was connected to the Women's Division, which did the most amazing theology in the church. Her world and her mind were expanding. My dad worried about her safety on the streets of the city, but really I think he worried about her expanded view from this churchly perch.

When I was in seminary, I wrote a poem about my own funeral. It was comic and surreal, in large part. I cast my mother as "theologian of the Board of Eschatological Discipleship"—which she received unfortunately as some sort of diminution, when it couldn't have been higher praise from my young seminarian head.

In the '80s, after Jeanie and I, and then my brother Jimmy, returned from Witness for Peace delegations to Nicaragua, Mom got the pull of the Spirit to go herself. She was beginning the process and arrangements, but my dad stopped it short. Just put his foot down in the name of safety. He wouldn't have it.

My mom always wanted to see the Alps. I think of it as a *Sound of Music* thing, but it may just have been in her blood. One Christmas, as a gift, my brothers and I put the money down on a Methodist trip, with our bishop no less, to Switzerland. My parents teared up upon receiving it. But then my dad (who had a fear of flying) reneged and returned the money. It was too extravagant, he said.

At a certain point, with arthritis making the basement stairs a trouble, Mom moved into a retirement residence in Grand Rapids, near my brother Paul. It was a Methodist facility, and many friends from Dad's early ministry lived on that side of the state, though she was attending their funerals almost as often as welcoming them at her table. She had a blessed year there, keeping a schedule of musical and theatrical events, even attending her first rock concert. On August 6, 2003 (I mark it as Hiroshima Day, and the Feast of the Transfiguration), she collapsed while weeding in the garden, of a brain aneurysm. She came to briefly in the emergency room, but promptly fell into a coma.

Though we didn't have a formal advance directive written in her hand, we did know she desired no extraordinary measures. We were all together in the decisions. The grandchildren were present for most of the discussion, but sent off for the conclusion to spare them any sense of personal responsibility.

Jeanie was present too, and participating fully in the discussions. She was then in the midst of her illness, so these questions struck close to the bone and resonated at another level of mindfulness. As a family, we actually worked really well together in consensus. If there were differences, we were not by any means strained or combative. We chose hospice, and my mom was moved back to a special wing at the residence where we could have access to our own apartment, coming and going down the hall from her room.

Those were remarkable days for us brothers (you may have counted by now that there are four of us still living, of whom I am the oldest). We vigiled in various configurations—singly, in assorted pairs, and all of us together. Around my mom's body, to the sound of her breathing, the memories rose up just as you'd wish: We were young, we were baking (a family tradition), we were in the car for this or that family vacation, we were playing sports on the field or in the backyard. We reconstructed the floor plans of various parsonages we had lived in, we renegotiated the birth-order blues.

My mom summoned it all in healing recollection. All four of us held her hands in the end as her breathing began to pause in long, apneic halts. I believe Jimmy prayed the final prayer. Another alleluia.

Decision and discernment

With Jeanie's illness, beginning to end, medical decision-making was a constant. Certain things we accepted as given, I notice in retrospect. The first surgery, for example. I don't think we hesitated over it, just set to work finding the one to do the task.

I take that back. There was a young resident at the first hospitalization who was privy to the diagnosis. He looked us in the eye and offered advice: "Don't be buffaloed. Think quality of life. It's going to be an issue."

He would be shocked, I'm certain, to discover the length of Jeanie's survival. And probably some of the decisions we made. And even in the end, how deep went the quality of life.

But it was a rare moment—an official of the medical system urging us on in our own freedom. That stuck. In fact, we didn't settle on the surgeon who first discussed the tumor's resection with us. Or the second. We went looking, or better, discerning, together. All that was so much a matter of feel.

Jeanie had one sense, but deferred to my intuition in this instance. Ironically, the guy I chose sent his partner at the last minute, and we couldn't have been more pleased. Jack Rock is a brilliant surgeon and a remarkable human being. For all our heed, we got to the right doc despite ourselves. Such are the mysteries of providence.

You'll recall the impairment of decision-making facilities from my upbringing, plus the balancing act which Nines on the Enneagram generally go through in making choices. Combined with Jeanie's decisiveness, the process between us prior to her illness worked pretty well, serving both marriage and family. In this new period, however, especially as Jeanie faded in and out of capacity, I was compelled to step up and lead. It took an inner effort that was a choice all its own.

Decisions seemed to come quick and incessant—clinical trials, alternative therapies, the standards of chemotherapy and radiation—and they all have invisible pressures behind them. Doctors commending clinical trials are not offering disinterested advice, they are also invested researchers tending not just a project, but a career. Hospitals are capitalized heavily into radiation devices they need to pay for by billing insurance companies. Alternative therapies make big claims, often selling themselves without benefit of independent testing or analysis.

Keeping your feet means dragging them sometimes—and kicking with them at others. Or, just turning on your heels and walking out of the room. Here's where community was an invaluable help in our experience.

At the suggestion of Ched Myers, a biblical scholar, activist, and dear friend who lives in Southern California (he was periodically able to sit as a member of the group), we began the process that Quakers call "convening a clearness committee"—also called a query circle or discernment group at various points in our journey. The idea is that the group doesn't insert itself with advice or leading, but poses probing questions to the ones seeking clarity—bringing our own inner leadings into the light.

Ours quickly morphed informal. It was a prayerful circle, generally convened in silence with a candle. Jeanie was always part of it, and often Lydia. The others were Tom Lumpkin, Martha Dage, Marianne Arbogast, Deb Choly, John Zettner, and Ed Rowe.

Their role varied over time. Jeanie and I bent the rules and did ask them for advice periodically, and they freely gave. They sometimes helped us diagram a sort of "decision tree," as we tried to sort the issues and the various paths offered. When we knew what we wanted or needed to do, but felt the life-and-death weight of it, they would confirm the choice and agree to bear the burden of the decision. We were in this together.

This group helped organize anniversary events and birthday celebrations. They also pursued resources, such as legal and medical information. They stood ready to raise funds when needed. And it was from that group (from Deb in particular) that help came in scheduling community caregiving for Jeanie when I was out of town.

We asked of them way more than thinking up deft questions. They were the constant presence of community to our healing and dying. In that sense, they were the seed of what would become our hospice community.

They also gathered a wider, invisible community prayerfully attentive to our needs. The correspondence we posted was at once a public narration of the saga, tracking and making sense of our treatment avenues, and an embodiment of extended community as defined by readership or intercession. These too bore, and bore with, our discernments.

And so now, on to the letters ...

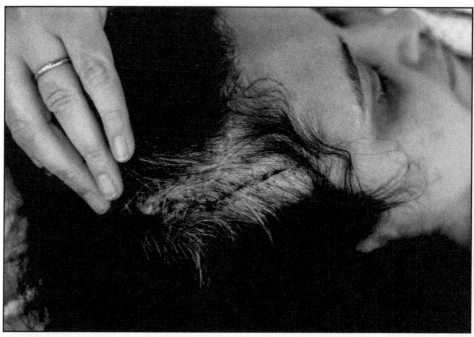

Jeanie's scar from the first surgery, fall 1998. Credit: Bill Wylie-Kellermann

Jeanie with her best friend, Meg Graham, and her partner Bonnie, December 2005.
Credit: Family collection

9

'Pulling Hope through Knotholes'

The first posting is from Jeanie. Speak to us, dear heart:

November 21, 1998: First Surgery, First Update

I'll start at the present and work backwards. We've just settled on a treatment plan after weeks of agony, as we read technical documents and tried to become proficient enough to understand them and, better, to be able to read between the lines.

Over time it sunk in that, although the hospital was recommending/pushing chemo experimental protocols and radiation, the medical records don't show much result for either in the case of a glioblastoma—the most aggressive of brain tumors. In fact, all the prognoses were very dire.

We began to look into alternative treatments. It was difficult untangling the charlatans from the dedicated, and the hopeful treatments from the bizarre. At length we were put in touch with a doctor in Nashville, Tennessee (a lifelong Episcopalian, it turns out). He recommended two things: taking Thalidomide (the drug responsible for so many birth defects because it blocked the development of new blood vessels; good in the case of tumors) and ultrapheresis.

The latter is a treatment he developed that, with a dialysis-like machine, screens certain proteins from your blood, which he believes tumors use to cloak themselves, hiding from your immune system. Without them, the disguise goes down and the immune system can go to work. This involves the tumor growing hot and inflamed, dying and liquefying. He's in Phase III clinical trials with this for some kinds of cancer and just starting a Phase I trial with glioblastomas.

We've signed on. I started Thalidomide two weeks ago and start ultrapheresis on December 1. (We're also eating semi-macrobiotic, and I'm taking nutritional supplements to build the immune system.) Since Advent is our family's favorite season, I dread being away for three weeks in December, but on the chance that it will work, I'll go. (Friends and family are taking stints so I won't be alone. I'm kind of hoping I might feel well enough to rent a blonde wig and go to an open mic night near the Grand Ol' Opry.)

During the time we took to think, we began to get pressure from the hospital and from friends who felt we were taking too much time, since this kind of tumor can double in size in 10 days! Five weeks out of surgery, I asked for an MRI and was told it was unnecessary. Finally, I got one anyway and had to wait two weeks to have it read by a doctor in Canada (long story).

We've just heard that the tumor did not grow during that five weeks! This widely respected Canadian, Greg Cairncross, also holds out some hope that the pathologists who declared it a glioblastoma may have been wrong—possibly it's a slightly lesser-grade cancer. He'll let us know in a month, after they have done genetic testing on the tumor slices.

You can tell we've been all over the map from despair to hope. We're learning a lot. We are so grateful to friends and to others we've never met who have sent encouragement. We're grateful to those who remember the kids in prayer and in correspondence.

On the surface, the kids seem to be doing quite well, but this just means their terror is buried. Lydia, 12, said recently, "I just don't believe you are dying. Everyone's always crying, but I don't believe it." She pretty much said she'd revise her viewpoint if it became clear she needed to later—this seemed sane to me. Lucy has started writing short stories about a family with two children in which the mother has died, but she pins me in huge hugs and declares her love in clear hope that she can hold me here. Nowhere I'd rather be.

So here's the history:

At the start of Labor Day weekend, I was finishing up the October issue of The Witness. *I had already heard from Julie Wortman, who said, "What about shortening this article, moving this one, identifying your article as an editorial and cutting a page out of it ... ?" I agreed with all her suggestions, which was extremely fortunate, because a few hours later I would be having seizures on my bathroom floor and waiting 20 hours to be rescued by a wonderful friend who helped me get dressed and to the hospital ER. (Julie took over the completion of the issue with Marianne's help and did a terrific job.)*

During the hours I was alone, I figured I was having a stroke and wondered whether delaying getting to the hospital was a bad idea, but I didn't have the decision-making ability to call anyone, not even Bill, who was with the Kellermanns for Labor Day. (I was supposed to be going on a retreat that weekend, so no one in my family had any reason to suspect I was lying on the bathroom floor.) But our doctor says I couldn't have done otherwise.

At the ER they did a CT scan and told me they'd found a mass and would need to find out if it was a malignancy. Then they put me through every kind of scan they could think of, to see if I was riddled with cancer. The rest of my body was clear. The MRIs showed a sizeable tumor in the front right side of my brain, an area surgeons would call "quiet." My vital signs quickly returned to normal.

At this point, Bill and I started a long process of learning about brain tumors—worse than cramming for exams because my life hung in the balance. We cried a lot. We prayed. We consulted the Internet. We read the materials that friends sent our way. We called doctors and made appointments. Finally, we settled on a surgeon at Henry Ford Hospital. At the last minute, we learned that the surgeon would be this man's partner, but we liked him very much, so that was okay with us.

At the hospital and at home, we listened almost constantly to sacred chant. It seemed to go deep and beyond our fears and concerns. I kept thinking, "The monks hold the center."

The surgery was early the next morning. Bill stayed with me until I got wheeled into the operating room. Next thing I knew, I was terribly thirsty and lying on a mobile bed in a recovery room that was as crowded as many ERs. I wanted water and they said no. I wanted

Bill and they said no. At length, I got ice chips and the surgeon brought Bill in (over my nurse's protests).

Forty-eight hours later, I checked out of the hospital! I had expected to want to stay, but was startled to find that they would feel it necessary to check my vital signs and prick my fingers for glucose testing all night long. I kept asking, "Isn't sleep part of healing?" When it dawned on me that no would wake me up at home, I was excited to get out and willing to trust that we would figure out how to take care of me. (My mom came up to help for three weeks!)

There's more to say about the things we're thinking/ learning about prayer, but that can wait for another posting.

Way opening

Many of our medical decisions are named and narrated in the letters. Others are unspoken, but no less labored. Most involved strenuous effort, tedious research, and pure will. Many were won in the listening agony of debate and sleepless silence. Yet some fell upon us like rain from above. They simply happened as gifts. "A way opening," as the Quakers say.

We outright resisted the immediate pressures of conventional radiation/chemotherapy (with, as Jeanie noted, pretty thin advantage to commend them but tons of institutional momentum). Likewise with the manipulations of a clinical trial, in which Jeanie would be the test subject of a narrowly controlled experiment for a new approach.

She took the early lead in reading over and thinking through alternative treatments. Friends subscribed us to an online service that summarized and independently evaluated various strange and emerging options. Everything from crystals to vaccines made from urine to electrical devices designed to kill "the parasites that cause cancer" was closely considered.

Hope you're not laughing. In these independently detailed analyses, ultrapheresis got high marks, and here we also found the chicken vaccine that Jeanie would take for years. But I'm getting ahead of myself.

Early on, Jeanie and I made a trek to Evanston, Illinois, outside Chicago, to see an upscale herbologist recommended by friends, Rosemary and Vincent Harding. His regimen was adjuvant treatment involving pricey packaged supplements and a retinue of well-tailored dietary consultants. We were weighing the whole thing in a face-to-face conversation when it crossed my mind to ask him, "If it were your wife who was sick, what would you do?"

Without pausing a beat, he replied, "I'd go to Nashville and have her do ultrapheresis." I beg your pardon? Way was opening. We took a quick dietary consult, had Chinese food, and made travel plans for Tennessee.

Like many alternative or developing treatments, ultrapheresis is a little weird. As Jeanie explained, in apparatus it's quite like dialysis. A sophisticated filter screens a certain protein out of one's blood. This is the protein that embryos use to mask themselves from a mother's immune system, lest they be done in by it. Tumors, by this theory, use the same strategy.

This protein fits in the "docking ports" that killer T-cells ordinarily use to mark and access a foreign body. But deny the tumor the protein and suddenly it becomes visible and vulnerable to your own immune system. Brilliant, right? Then again, it hadn't yet been through clinical trials, wasn't covered by insurance, and was expensive.

Other providence would be required. In the short term, *The Witness* loaned us the money. Then friends, Laura Markham and Ron Williams who had started a newspaper of politics and culture (think back to the syndicate that published my basketball article) were selling their local operation. They did a capital gains gift transfer to our church, Central United Methodist (some of you will understand how this works—which is good, because I couldn't explain it if I tried), and we were able to draw the necessary funds from a health care support fund. It was a gift and a privilege.

Perhaps a little more on the privilege. We were, throughout this ordeal, able to draw on such resources and on the options of quality church-based insurance. These are, to be sure, an aspect of "life in community" in some broad sense. But when one in six of the people who live in this country didn't have health insurance, we must not be blinded to the privilege entailed. An account of this same illness told by one of our neighbors down the block might also be about the graces of dying well, but I wager the story would be shorter and more painful.

On December 2, from Nashville, Jeanie wrote to friends that "Bill and I both feel that we are in the right place and in the right hands," which was true. We brought Lydia and Lucy with us for the first night, so that they would know exactly where their mother was in the ensuing weeks. Jeanie reported that they "loved the hotel and discovering all the nooks and crannies."

She had a rough go of it after her first ultrapheresis treatment on a Tuesday morning. "I watched a lot of other patients come and go," she wrote, "but my blood pressure stayed really low. Occasionally I was able to sit up, but if they lowered my legs, I'd faint again. In all, I fainted four times. Each time, it took a while to get oriented again. I was the last patient out of the clinic at 7 p.m. and left in a wheelchair."

Undaunted, Jeanie reported feeling better the next morning and "eager to try it again." She ended that letter with "What a strange Advent. I'm really grateful to have Bill with me." She wrote again a few days later, during a brief stay at home in Detroit:

December 5, 1998: Writing from Home

It feels great to be home, even just for the weekend (Lucy's 9th birthday!) My first week of treatment in Tennessee has been good. The doctor ordered another MRI, since it had been three weeks since the last one. The cavity from the tumor removal is smaller. There is still an enhanced area around the cavity that could be either tumor growth or, more likely, the formation of tissue that will eventually be scar tissue.

For treatment, I had a catheter installed under my collarbone on the right side with two tubes that dangle from it. I sat beside a nice, new-looking machine and got the tubes hooked up to it. One draws my blood out; the other replaces my filtered blood, along with a saline solution and, I think, plasma. Afterwards, patients tend to sit in recovery for an hour or two before leaving either on foot or in a wheelchair. I've done both.

Tuesday was the most dramatic (and frightening) day. I passed out four times! Now they are doing a few things differently, and I am too (like eating a high-protein breakfast). I've stayed conscious, but it's becoming clear that I won't be dancing the Two Step at any country bars!

What we're ultimately hoping for, I believe, is for the treatment to inflame my tumor remnants and for me to get a fever. They say 103 is no big deal and even 105 is just fine.

When it's clear that I am reacting to the treatment, the doctor plans to flush my system with a chemo ingredient (a one-shot dose) that's supposed to give the tumor a double whammy. I assume I'll get laid low by that, but soon after I'll be considered finished and get to go home. Quite likely all that will happen in the third week, but there's really no way to know for sure.

Most recently the doctor said, "If you can get through this with no headaches and not even a low fever, that's great." So I'm a little confused. But I'm grateful that I really like the doctor and his whole staff, so I'm content not to think too hard and to trust their interpretation of what happens.

Thanks for your continuing love, prayers and support. It means everything.

And her last from Tennessee:

December 17, 1998: Community and the Chemo Flush

I'm tired.

I'm also encouraged but won't really know much for another month.

The treatment has gone well. I continue to really like the staff, which helps a lot since I am so far from home. I also feel very connected to the other people with morning appointments. Two of them have left with clear CT scans—no more tumors!

It's interesting how close we feel to each other, even though we've hardly spoken. We've spent a couple hours each morning hooked up to these machines, and another hour recovering. But more than that, we are all praying for our lives and are necessarily pretty humble about what that will yield.

I find myself thinking often of the courage in the AIDS community. It's a strange edge to walk—am I living or dying or both? (And how do I avoid that Mack truck in the meantime? I use my seatbelt more faithfully.)

I haven't fainted since that first treatment. I really found that unnerving. (So did the nurse, who said later he'd have thrown himself between me and the floor if possible when I nose-dived from a low stool flat on my face.) We watch my blood pressure carefully. I eat more protein. I always eat breakfast.

Today I had a Carboplatin infusion. This is a chemo agent, but the treatment is a one-shot deal. The doctor says I will be exhausted in a week and may need a blood transfusion (so much for my fantasies that I'll get free of medical procedures as soon as I get home). During that week I'll also need to lay low so as not to risk infection—we'll probably head for the cabin in Port Sanilac and spend that week in the woods! He also says he's 100 percent sure that I will lose my hair in three weeks. One of the nurses says that it is more 50-50. I try to stay calm lest anyone think that my vanity outweighs my will to live.

Last night I was terrified about the Carboplatin (Would it hurt? Would I spend hours throwing up?) and about resuming the Thalidomide (Would I be hopelessly groggy and bloated? Would my blood pressure drop and cause me to faint again?). To my surprise, Bill decided to fly down, just for the day, to see me through. Having him beside me was wonderful. We even dozed side by side in the clinic's reclining seats as the IV dripped the Carboplatin into me. It was hard to let him go at the airport in the evening, but I could hear the kids' delight to have him home when they called tonight.

Spending last week with Meg Graham, my best friend from pre-school, was great. She's quite knowledgeable about glioblastomas and nutrition. She took good care of me, and we even got to work through the elements that made our friendship hard in junior high! And we are probably the only ones in the world who share memories of each other's homes and schools.

At the end of that second week, I nearly refused to go home. We were over-scheduled, and I was afraid I would die simply of exhaustion. But the whole thing was wonderful. I felt like I was given the wind I needed.

I even found it good to see a lot of people. Sometimes people's compassion and concern just dissolves me, and I can't cope; other times I run kind of cold, because I don't feel like being wholly vulnerable in a crowd. But this time it was all a gift.

We celebrated the Kellermann Christmas. It was really nice to be with family, to sing Christmas carols, to have a low-key gift exchange (the nieces and nephews are mostly teens now!), to check in with each other, and to curl up together in front of Bing Crosby.

Bill and I also went to a memorial service for Mary Durham, 89. She's a wonderful spirit—genteel and vigorous, able to tell the truth and to be unexpectedly funny. (Mary once confided, "When I need to tell someone something, I often say, 'Do you read The Witness?' If they say yes, then I know I can speak freely"!) The service was beautiful—Anglican, hymns that I like and a good sermon by Bishop Coleman McGehee.

The next day, we went to church again at Central Methodist, where Dan Berrigan preached and Ed Rowe called for healing. Ed did it really nicely by inviting forward everyone who wanted healing, including those who had prayed about city shootings and knifings during the intercessions. Then he invited everyone who wanted to pray for us to come forward, so I didn't feel conspicuous. Dan preached about pulling hope through a knothole in these hard days, then he said maybe even through the eye of a needle.

I loved being at church. It felt like a place that holds the center together. These days I am entirely aware of

*how I am dependent on God and on those of you still
pulling hope through knotholes—especially today with
news of the bombing of Iraq. Your love and faith hold
me. I get to go home soon! (The girls sound good on the
phone.)*

Jeanie was most eloquent and reflective about her experience
in the annual Christmas letter she wrote that year to readers of
The Witness:

Third Sunday of Advent 1998

"Be patient, therefore, beloved, until the coming of the Lord.
The farmer waits for the precious crop from the earth, being
patient with it until it receives the early and the late rains. You
also must be patient. Strengthen your hearts, for the coming of
the Lord is near. Beloved, do not grumble against one another,
so that you may not be judged. See, the Judge is standing at the
doors! As an example of suffering and patience, beloved, take
the prophets who spoke in the name of the Lord. Indeed we
call blessed those who showed endurance. You have heard of the
endurance of Job, and you have seen the purpose of the Lord,
how the Lord is compassionate and merciful." (James 5:7-11)

*Two weeks before my body succumbed to seizures in early
September, an episode that resulted in the diagnosis of
a brain tumor, I lay on my living room floor crying as
I listened to "God Help Us" by the Miserable Offenders.
I had studied the new arrangements of traditional
hymns and the original pieces, all dealing with the
crux of our faith, the business of living and of dying,
the need to pay attention to our lives, the welcome
held out for the sinner. Listening, I wondered how we
ever forget how fragile life is and how immanent our
encounter with God. Not bad thoughts for Advent.*

*By October, after a craniotomy to remove most of
the tumor, these thoughts were more constant than I
wished. My brain tumor was diagnosed as a Grade 4,*

extremely aggressive glioblastoma, and the projections for the length of my life were dismal. I've spent much of the fall crying. Crying for my kids (9 and 12), crying for Bill, crying for myself.

I've had grace-filled moments, prayer relief, moments of being carried by other people's love—and then those bone-chilling, fear-filled moments when I am clinging by my fingernails to this familiar life. It's still my intention to die with my eyes open and my spirit willing, whenever that moment comes. I will honestly try to do that. But, God, it's much harder than I had imagined.

So what is it that is offered us in this season of preparation? If not security and permanence, what does God promise and what does God ask?

Patience, according to James, and a willingness to listen to the prophets. What do the prophets say? It seems that over and over again the prophets ask us to acknowledge the widow and orphan, to do justice, to stop making animal sacrifices and instead offer up those things that we substitute for God—wealth, immortality, power.

And, always, there's the Judge waiting at the doors. Coming. Like the thief in the night. Coming. Like the bridegroom who is awaited. Coming.

Do our hearts rise? Or do they cry out, "Not yet!" Or "Oh Lord, this was for real." It's for real. It is coming soon. In my case, maybe sooner than I would like.

This Advent, as we light the candles in the dark and sing for Emmanuel, let's be even more intentional than usual in clearing the commercial Christmas assault from our minds and hearts. Whatever God is calling us to has little to do with shopping and driving ourselves into a frenzy creating the "perfect" holiday.

We need to honor the silence and the dark, to remember our stories, to teach the youth in our lives what we believe matters. We need to recall, to intuit, to dream the life we're called to and then make a plan that allows us to strip down enough to have it. In the course of that, of course, we need to give thanks for all that we are and for those traveling in our circles and beyond.

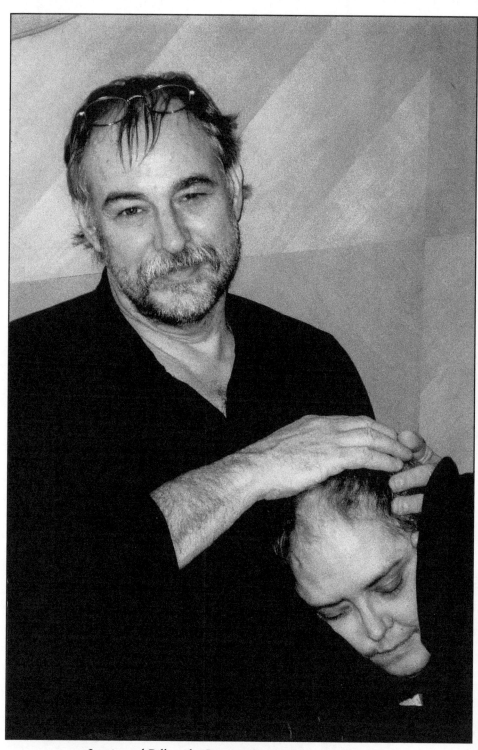

Jeanie and Bill at the Leaven Center, Lyons, MI, 2005.
Credit: Family collection

She Likes Jazz!

We were grateful that friends and family gathered around Jeanie in Nashville. In addition to her preschool friend Meg Graham, Deb Choly, Jeanie's older sister Irene (Rene Beth) Rodgers, and sister-in-law Carol Larzelere-Kellermann took turns being with her and getting her to appointments. When Jeanie felt up to it, she and Rene Beth even managed a trip to the Ryder Auditorium, which had housed the Grand Ol' Opry for decades.

Jeanie had seizures again, for the first time since the beginning—likely the result of a contrast added to enhance an MRI. They were terrifying, but soon abated with Dilantin and bed rest. Blessedly, the MRI showed no tumor growth. Jeanie picks up the story again here.

January 2, 1999: Half-formed Thoughts to Come

> I wanted the doctor to announce that it was time to celebrate. But he remained sober, saying that a glioblastoma is a very aggressive form of cancer and that he wanted me back in three weeks for two more weeks of treatment. I couldn't face the prospect then,

and I am not sure I can face it now. I don't like leaving my kids at all. (Okay, I get the irony.)

Arriving home was wonderful. We spent Christmas in Port Sanilac, which kept me secluded when my white count was lowest and I was most vulnerable to infection. We watched the stars. We walked in the woods. We stared at Lake Huron. We read to each other, and the girls baked cookies.

Now we are back in Detroit, and I find that I am restless. I still don't know if I am living or dying. I still cry a lot. Finally it dawned on me last night that I need a forward focus aside from medical stuff like the next MRI. The next issue of The Witness that I am responsible for is May's, so I look forward to turning to that. It makes me believe that I am getting my life back.

I continue to be grateful for prayers. I have lots of half-formed thoughts on prayer and healing, cancer and mortality. I'll be glad if I have the time to sort these through and write about them. Better yet, I'd like to be around to stand beside my daughters as they grow up. They are truly wonderful. And what about long walks in the woods with Bill in our old age?

11 February 1999: Complying with the Will

Another update: I've been sick as a dog for the last three weeks. I was surprised because the treatment plan I have chosen works with the immune system and is not very toxic. But later I learned that they've added a low dose of chemo over the first five treatments and I get a large dose at the end, so I assume that's the issue.

Today I'm up, finally. It's nice not to feel completely overwhelmed by even the small things I'd like to do, like unpack from the last trip to Tennessee.

Despite the fact that I felt lousy, the reports are that the treatment is working and that we are "challenging the natural course of disease." I thank God for that, because the natural course is dire indeed (with only 50 percent of those diagnosed surviving the first year). I'm continually grateful for prayers. I know they sustain me. I've been so glad to have been spared any feelings of fury at God about this. In fact, just as the Christmas Eve service began, I was flooded with a feeling that it wasn't God's will that I die. This was very helpful, because I'd been feeling that if it was, I would want to comply somehow, but now I'm free to fight it fully.

There's talk of a third round of treatment in March, but at present I don't feel nearly strong enough. Plus there are things I want to do at home to strengthen my heart, like take walks with my daughters, stare at Lake Huron, join in a circle of drumming women, go on dates with Bill, sing hymns.

February 16, 1999: Weak and Refocused

I am finally recovering. For nearly a week, I have been able to keep food down. I am able to get out of bed and to think a little. (I was startled to realize that there were chunks of time during all this that I couldn't recall at all.) I have never felt so weak and so thoroughly dependent on prayer.

My doctor checked in, and when I told him how sick I had been, he said, "Let's say no more chemo. Let's focus on building your immune system up." I was delighted. In addition, when I told him I didn't feel physically strong enough to come back as requested on March 1st, he didn't push me (as he has always done in the past).

Therefore, instead of another round of treatment in early March, Bill and I have decided to take the kids (who have been getting short shrift lately) to see their grandmother in Florida the first week of March! We'll hang out together and play cards, swim if it's warm enough, eat with their grandma and just enjoy being a family ...

People ask often about the girls. Right now they are full of music and dance. They auditioned for a musical presentation of Jack and the Beanstalk. Lydia got the lead. Lucy is in the chorus, but she has been asked to fill in for the cow, who has missed a lot of rehearsals. It looks as though she may get the part, which would make her very happy. It's a singing cow. In addition, Lucy has auditioned for her school spring performance and landed a solo. I love them so much it takes my breath away.

Bill is back to teaching in Chicago, so we are in our rhythm of sometimes here and sometimes not. Now that I can get out of bed, it will be easier. Last trip, my mom came up and stayed with us, which helped enormously. Bill has been terrifically supportive.

Things then took a difficult turn for Jeanie, and so I began to add my own voice here:

March 19, 1999: Not Dying in my Arms

"Is everything OK with Jeanie? I'm just calling because I began to feel troubled a couple hours ago that she wasn't all right."
—A friend in the woods of Michigan's Thumb

Several of you have written or called, even presciently, for another round of news. Herewith. It's hard to know exactly what to make of recent events.

Two evenings ago, Jeanie began to have seizures in her left arm. Though her own willful inclination was simply to lie down and take additional medication, they came faster and more furious and began to involve her legs. By the time we got a wheelchair and help organized to get her to an Emergency Room, she had a major seizure, which left her unconscious and the rest of us in a panic. I, to be honest, nearly lost it imagining I might be losing her right there in my arms.

The girls first fled the chaos, then held one another in tears nearby on the couch. Friends on the block tended to them promptly with care and prayer as we finally went off with EMS lights flashing.

A CT Scan showed clear (no new or acute tumor activity, and no bleeding), but Jeanie's Dilantin levels were unaccountably low. They leveled her off with a drip and sent her home at 2 a.m. Things began to repeat, however, the next morning.

So another ER run … An EEG proved pretty normal and reassuring, leaving mysteries unresolved. Today they sent her home, but now with Phenobarbital added to her med regimen. As she says, "It hardly seems fair to be made to edit an issue [of the magazine] under the weight of three sedatives."

Actually, this latter may indeed bear on matters. March for our family has been unduly overscheduled. Stress can figure in the seizure formula. In the midst of such a month, Jeanie is back in the editorial chair, putting together a Witness on "Eldering and Mentoring."

This, of course, is to reference the flip side of things: she has been doing incredibly well, and our sense of her healing progress may have been arrogantly complacent … She's been looking like the poster child for this kind of treatment. Our proof in the pudding (and the prayer and the providence).

So, we are nonplused by the recent humbling and reluctant to say too much definitive. We are trying to seize the miracle and notice the fragileness of things precious ...

I guess this ends up being another call for prayer. Please post silence and intercession. And thanks for the inquiries and intuitions, the light summoned, the plenteous support (both material and spiritual), for coming alongside in these ways and more. We can only confess our love.

As we tried to figure out what had caused the seizures, the neurologist calmly explained that, because Jeanie had scar tissue in her brain, she would always be subject to seizures. Which also meant she would always be taking anti-seizure medications. Swelling in her brain raised our fears once more. She speaks again:

April 16, 1999: Learning to Trust

"You have had too many ups and downs on this medical opinion thing. Walk slowly and don't put too much stock in any one diagnosis. You do not walk alone."
—A friend in California

We've been through hell and back, again. We're hoping to have saved most of you the latest loop on the roller coaster ... At the moment I'm on Dilantin, Phenobarbital, and Thalidomide, which makes it hard to know whether my occasional memory lapses are drug-induced, seizure-related, or just middle age kicking in ...

Bill moved mountains to get the MRI films overnighted to our doctor in Tennessee, who was in the office one last day before leaving for a two-week conference. At the end of the day, he told us that the "suspicious" swelling in my brain could be from healing or from new tumor growth, and he leaned toward believing it was the latter.

At first, I had a rebellious bravado. But it quickly crumbled into a true fear that I was going to disintegrate over time in front of my husband (who would be stuck with caring for me) and my children—until I finally died. (We see lots of people in the neurologist's waiting room that give real meaning to this.)

When I confessed my fear to Bill, he said, "That's the fear I have all the time." But he adds that while we are under the shadow of fear, we try not to be consumed by it. Bill manages to be incredibly present and we laugh often—even about all this ...

I did finish editing the May issue, but talked with Julie about changing some of my responsibilities at The Witness. *In the meantime, my biggest challenge seems to be learning about seizures.*

A good friend, Jenny Atlee, who is studying acupuncture, visited and showed me a spot in my palm where if pressure is applied will stop a seizure from progressing. We've tried it repeatedly and it works. But there are lots of new questions about where I can go by myself, whether I need an ID bracelet to inform strangers about my condition, what the kids need to know in case they are alone with me in the event of seizures. Tough stuff, on top of tough stuff ...

I don't want to sound hokey or like a Pollyanna, but I do find the faith of women in this God-forsaken city a really helpful witness. Through all this, I continue to be learning an enormous amount about myself (starting with my foibles), about what is really important (remarkably little), and about God (who it turns out is more generous and warm than I had imagined). So, at least for me, it has been worth it.

Another good friend, Debbie Mast, assures me that I need to be able to imagine that the kids are gaining strength and self-respect through this, too, because they are helping me so well. When I told them they would each get a half hour with a counselor next week, they looked shocked. Lydia said, "I thought this was family counseling!" Lucy explained, "We thought we were going to be supportive of you because you needed counseling!!" I like these kids.

My current challenge (okay, one among many) will be learning to trust that God is looking after Bill and the kids too …

June 4, 1999: Bill's Jubilee

… You've heard a lot about me. This update is about Bill. He turned 50 on June 2nd. He spent a fair amount of time readying himself for this transition, even before my health crisis kicked in.

We've planned a party for June 12th. I know that many of you can't make it, but if you'll send a card or a note that would be lovely. And if you can come, please feel free to bring kids, bring food, bring drinks. The party will start at 7 p.m. and it will need to end by 11 p.m. (That should give us time to clean up before midnight.)

It won't surprise you that Bill has been terrific through all of this. (He's more of a pain when he's asleep on his feet. Crisis brings out the best in him, I think.) There isn't anyone I'd rather see at my bedside than Bill … There are lots of ways that we are at our best when struggling to deal with something as life-threatening as all this. We pray well together. We seek out each other's eyes. We often know what the other is thinking.

Bill approached his Jubilee Year by spending solitude days (on a rhythm of every 50 days since his 49th birthday) at our cabin in Port Sanilac, adopting disciplines of morning prayer, tree-tending, walking, maybe dancing some—definitely clearing work concerns out of his mind ... By spring, I started doubling his solitude days so that he could go every 25 days. It was so good to get him home again! So refreshed! ... He's carrying a considerable load worrying about all of us.

So, finally there is a chance to invite letters from Bill's loved ones. Write long, write short, draw a picture, send anything at all. Most of all, please know how much we all love you!

June 14, 1999: Back with a Vengeance

So, that wasn't much of a lull, here comes a letter about me ...

I had an MRI on Saturday, June 5th, which was not interpreted until just before Bill's 50th birthday party on the 12th. So, now we're in for the long haul.

The preliminary reading on the films was that I have a tumor the same size that I had on my right side last September, now on the left side of my brain. After a brief hesitation, we decided to go ahead with the party and just dance in the face of it.

We were reassured yesterday that the entry point for a surgery could be similar to the one used previously. They could just go in from the top with as much precision as possible and remove the evident tumor.

*Bill is asking the hard quality-of-life questions—
"What happens if ... ?" He is also keeping me
up-to-speed on the limits of my own abilities. For
instance, writing these few paragraphs has taken me
perhaps three-quarters of an hour!*

I picked up the thread:

*Let me pick up where Jeanie leaves off: joining a call
to the redoubling of prayer.*

*We do indeed have new tumor on the left side. The
doctors here say that though the treatment worked well
(the original tumor bed remains clear), these things are
relentless in figuring a way around therapeutic blocks.
This one has pretty much mushroomed in nine weeks'
time, since the MRI (following her seizures the end
of March) that was scrutinized so closely. They also
say that for someone who consciously ducked radiation,
her progress has been remarkable up to now. And so
also hard to predict.*

*We are in the midst of difficult and quick decisions.
Please include that in your intercessions as well. We
are left facing options, some of which we have worked
mightily to avoid.*

*Jeanie is incredibly brave and sweet-spirited. The
doctors would guess she will become increasingly
lethargic and indifferent. I'm not ready to bet on it.
But she does move slow and linger long over small tasks,
like calling on your love as above. I add my own.*

Another from me:

June 22, 1999: From Worriness to Light

"And if the earthly fades and has forgotyou, whisper to the silent
Earth, 'I flow.' To the rushing waters say, 'I am.'"
—Rainer Maria Rilke, transcribed and sent to us by Dan

"While you were dancing at the 50th party, we were dancing our annual Eagle Dance ... I danced to the Tree of Life for you and the girls ... We did a round of dedications, where each dancer names someone in need of healing or help and the entire circle dances for that person. At that point we all danced for you. I continue in my heart."
—Email from a friend

"Oh, there are angels. So many angels everywhere. Their house is set in a wide space, filled with angels."
—To Jeanie's mom, from a charismatic friend in worship

> ... *Though the new tumor is in another "quiet area" of the frontal lobe, Jeanie is experiencing its effects in short-term memory and sequencing (She can get stuck or distracted in the middle of a process as basic as dressing). Happily, it must not come anywhere near the "humor center," as hers is fully intact. Nor could she be more sweet-spirited, giving and receiving love without limit.*

> *We have decided to do another surgery. It is currently scheduled for June 30 at Henry Ford Hospital. Though it is an admittedly aggressive approach, all the diverse physicians with whom we are in touch urge it. As previous, the tumor is accessible without going through healthy tissue, and they anticipate getting 90 percent. It should, for a time, forestall further change, and there is a small chance that any deficits caused by swelling pressure may be alleviated.*

> *They will also leave behind a chemo wafer, which will dissolve over time, giving the tumor site direct therapy without any of the ordinary side effects of chemotherapy. We will need to make further therapy decisions as we go. For a variety of reasons, it's not clear whether Nashville is a useful option any longer.*

I walk around with a rock in my stomach, though its size and weight seem to change with moment and circumstance. Generally, it's about the size of a softball. I confess it was dragging me under, spiraling quickly down into dread and despair. Lucy warned me that I was filling up the house with "worriness."

Since then, I've asked the girls to help me fill the house with light. (That is part of my request to you as well.) We are trying to sing every day together. Perhaps the messengers of light seen above are reply.

Lydia, from question upon question put to me over a lovely Father's Day breakfast of her own making, knows all—at least all of what the doctors can see and say. Our conversation that morning turned theological—to theodicy, meaning and hope. We agree that all things work together for good in those who love God. Her view is more supernatural than mine, but she was firm with me that I should speak always out of hope. I'm trying to listen to my daughters.

The other night, between fits of sleeplessness, I dreamed I'd forgotten to prepare for a class of children. When I walked in, they were already waiting and singing. What was the lesson last time? Beatitudes? Those who morn? I'm madly flipping the pages in search of a text. Then in my ear, practically with music: "The Lord is my light and my salvation." The whole of Psalm 27 may be commended to us all.

Please pray us light and hope. Remember Jeanie (and Dr. Rock) on the 30th. And those of us who gather round in love.

July 4, 1999: At Least Now She Likes Jazz

Jeanie arrived home yesterday, a Block Island baseball cap hiding her staples. She looks terrific. Prior and since, she has had some disturbing moments of confusion (looking me in the eye and asking urgently, "Where's Bill?"—though she was subsequently able to remember and process that strange moment). The CAT scan showed predictable swelling, but nothing untoward.

Actually, she is more talkative now than she has been for weeks. One interesting change: Jeanie now likes jazz! She only used to listen to it when I was out of town, for associative comfort in my absence. Now she thinks it brilliant. The girls are up at camp with community friends. Lydia, by phone, laughs out loud at the jazz news, saying: "Put on the Celtic music and see if she thinks it's boring."

We won't know the true outcome of surgery for a couple weeks. Meanwhile, the medicos are rushing us toward radiation, on the premise that the chemo wafers they left behind on the tumor bed have a synergistic effect with it. I'm still trying to find my breath and weigh the rock in my stomach.

Thanks to friends, we came home to the tall pine in front of our flat lit thick with tiny white Christmas lights. One answer to "Fill our home with light." Each sparkle summons for me the host of pray-ers who surround us. Please persevere, dear friends, as do we in thanks and love.

Another from me, begun with a poem I wrote:

July 22, 1999: A radiation therapy warfare prayer

In the grove, a drizzle
filtered by green needles
leaves its tears upon my page.

Later, in a hall outside
the sealed room, my back straight against the wall,
I close my eyes and see you on the techno slab of an
altar,
an accelerator pivoting
about your sweet head,
laser-lined to the cross mark
so precise upon your temple.

Lord of the Universe,
galaxymaker and tender of sparrows:
Filter photonsthrough your fine needles, green of chaos
and cause,
to protect my lover's living flesh,
renewing at once her mind
and shrinking death's dominion,
wiping it away as a tear.

"Each of your epistles is carefully placed on the 'bulletin board' in the middle of our dining room: a double-walled, metal fireplace that provides a central location for the most important communications that come through the community ... We are cheered by the good reports, led to prayer on your behalf when the reports are not so good ... I wonder if any couple has ever been followed by so great a group of well-wishers and loving supporters! I don't think I have ever known of such a thing."
—From friends at Jubilee Partners in Georgia

By way of preface, let me say that if these letters come to seem self-indulgent, we'll trust our friends to stop thanking or encouraging us and let us frankly know. There are, to be sure, tacit dangers in over-narrating our struggle. But in addition to summoning prayer, it has simply been one of the ways I process and cope with it all.

What to say about where we are? That Jeanie Wylie is dying? That Jeanie Wylie is fighting for her life? That Jeanie Wylie is free to die? That Jeanie Wylie is full of life and hope? All, in one respect or another, are true.

We have begun radiation. It was the hardest decision of this entire journey. There are permanent consequences of brain radiation, but these are a year or more off, and the doctors of conventional medicine regard that as a moot point in our situation. We had help from a clearness committee of gracious friends, and monkey wrenches from a radiologist who ought to appear before an AMA tribunal. There were 180-degree reversals, more rocks in the stomach, and dark-of-the-night second guessings. But we are doing it. Every working day for six weeks.

Blessedly, Jeanie was able to participate actively in the decision. Following the surgery, she was back with judgment engaged and opinions strong. As the neurologist said in amazement, "That woman has a pair of frontal lobes!"

In the course of my own decision-making angst, she turned me down a dirt road to pull over and park, looked me in the eye, and explained that she was, in fact, free to die. We held one another and wept.

This is not to suggest that we are resigned or giving up. (In fact, it means just the opposite. Free to die is free to live, free to fight, free to bet the farm.) We are exploring some new alternatives, including some exotic long shots. The radiation gives us some time to think.

When the clearness committee met, Lydia got clear, too: "If people in the community know about Mom's time, then you have to tell Lucy before she hears from somebody else." More 13-year-old wisdom. Early Sunday morning, on a cereal run with Lucy, I began to talk. Then on the way to church, as the reasons we might do radiation got spelled out, she wordlessly climbed into the front seat and quietly cried in Jeanie's lap.

In all providence, the Eucharist turned out to be a healing service. As Jeanie knelt for the anointing, Lucy began to sob uncontrollably and continued unselfconsciously in our laps back in the pew. The congregation was loving and prayerful. I can't imagine a better place for a child to process hard truth than in worship and prayer.

At present, Jeanie and I are alone at the cabin, having moved treatments to a hospital farther north. The girls are in final rehearsals for a youth theater production of The Sound of Music. (They play two of the daughters. "Like a lark who is learning to pray ... ") In the past week, Jeanie has had some unassailable head pain and seizures that overtake her as she walks, but we seem to have finally passed through both with medication and wheelchairs waiting in the wings.

Today was wonderful. Walks and talks, kisses and the banter of humor. As I write, Jeanie of the Frontal Lobes is answering correspondence, her fingers flying on the keyboard, writing once again faster than I can think. I couldn't be happier in the moment.

The decision about radiation remains the hardest judgment call of our long saga. Jeanie was dead-set against it. I remember sitting together in the car that night on the dirt road, praying and deciding to let the course of things play out. It was in a way the first choosing of hospice.

But then I couldn't sleep. Or eat. I reopened the decision process and made the case for reversal. And she assented. Jesus. It's the one choice I work hard not to regret. In part because the initiative was so categorically mine.

Radiation has long-term consequences that were presumed to be irrelevant in her expected lifetime. But then she stuck around for the longer haul. I always wondered quietly how many of her later deficits were related to radiation necrosis rather than tumor growth. We'll never know. I have prayed to let it go.

There's confession in this. I aspired to the freedom already named, but grasped it unevenly and only in part. And yet, decision by decision, in the mysteries of providence, and borne by community, we went forward.

Jeanie with Dr. Tom Shaw upon receiving an honorary doctorate from Episcopal Divinity School, 2000. Credit: Bill Wylie-Kellermann

Not So Good for Chickens

Another update from Jeanie:

August 29, 1999: The Budapest Option

After the last letter, you probably picture me six feet under. It's a strange see-saw. Anyway, strange as it is, we are okay. In many ways, better than expected.

I know Bill wrote about me fighting for my life and being willing to die. All true. Before the second brain surgery at the end of June, I had started to think often of dying. In my heart, I had let go of the kids and Bill. Dying did not seem so bad.

Our friend Ed Rowe took me out for lunch and was concerned about my death talk. He attributed it to the meds and told Bill he expected that I would eventually be livid about them. I was just getting fuzzier and fuzzier, forgetting things, losing time. I heard Bill ask Henry Ford's staff whether radiation would bring me back, or was this the best we could hope for?

Anyway, I was surprised to discover that when I woke up after the surgery, it was three days later! The first time, I startled everyone by waking up so soon—less than two hours after the surgery. I must have done something similar this time— I've been told that I talked, moved, and seemed to understand things—but my soul didn't rejoin my body until a few days later.

The good news is that over time it came clear first to me, and then to Bill, that I was much better! I can't tell you how glad I was finally to hear him say so. Anyway, there's not much that I cannot do now—I can walk, talk, write letters, make decisions. I seem to be in pretty good shape. Considerably better than before!

I started radiation in the middle of July and completed it at the end of this week. If I understand it correctly, I've maxed out brain radiation forever and am now free!

None of the potential side-effects kicked in, except that the affected area did start to burn (after two weeks) and my hair started falling out in clumps. I now have hair in the back, but the front is very bald. I've become adept with scarves and hats …

Next week we'll go as a family to Budapest. There is a chicken virus that researchers in Budapest have been experimenting with for the last decade or two. The word is that it's not so good for chickens, but seems to benefit some cancer patients. It takes time—up to a year—but we're eager to try it.

I began our next update with a recalling of our wedding vows:

August 29, 1999: And Even in the Face of Death Itself

"Jeanie Wylie/Bill Kellermann: In solemn delight and the
fullest freedom I am able to receive from our God, I take you,
foreswearing all others, to be my wife/husband, in joy and in
sorrow, in sickness and in health, in freedom and captivity,
and even in the face of death itself. I honor you as a child of
God, and commit myself to the working out of our salvation
within the vocation of marriage. I join you in a life of simplicity, renouncing waste and violence and endeavoring to
preserve creation. I pray that our marriage will be a sign of
faith and fidelity, a service to our sisters and brothers, and
in hope of family and future. All this in the name of the One
who is Creator and Sustainer of life, the Lord and Servant
of all creation, and the Spirit that binds us together as one.
Amen."

*September 1st will mark our 15th anniversary. It is
now just a year since Jeanie collapsed under the tumor.
Somehow these days co-mingle for us in memory and
meaning. Our vows cover it all in ways providential
and unforeseeable. Together we choose it all yet again.*

*Today Jeanie finished the course of radiation, and we
are joining that to our celebration in an overnight
away at the cabin. We're about to go for a walk under
the full moon. (Since it was full the time we got
engaged, and we mark those so, it's a kind of double
anniversary.)*

*The radiation treatment, be it due to prayer, nutritional
supplements, or pure will, has been free of illness or
fatigue. Jeanie did have a periodic fever that left the
doctors anxious, since the steroids that she takes would
mask any infection. Being hospitalized for a couple
days of testing drew only the conclusion that it was the
heavy-duty meds themselves that were taxing her liver
and prompting the spikes. We really like the smaller*

Mt. Clemens hospital, and all the folks who have been treating her there.

So what's next? We go to Budapest, no less, for a viral treatment that our oncologist here is gladly supporting in lieu of the blunt and useless tools he admits having at his disposal. It's a chicken virus/vaccine, harmless to humans. They discovered this thing when the chickens died and the farmer got better ... There is a scientific letter about it in the May 5 Journal of the American Medical Association. Which means it will be eventually available here in trials, but not soon enough for Jeanie.

The other providence is that, against all expectation, the Nashville doctor gave us our up front money back ... Since the insurance company paid, at least sufficient for the doctor's needs, he sent the reimbursement to our Central Methodist health fund. That is what is enabling us to go, and even take the girls along.

The treatment there will be in large part out-patient. Jeanie is doing so well that we are looking forward to a spirit of vacation in this. My Mom, who has never been out of the country but yearned to travel all her life, will even accompany us. It feels full of life and adventure.

I'll confess that my last letter was written having just turned a corner of despair. The radiation decision had left me in deeper resignation than I knew. I was explaining to a friend (in front of Jeanie) that what we, and the doctors, were hoping for was six months of stability, when Lydia stomped her foot, threw her pencil across the kitchen, and ran out saying, "I told you I don't want to hear this kind of talk anymore!" It was like another Zen whack, or a Word anointed.

I woke in the middle of the night and journaled my confession. Next morning, Jeanie allowed she was ready, in the aforementioned freedom, to keep fighting, and we cranked up the alternative search again in earnest, settling upon this strange and exotic, long-shot approach.

A couple evenings ago, at the behest of, and brokered by, a good friend, we took Jeanie to a sprawling, working-class, charismatic church to be prayed over by a circle of tongued warriors. It was good. I almost always delight to be in the midst of tongues, experiencing it like being washed in rainfall.

I'm generally able to mingle my own silent praise and intercession in the sound. For one woman in the group, however, we were way too peaceful, quiet, and receptive. Well, perhaps not "receptive"—I think her measure of that would be for us to break down in sobs, or burst into tongues ourselves. I suspect she doubted our salvation (it's probably just as well there wasn't time to talk politics).

But that was not our experience of the others, vulnerable and sweet-spirited, who pressed their hands upon Jeanie in anonymous love. Yesterday, she slept the morning through. Our friend declared this good, saying, "If this tumor is gone, I hope you'll credit the prayers at least as much as the chickens." Hey, count on it dear friends. And also our love.

September 30, 1999, from Gethsemani Abbey:
The Hungarian Tale

"You will not fear the terror of the night
       nor the arrow that flies by day,
nor the plague that prowls in the darkness
       nor the scourge that lays waste at noon."
       —Psalm 90, sung Gregorian by the monks at compline

Gethsemani and home

Out the corner of my eye
The Pleiades loom light in the moonless sky.

Nevertheless
I count our moons since beneath its fulsome face
we sealed here our kisses with engagement.

Now, though the fire tower
with its missing and riskier steps, is long dismantled,
a brown and brassy hawk steps off another height
to hover still, as then, in the wind.

Ancient reeds which rustled once when this was shore
turn up again as though in endless supply,
in fractured perfect rings, fossils at my feet.
Without a second thought, in decision ever so easily made,
I would thread this stone and take it for a promise
again and ever again.

You are here
in the gate, now thick with new paint, opening on the close
where you posed with a brassy smile
and a threaded stone ring upon your neck.
The cathedral of white pines where you wept, beloved of God,
burned to the ground a decade ago;
the sculptures took the heat and stayed.
Here where disciples drowse and Jesus pleads this cup to pass,
you are beloved again in tears
while hurries my heart to you.

I'm much on the road since we are back from Hungary. Last week, preaching and speaking in seminaries of Michigan and Indiana; this week in Kentucky. A good friend staying with Jeanie pulls the phone into the other room, drops her voice, and suggests it's time for me to be done with the road work. She may be right, but I'm not fully convinced. I can't hear it yet in Jeanie's voice on the line, so strong, or see it in her face across the table, so completely herself. Perhaps it is another cycle of denial, but if so I'm happy in it.

How's Jeanie? A neurologist declares her this day "clinically quite good." My very sentiments, more or less. At present she's working on and off at the December issue of The Witness on "Healing from Human Evil." And she marked up this letter, correcting for typos and improvements.

The Budapest trip went well. We stayed in an apartment just across from the largest synagogue in Europe, entranceway to the Jewish ghetto in the '30s and '40s. A Rosh Hashanah crowd overflowed into the street. We even went to a Klesmer concert there. Its onion-topped towers across the roofs made our kitchen window view an easy place to pray.

Treatment, especially, went very well, with the doctor coming to our flat daily to build up the injections. This virus works genetically to alter tumor cells, "allowing them to die," as it were.

Through the course of things, Jeanie felt fine enough (with appropriate mild fevers) that we were able to get around the city in vacation-like forays to castles and Danube boat rides. The girls came home with chess sets and secret-keyed jewelry boxes from the tented vendors. Lydia, who was the best street bargainer of our lot, was also unaccountably astonished when everything was in Hungarian instead of English. Lucy kept a daily journal, answering questions put by her teacher.

One blessing of Jeanie's illness is that my mom was able to join us (at 83!) and fulfill a lifelong dream. We rented a car and made a side trip to Salzburg and the mountains of Austria. When we turned a corner and the Alps came into view, Mom quietly wept.

I weathered the stress of logistical anxiety, arranging hedges against every possible medical crisis in a foreign system. In the end, as a Vonnegut character says upon returning from a free trip to the Chronosynclastic Infundibulum, "Everything was wonderful and nothing hurt."

What we hadn't foreseen was how complicated and tricky it would be to bring back a non-FDA-approved treatment into our system. We'd gone with the blessing of our oncologist, who signed off on papers of non-objection and post-return monitoring, so we didn't imagine how difficult it would prove to acquire basic services and materials (like syringes and ports and the necessary orders that go with such devices). In the interim we've had to scramble for a fallback and less efficient way of delivering the vaccine, as we figure a way around the barriers. And lots of this figuring has been managed while I am roadbound.

The other night we had a gathering of folks from around the Worker to think about logistical support in the next several months. What a wondrous circle of friends we are granted (including you, dear readers, at a distance). Food came in the door like a potluck unannounced. It felt more like a party or a prayer time than a planning session. I guess we go forward in a mix of all three, and in gratitude for each.

Christmas Day, 1999: While Dragons Sleep Beneath the Floor

Dear Friends:

What a gift to celebrate a feast of the Incarnation, while thinking on you in the same moment. We are at the cabin ("the cabbage," as one of our goddaughters has dubbed it in word-crossed fusion with "cottage"). That luminous solstice moon has encircled us, lighting up the landscape for nightwalks.

This morning we wove wreaths from seven varieties of pine branches, plus pods and cones and berries, harvested in a hike about these woods. (One of these lies now beneath the tree, a present for Jeanie's Mom, immanently expected.) Actually, we all had homemade gifts for one another this morning. This gift-of-our-hands way of marking the day makes my heart glad.

Last night Jeanie had a seizure about 5 p.m., which not only sent us scurrying in near panic to find among these small towns a pharmacy still open Christmas Eve, but also foreclosed our plan for candlelight Eucharist with the Episcopalians. This turned out to be an odd and lovely providence, as we ended up at the kitchen table in a candlelight caroling and intercession service of our own, reading the gospel from a store of favorite children's books and taking communion from a bowl and mug. In luminous sacrament, we were given one another in a way I'll never forget.

OK, this seizure. We are convinced that it, like a bigger one 10 days ago, stems from a medication imbalance rather than new tumor growth. A course of antibiotics, prescribed some weeks back in the wake of superficial corrective surgery, taxed Jeanie's liver and sent things *out of whack. It's compounded now by a transition from one anti-seizure med to another.*

In point of fact, Jeanie has had a very good autumn, not without bouts of symptom or deficit. But she edited an amazing issue of The Witness on "Healing from Human Evil"—soliciting and shaping the articles, choosing art, sizing photos, doing layout, and summing it all up editorially—the entire shtick. No issue is a single-handed affair; it involves a skilled circle of friends. But Jeanie did what she does—something of a minor triumph.

Need I tell you this is one remarkable woman, caring for us and exercising wisdom in the midst of it all. She wrote the meditation below for the January issue on "Time." To be honest, she had forgotten she'd promised it, then sat down to the keyboard and poured it out of her head and heart in an hour. The way I labor over similar things, you'd think I had a brain tumor.

On the complicated medical front, we did arrange (yet another tale of providence) to get a Groshong catheter put in (yet another surgery), which we self-manage with a highly ritualized sterile procedures of care. (Feature me in a mask with surgical gloves and you get the picture.) We do daily injections of the "chicken virus," NDV (Newcastles Disease Virus).

You'll recall that we had completed the radiation end of August, and this period falls within the six-month benefit the medicos would hope in consequence. But several weeks ago following an MRI showing no new growth, when I asked one of our doctors if he credited Jeanie's well-being to radiation, he replied, "Well, you're also taking that vaccine. You know I can't tell you to do that stuff, but I sure wouldn't tell you to stop."

So far, I've been present for each of this recent series of seizures, holding Jeanie and riding them out, but I'm praying for an even medication keel as we begin a new term at SCUPE in Chicago and my teaching kicks in. I continue to walk the line between commitment to the program of hope in which we live, and making mental preparations (usually late in a sleepless night) for more dire outcomes conventional medicine would call "realistic." I know I often stuff the emotions that accompany the latter trains of thought.

The staff at SCUPE is remarkable in its willingness to accommodate our uncertainties. In Chicago we have begun a new program, "Nurturing the Call," which recruits working African American pastors in the city (from storefronts and big congregations both) to use the SCUPE program as an entree into seminary training. It's an exciting year at hand, with new and gifted colleagues at the table. I'm working on a lecture for the first go round, the January term course, on "The Gospel as Urban Nonviolence."

In a related connection, I was pleased to do a training several weeks back for a group of friends traveling as direct action from Detroit to Iraq, bearing medicine and wide-eyed witness. (What a time to be there, no?) As for Detroit, the casinos have arrived big-time in "temporary" digs. Last week when I went to do the homily at Day House, it was in a sea of cars—employees parking blocks away and shuttled to the old Wonder Bread factory, now "converted." This is an economy?

The girls flourish. Here at the cabin, Lydia, with Lucy's attentive help, has been working on a new Epiphany play for our community at the Catholic Worker. Her script from last year (a talk show interviewing all the principals, including the "wisewomen" and the donkey), got picked up and performed at several churches and for their own school performance. When she saw the fifth-graders rehearsing, she came home downcast: "Dad! They've added commercials!"

Theater remains her activity of choice. She's just been in productions of A Charlie Brown Christmas and a fractured musical version of Sleeping Beauty. She's in all her glory as an eighth-grade student, something of a senior year for middle-schoolers. Which also means, we are trying to figure out high school for next year.

Lucy does the theater too (she was Sally and Woodstock variously in the traveling Charlie Brown), but basketball is her new love. Wish I could say I'd been working with her, but any credit I could claim would have to be genetic (who can claim credit for that?) She's learning it all from scratch. Signing on as a fourth-grader in the fifth- and sixth-grade community league, she's nonetheless fastest among her teammates. As a guard, she is tenacious as the "last line of defense" against a fast break of girls often twice her size. Lucy has also latched suddenly and unrelentingly onto the piano, though she declines lessons on the premise that Mozart taught himself.

I can hear the girls talking quietly upstairs. It's late now as I finish this. Another log goes on the fire. I think of the sleeping calm in Fritz Eichenberg's Catholic Worker print, above, which we enclose as a greeting and meditation. The dragons in the floorboards sleep quietly, too. But like Herod's troops—or cruise missiles or malignancies (economic or otherwise)— they can wake with a start. When they do, we trust not so much our own wits and resources, as the dreams and messengers of grace who open the Way. Like you, dear friends. Thank you. Bless you. You are sacraments luminous.

Here, Jeanie's meditation for the midwinter issue on "Time":

Midwinter for Witness Readers: Wisdom of an Old Soul

"We may never pass this way again ... "
—Seals and Crofts

I had the misfortune to finish high school just as this song peaked in its popularity in my small Michigan town. At an all-school assembly, it was announced as our class song, and I fled. A friend tagged along. She knew that my father had just died. I was glad for the company but also frustrated that she seemed self-absorbed: "I've never been this close to death before ... "

"Yeah, well, get a grip!" I wanted to yell. Or, had I known it then, I could have quoted Julie Wortman's favorite Emerson line: "Life is real; life is earnest."

So now I'm about to turn 43 and have a high-grade cancer in my brain. I spent the whole last year struggling to digest the news that the seizures I had Labor Day weekend in 1998 were caused by an anaplastic glioblastoma. I fought believing that it was actually cancer until there was no other conclusion. Until that moment, I kept thinking, "Unh-unh, I won't join that club 'til I have to. I'm not the cancer-personality type!"

Since then my partner, Bill, and I have read more than anyone wants to know about the theories on cancer, the composition of cancer, the treatments for cancer. I was quickly overwhelmed even on the lack of agreement about what cancer is. And then there is lots of literature on how to develop the right attitude, how to grip something in this world so strongly that dying is not an option. Some people refuse to die because they have kids to raise. One farmer-type said, "Nope, I got to get home to my garden." Doubtless some people live for their pets or the view or their neighbors. Perhaps they simply want to praise God in some particular way.

Recently I was sitting at my kitchen table talking with my 13-year-old. It's easy to forget that she's 13. She is extremely attentive and has always had a mind like a 35-year-old. She's good on details and usually right. It's hard when parenting her to try to recall that she is a child and needs to be protected like a child.

So, there I was in one of those judgment spirals, when I was having an insight and she was my companion. I said to my own kid, "You know, I've been thinking about time. While it matters whether I die at 42 or at 82, in many ways it doesn't matter at all."

Ever so gently, testing what I could bear, she said, "Mom, do you want to hear some reasons why it does matter?"

As it crashed in on me that I was having this conversation with the very last person in the world who should hear my philosophizing, I nodded. She told me that if I live to be 82, I would meet our grandchildren (should the girls choose to have any). I would have time to walk in the woods.

She tailored the list to the things I love, with a strong but gentle bias toward being there as she and her sister grow up. At the same time, she managed not to put pressure on me. She was artful—as usual. It's challenging parenting a child who is often older than you.

(Lydia does have her faults, not to worry. And her sister Lucy is a bundle of joy and challenges of a different type. Lucy is much less likely to tell you what's on her

mind. You have to notice. And she'll notice you notice! Both girls are smart and loving in radically different ways.)

But, despite my regrets for announcing my great insight about death and time to my oldest child, the thoughts remain true. Daniel Corrigan preached at my Dad's installation at the Church of the Advent in Boston in 1960. I've heard that he leaned forward with a twinkle in his eyes and said, "Sam Wylie is my best friend and I don't care if he lives or dies!"

It's the great tension of our faith. What is it we are about? Are we living or dying? Does it matter?

Knowing some of the stats on cancer, I look around rooms now and wonder: if indeed it's one out of three, who else shares this ailment? How can we help each other? What worldly things need to change? Which factories close? Which pollutants get screened out of smoke?

How can we learn to walk in beauty and trust, while also fighting back? To model what it means to be an elder, yet also be effective at bringing change? And most of all, how can we praise God without ceasing in this time-bound world?

(The Witness, *January/February 2000)*

Jeanie and Bill at Leaven Center, 1998. Credit: Family collection

12

A Yearning for the Absent

I picked up the thread once more:

February 15, 2000: Passed Worries Unknown

Friends:

Light a candle. Give some thanks. But don't cease the intercessions.

The cloud under which we've been living for a week has only this morning been lifted. Actually, at the Worker when I asked for prayers and said we were anxious for the outcome of this Sunday's MRI, Jeanie corrected me: I might be anxious, but she was confident, clear, and hopeful. And as it turns out, right so to be.

Last Wednesday morning Jeanie had a seizure. It was a long one, but she retained sufficient consciousness to recall me in tears holding her. Since the girls were just then preparing for school, they witnessed it all yet again. When they finally went off late with our neighbor to school, we headed for the ER. This time bloodwork showed, disconcertingly, that her level of

*seizure medication was on the high end of normal,
indicating this was some kind of "breakthrough"
seizure, overriding the meds. I did indeed imagine the
worst (as did the neurologist) but don't believe I gave
myself over to it.*

*Friday morning, same hour, Jeanie crashed to the floor
in a faint. More fuel for my inner fretting and late-
night sleeplessness. I'm from a family line famous for
wrestling worries. Lydia rolls her eyes and sides with
Jeanie's resolute confidence. When Lucy couldn't sleep
the other night and requested the light on, I sat with
her and asked if she was worrying about Mom. "Not
that I know of, but sometimes you worry deep down
and don't even know it."*

*Then today, we got the radiologist's read of the weekend
MRI: no new tumor growth. We still don't know what's
behind the seizing, but the doctor adds another layer
of meds in the interest of prevention—and, above
all, we can rule out the hastening fears. Nor do we
know to what the tumor's stability may be attributed
(radiation, viral treatment, prayer, all of the above?)
But we are content to light a candle, give thanks, and
send out this day's good news in tears and love.*

April 1, Feast of Fools, 2000: With a Wordless Grace

"O God, the strength of the weak and the comfort of sufferers:
Mercifully accept our prayers, and grant to your servant Jeanie
the help of your power, that her sickness may be turned into
health, and our sorrow into joy; through Jesus Christ our Lord.
Amen."
—Evening Prayer, March 29, St. James Cathedral

*Jeanie had emergency surgery last night. Her brain
was filled with fluid pressure: hydrocephalus—water
on the brain. My older brother died of it at two weeks*

old. She woke up this morning with a shunt draining the excess into her belly and a smile wide as her eyes are bright.

Since the several days of intensive work last month, when she put final touches to a discipleship issue of The Witness (with major backside editorial coverage from the staff), I have watched her decline and slow. Progressively nonverbal. At the neurologist's office Monday, she couldn't add 9+3, draw the face of a clock, say the day or date, or even where we were—try hard as she might.

When my bishop asked us to serve communion at a Methodist gathering Tuesday, she offered the cup with a grace not wordless, but silent. At an Associated Church Press worship service on her behalf in Chicago last week, and at the Episcopal Communicators' luncheon (where Lydia and Lucy handed out the awards with a grace all their own), she would tire quickly, fail to recognize friends, lapse into a stare, or merely nod and smile in earnest attempts at conversation.

These weeks have been full of grief for me. I hadn't stopped working or doing the tasks of our life together, I just did them with tears streaming down or cracks in my voice. Dishes and driving, faxing and phone calls. Lydia took it as the first time I had "given up" (and set her hand to encouraging and caring for me). But in truth, not so. It never seemed to me resignation or despair, simply the cleanest and most open response to what was slipping away before my eyes. A yearning for the absent. And the ceaseless prayer which love is.

We returned early from Chicago, as Jeanie was requiring constant assistance for the most basic of functions. I'd found myself necessarily holding her fork or toilet paper or shoelace, albeit as loving intercession mingling frustration and grief. We went the next morning, Friday, to the hospital for pictures and tests. In the car on the way she didn't talk, but she was able to sing with me.

The surgery decision was urgently simple and well advised. She looked me in the eye and nodded as I signed consent. (To forego it or delay would have meant quickly blindness, then stroke, then respiratory failure.) And yet it betokened and presaged other decisions which one day might forego "heroic measures" and technological false hopes. She made her living will long ago. At the very least, true hope includes not dreading such choices prematurely.

Opening the ACP/EC worship service at the cathedral in Chicago, our friend Herb said, "It is not death which Jeanie Wylie resists, but the power of death. Her wisdom is to show us the difference." She surely does show me.

At the conference (and at the Methodist meeting) people introduced themselves who had previously known Jeanie only in prayer. What an amazing way to meet. In the company of the wide communion of all who have ever prayed and all who will. Thanks for being in that communion.

'Til every tear is wiped away ...

April 2, 2000 Postscript: *Jeanie, while still a little disoriented and agitated, is talking a mile a minute. Completing her sentences. By afternoon she should be out of ICU and into a regular room. Home, if things proceed as hoped, in a day or two.*

April 3, 2000: ICU Crash

Our Jeanie is still in the ICU. As they were preparing her for the room transfer, she had a brief seizure while on the commode unattended, and took a nose dive. It's clear setback, and she is recovering way more slowly than my heart yearns. I like this hospital, its human scale, and the doctors for whom we choose it, but at the moment my grief renewed is mixed with anger.

The seizure could have been caused by any number of things: aftermath of surgery, the shunt itself, or an anti-seizure medication change just then in transition. A CT scan last night shows nothing untoward. Her eyes open and her smile follows, but she talks little and then barely. The neurologist is hunting clues and saying that time is what she needs. The fruitfulness of time and prayer are equal mysteries to me (and notably related). God grant her both.

April 11, 2000: Upturn in the Dark

Jeanie Wylie's sweet head, now wounded again, looks like the map of a warzone—scarred, cross-stitched, overlaid with the subterranean shunt tube, and now a third shaved and fuzzy length of hair—yet she remains unaffectedly beautiful. One of the nurses declares her gorgeous and brings in a turquoise scarf to cover the battleground and make her practically beatific. This morning her countenance—quick smile and eyes full of thoughts she can't yet say—was so sunny it turned my mood rightside up. It has not always been so this last week.

Yesterday was actually the worst, though perhaps I gave in. She: sluggish and slack, utterly nonverbal, acting only on command. Me: dragged under with grief. I summoned my brother Jimmy out of a Methodist meeting in sobs over the payphone.

The recovery for which we pray has been slow and incremental at best. Doctors, even those we like and trust, render diverse opinions, some dire and dead-end: "If I had to classify her state, it would be 'dementia.' This may be what we're going to get."

Short-term memory seemed to be withering rather than improving. Over the weekend, her Mom, sister and brother-in-law, on a marathon visit, would engage her joy. Then returning from a bathroom break, she'd open the door, suddenly so pleased and surprised and full of welcoming smiles all over again.

Today she rallies unaccountably. Initiates conversation she can't even finish. Pushes me physically toward the elevator on a stroll through the hall. Let's blow this pop stand, whatever it may be.

She is strong and stable enough to come home in the next day or two. To that end, we reconvened the famous clearness committee to figure the possibilities for 24-hour care (at least for the time being). Personally, I believe being home will ground her in place and time, allowing the brain to more safely reroute its signals.

I'm six days into a fast. I know it's counterintuitive, when I need strength for Jeanie and the girls, but intuitive nonetheless. As a form of prayer, it seemed most in accord with my sense of powerlessness. And a way of honoring the emptiness already in my gut.

When I've felt tired and weak, it's really been from sleeplessness. If anything, the fast has lightened and energized me. I'm verified in the late-night impulse. And when that woman finally walks up the stairs and in the door here, I will feast in ways more than one.

Downstairs (I'm writing in the attic) the girls are noisily dragging furniture—their way of preparing space for Jeanie's mom, Grandma Bea, to come for a longer stay. Earlier, I found Lucy quietly crying in Grandpa Sam's sermon-writing Morris chair by the front window. "Just too many changes!" she explains. O sweetie, you don't have to give up your room.

But, of course, I've barely touched the real change. "No, it's Mom needing so much help and care." We hold one another and cry in complete agreement. Later on the phone, Jeanie freely holds up her end of a conversation with both girls. And now the furniture gets energetically pushed.

I don't know. Usually, to be frank, I wait for an upturn of some sort (like this morning) to write you all. But I don't honestly know if what we get is increments turning a corner or simply what we get.

But you know what, dear friends? What we get is Jeanie Wylie through and through. Even sluggish and weighed under, it's she. So far, even at the worst, she knows she's loved. Even at worst, she loves from somewhere so deep it can't be covered over or knifed away. With nothing more than that (but thank God blessedly more), we can live.

'Til the darkest glass clears …

April 13, 2000: Soar We Now

Two simpatico notes from California:

"You are chronicling a *via crucis* of the most intimate kind, and your words, like dropped tears, pave the way for all of us to follow. Tomorrow, I'll fast with you."

"I will think of you especially during Holy Week and know you will be relating to the passion and suffering in a most personal way. I can only hope for you the resurrection too. I love you."

Jeanie Wylie came home last night. I broke my fast on Lebanese take-out (I'm up at 3:30 a.m. with guts roiling). The host of tiny white lights that adorn the 60-foot tree before our house burn now in celebration, as they have in vigil the last two weeks. Tomorrow the circuits will get their rest.

Yesterday when I went into the hospital, Jeanie was up and about, packing unprompted for home (!), everything laid out in tidy piles on the bed in preparation. After a proper greeting, she turned toward the Betty LaDuke poster we'd hung on her wall and said, "Isn't that painting beautiful? There's so much going on." Sentences effortless, lucid, and complete.

For 45 minutes downstairs in rehab, she was completely focused and coordinated, climbing stairs, getting in and out of mocked-up car doors, and otherwise demonstrating her readiness. Doctors paraded through with smiles agog and tears welling in their eyes. It seemed we were all suddenly looking back on the corner we'd been praying she'd turn.

She still gets stuck mid-sentence, searches for words, or forgets she's already listened to the phone messages, but Jeanie's clearly busy rerouting circuits to her brain's place of naming. Day before yesterday, Lucy and I sat in the Morris chair discussing how we'd get her some weekly counsel time; today the girls dance giddy, and Lydia runs house to house on the block with good news she never really doubted.

Two days ago, I was fighting not to be haunted by a string of second-guessed decisions; in the light of today, I think we made some good calls and know once again that second-guessed self-accusations are pointless, if not faithless. Two days back, I was turning my head away in tears as we discussed the merits of hospice with physicians and social workers; this morning I can fully imagine Jeanie editing yet another issue of the magazine. Then, I figured if she joined the Peace Community's Good Friday Way of the Cross streetwalk, it would be in silence by wheelchair; today I see her on foot, reading prayers aloud at each stop and later at her favorite service of all: the Easter Vigil.

So what turned this amazing tide? Lord knows. It coincides with several things. I began surreptitious resumption of the NDV (chicken virus) treatment. She and I would repair to the bathroom and shoot up. (Actually, I did alert one of the doctors to my intention.)

Based on high blood levels, they also began reducing the dosage of Jeanie's new seizure medication. There is, needless to say, the coincident mystery of "time," which one of the doctors persisted in urging us to wait upon. And, of course, that other mystery: prayers more numerous, more numinous, than lights upon the Lenten tree.

Thank you, dear friends, for vigiling with us yet again. Forgive us the changes we must put you through. You, however, hold us steady and lighten our hearts.

'Til we walk those streets together ...

June 1, 2000: Shadows and Feathers (written over several days)

Wisdom from Emily Dickinson:
"Hope is an unbearably precious thing, worth its weight in feathers."

"The happiness without cause is the best happiness, for glee intuitive and lasting is the gift of God."

"I find ecstasy in living, the mere sense of living is joy enough."

Where are we? At just the moment I begin to write, up in the air between Chicago and Detroit. Jeanie came along for SCUPE graduation and to see the Betty LaDuke Eritrea paintings exhibited at the Field Museum. By the time we kiss the girls and turn in after midnight, she won't be able to recall the day's events unprompted.

Ten days ago she had another seizure, a considerable setback from which she has recovered more slowly than before. Perhaps as much to the point, an MRI the day prior had shadows "suspicious of new neoplasm," as they say.

She takes my hand across the empty seat and her eyes are bright. Her face is a little drawn and she tires easily. She forgets phone messages, sometimes as soon as hanging up (be warned and ask her to write it down). She is simple, direct, inclusive in family prayertime. She picks up a novel and begins reading yet again from page one. Getting out of a car in Chicago she panics slightly looking for Lucy (home in Detroit). She laughs, and my heart rises with its ripple.

She gets lost, but in a winsome kind of way. Losing a thought, she is gracious with herself and others. She puts her head on my shoulder, holds tight, and sinks in deep. Her kisses are long and tender. She loves and knows and receives at a depth. She "bes" freely herself.

How did we get here? For those wanting the saga in detail: She did walk the Good Friday Stations (with both our mothers). At the Easter Vigil, she covered last minute for Lydia, who turned up with a sore throat. Waving off all proffers of assistance, Jeanie took the lectern and, as we held our collective breath, read a full chapter of Exodus, leaving Pharaoh's army and death itself drowned in the tide. It was a stunning moment. Miriam herself might have danced.

A week later she seized while alone. I'd gone to fetch something from the car and ended up in sidewalk conversation with a close friend (about the Holocaust and the New Testament causes of anti-Semitism, no less). I was heartsick to find her recovering wide-eyed on her knees, forehead rug-burned and a black eye begun. Next day, her memory was not so hot, but she bounced back—doing cognitive, sequencing, and memory exercises with a home therapist. Time story problems and checkbook balancing sheets (hell, I should have her do mine).

The week of May 15, the week of the MRI, I was giddy with joy. The doctors, in progression, all smiled or teared and declared her a walking wonder. Enroute home by car, I asked about the novel she's reading (the one now begun again). To my amazement, she details plot and character, imagining what's to come. We agree the time is ripe to think on a next magazine issue topic for her to edit.

That very evening she seizes again, this time with 10-year old Lucy the one on deck. Lucy had dreaded this prospect, alone with Mom, but Jeanie's been so good I thought nothing of a pick-up run to get Lydia. Lucy rose to the moment, getting a pillow beneath Jeanie's head and phoning a neighbor. Actually, the numbers by the phone "went all blurry," but she called one by heart, a block friend whose mother came running.

Now recovery goes more slowly or levels off, fluctuating on the slope of slippage. I don't know how many more times I can bear to watch Jeanie slip away, but Lord knows she's so far bounced back an equal number of times. (Sometimes I'm not even sure how many more miracles I can bear.)

Tomorrow I head off for five days of conference and teaching, plans confirmed in the giddy days of her wellness. Mothers and friends piece together a schedule of presence and care. Tomorrow is also my 51st birthday. My jubilee disciplines have, to be honest, deteriorated—all but abandoned. A journal and these letters about all that remain.

I know I'm not taking care of myself. Friends notice and step in. A new one from Bartimaeus Cooperative Ministries in Los Angeles appeared a few weeks back to do "bodywork" a few days with us all. Lucy, poor sweetie, was on the table relaxing beneath the healing touch of a massage when a tornado blew through town, setting off sirens and driving us with books and candles to the basement. (You'll think I'm contriving some sort of metaphor.)

Lucy, by the way, is asking for weekly counseling, which is being hooked up right here on the block with a therapist in the Worker community. Lydia, meanwhile, is in the final throes of eighth grade, back from a D.C. trip, orchestrating talent shows, and braiding flowers in her hair for graduation.

I guess that's it. We make summer plans on uncertain premises. We rest in the rhythm of day by day, step by step, trying to pay attention. It dawns on me that these letters are themselves a form of prayer. You know they are a summons as well. Please and thanks.

Death be drowned ...

From Lydia:

June 14, 2000: Young Eyes and Eagle's Wings

> *Dear Friends (as so commonly written by my dad),*

"And he will raise you up on eagle's wings,
bear you on the breath of dawn,
make you to shine like the sun,
and hold you in the palm of his hand."
—Song by Michael Joncas based on Psalm 91 and Isaiah 40

This Psalm fits well, for it is true that God has raised my family up so many times in the last year and a half. I decided I needed to take over and write a letter myself. Every time I read my dad's letters they make me cry. They make our life sound so depressing, when truthfully I wouldn't trade my life for the world.

My dad was gone for the last couple of days, and in those couple of days I noticed an incredible change in my mom. She speaks clearly, her short-term memory is much better, and she is able to speak complete thoughts. She's like our mom again, the one in charge. She has favors to ask, the kind you can't say no to. Lucy will occasionally break out into tears because she doesn't want to do something my mom says she has to. If that's not mom power, I don't know what is. This is the first time in months when she has regained her power.

My mom is sweet, strong-willed, spiritual, gentle, loving, and my mom. Some of these qualities have been hidden for a while. I can sit with her and she will bring up a topic and she can hold her own in the conversation.

Although the MRI says there is "suspicious" growth of the tumor in the middle of the brain that would be impossible to remove, I can't see it! She is strong and healthy, and I can see that God will lift us up on eagles' wings yet another time. To do this we are counting and praying for your prayers.

I have to admit that if I were to go back in time and there was some way to take back the cancer, in a way I wouldn't do it! I feel that ever since my mom was diagnosed with cancer, I've been born. I started my life. I was reborn. I appreciate my life and I feel like I am living it every second rather than the past. I also finally found God, who is my best friend, the one I tell everything, and for me that is enough. I love my life and my family so much.

I feel a great compassion for my dad. When he leaves on business, I get this empty feeling in my stomach. I know I have this responsibility for my mom. There is always someone with me, but I still feel like the one in charge, the one who knows what to do. If anything happened, I would be the one that would have to take charge.

When my dad comes home, the empty feeling disappears. He is there and I trust him with my whole heart. When I then put myself in his position. I realize his empty hole and the responsibility that was given to him on that sunny September 6, 1998. Whether he is here in Detroit or somewhere else in the country, the empty hole remains and will probably never go away (especially since my mom promises me she is going to live 'til she's 83). I can then understand the pain he feels that he lets out through many of the letters he writes to you.

Every time he says "I'm watching her slip away," my stomach does a flip flop, and I either want to give him a hug or scream at him. I feel like I know what's coming. I feel like God sends me the truth and hope and that I am God's messenger. I feel incredibly close to God, who is in me, the one that truly knows me and who gives me strength and tells me of my struggles and challenges.

My dad continues to be tired and stressed out from work and life at home, but in the last week it seems his spirits have enlightened. I hope that the summer is the best rest and medication for him.

About a week ago, I woke up early, lying in bed to the sound of laughter and the smell of coffee. My dad was telling jokes and stories that my mom was able to interpret. They were both laughing so loud. My mom was laughing the laughter that makes your side hurt, and my dad was laughing the laugh that brings tears to his eyes. This event was rare in the last year and brought back memories of childhood. As I read this to Lucy, she smiles remembering the same day I am.

My mom seems younger and stronger again, always smiling with a "hello" or an "I love you." I feel she gets bored, though, being in the house 24 hours a day, seven days a week. She kind of just is lazy. She does what most of us wish we had more time for—sleeps, eats, reads. She always wants to help or be useful, but we run out of things for her to do in the house. I hope the summer gives her more time to be with us and time at the cottage and out of the house.

So, from my perspective, our life is strong, healthy, and happy. I think we are ready to face any challenges that come our way. I hope all of you can soar just as high in God's palm.

Love always,
'Til next the eagle soars,
Lydia Irene Wylie-Kellermann

June 15 P.S. Sadly, I have to add that this morning my mom had three seizures in a row, including one that made her mouth bleed and one in the car while my dad was driving madly to the hospital. She does not remember the seizures (never does), but she did recall a hymn sing that was put on for her the night before. There are two possible causes for the seizures. One was that we found some of her medication on the floor a couple days ago. How long had it been there? Did she forget it sometime, or that day? We gave her the pill anyway. She swallowed the pill and we swallowed our questions.

The other thing is that when they took a CT scan, the place where the fluid is, is larger. This could mean that her shunt is clogged. They are going to do surgery on the shunt. (My dad will probably write you about all that.)

But for what she's been through today, the doctors are amazed that she is so alive and clear. I'm not surprised. I knew God would fly us again.

Jeanie leading Advent liturgy at Williams International, 1985.
Credit: Bill Wylie-Kellermann

13

Walking in Dreamcatchers, Wishing for Rabbit Tracks

June 23, 2000: Tree/Surgery

The Tree

If I were to study a tree
I would say it's like my Mom.
There are troubles like dead branches,
but it always keeps growing.
A tree always sways with the wind
showing its many leaves,
like my Mom shows hope.
I believe in this hope.

Flowers in Delight

Watch a flower in the day,
Watch it lean or even sway,
Its colors so bright
Like dancing in delight
Watch it sway in the shimmering moonlight.
Its reaching hand
petals land
on the hand of deep compassion.

—Lucia Jeanne Wylie-Kellermann

Most of you will have read the last update sent by Lydia Irene, who finds my own missives unduly ambiguous or even bleak and so set the record straight with her personal testimony and take. Only fair to begin this follow-up with recent poetry by 10-year-old Lucy.

The first of these was written while Jeanie was in the second of three back-to-back seizures Wednesday morning, June 14. Lucy "wanted to be supportive but not have to watch." And she couldn't think of another way to be "useful."

While others held Jeanie, administered emergency measures, or dialed doctors, she made for the upstairs porch to contemplate what was right before her eyes. (She does know she can rise to the necessary and has proven so to herself.) Lucy has begun her sessions with the IHM therapist friend on our block. She now takes along her "poetry and dream journal." Albeit in ways different from Lydia, she is coping, and then some.

Jeanie's third seizure took place with her mom in the backseat, en route to the hospital as I drove outrageously illegal speeds, harboring hopes of being spotted and accompanied by the cops. No such luck. EMS had arrived after Jeanie was up and talking. Their choice of hospitals was narrowly complicating, so we waved them off and set out for the small place north of town where our doctors are connected. As the endless string of judgment calls go, this one was wrong, but not disastrous.

After a day in ER, including a CT scan showing ventricles once again enlarged, Jeanie was moved back downtown for next-morning surgery. I didn't think we'd submit to another cutting intervention, but the shunt draining excess fluid into her belly was clogged and misplaced. I couldn't imagine watching Jeanie seize continuously, never mind the great decline.

We signed off. Then in the OR prep room, the anesthesiologist asked if this was the "first revision of the shunt," an ominous question with serial import new to us. When does the point come when we wave off the endless cutting?

Meanwhile, Jeanie bounces back yet again, lush and verdant. Willful, wise, and wonderful. She's home now a week and plotting the summer. Even though it overlaps with our community camping time up north, she is stubbornly set on attending the Witness events at the Episcopal General Convention in Denver. I can't decide whether to wince or smile, but I make reservations in the air and on the ground.

Who can say what summer holds? I'm beyond second-guessing this woman and her hope. Yesterday she vigiled downtown with the fasters against Gary Graham's execution. Today she journals about "another eventful day at the cabin." Here the girls rehearse loudly their parts for The Music Man (Lucy belting out her Winthrop song with a thplattering lithp).

The place has gone feral, the grass a sea of daisies (gift of a broken mower). Beneath the moon they close hands tight, but come the sun there is the dance, its sway of our delight. Love in poems and prayers ...

August 8, 2000: Heavenly Signs: Trailing Through the Luminous Dome

I begin this letter on the waiting side of dread and hope. By the time I finish it, we'll have crossed through the news of last Friday's MRI. You're welcome to jump ahead. Wish I could. Dread has the upper hand on my guts.

While waiting, the interim news: We did go to Denver for General Convention and the Witness events. It was a far flyin' piece from familiar medical support, but once home, I was glad we did it. So many folks startled with joy to lay eyes on Jeanie. Momentously, at a board meeting there, her torch officially was passed. Julie Wortman is now editor/publisher of The Witness, as Jeanie intuitively fore-maneuvered long ago. The magazine reception was not designed to honor her, but one of the honorees, a good bishop, did—calling Jeanie into the light of a standing ovation.

The camping vacation with Peace Community families up north at Camp Chick went wondrously well. We kept (and furthered) the tradition of swimming the lake lengthwise by skinny-dipped moonlight, though Jeanie accompanied in a rowboat. The kids put on a talent show, with our girls reprising numbers from Music Man.

On the last day, however, Jeanie seized, and frighteningly so. Her right side was left slack and useless, looking for all the world like a stroke. I freaked. We were back-road miles from even a small hospital, but a neurologist by payphone reassured: this was not uncommon, simply Todd's paralysis—a typical short-term consequence to which we'd just never been alerted. Jeanie revived quickly, though it recurred with subsequent seizures, shifting now to the other side.

A friend of ours, actually knowledgeable and experienced in such things, was recently shocked to understand that these are full-blown grand mal seizures. I'll spare the description, but they can last five minutes or more, wrack her body and leave her exhausted. Recovery can take days. The one at Camp

Chick was the first of five in a little over a week. A new anti-seizure med has been added.

Coincident, some drop in function: disorientation to time and occasionally place; more sentences unfinished; wires crossed, even comically so; a couple days of low initiative and motor loss (these seem to accentuate when I'm out of town). No pain, thanks be.

But you know what? Still, thanks be the more, quick of smile; bright in her eye and presently perceptive; full of responsive love; funny and sweet as ever. Still gets overwhelmed with emotion, tearing up when her East Coast nephew and niece depart from their visit or when young people sing the offertory in church, or as I read her certain parts of this letter. Can you imagine? A constant amazement to undercut the darkest dread.

So then. Is the change in state related to new medication, with which it correlates? Or with breakthrough seizures, likewise? Does it stem from new tumor growth, so foreshadowed in the May pictures? Does it stem from shunt blockage? Is radiation catching up with us? Or simply the cumulative effect of repeated interventions on her poor skull? Answers to some of these hang in the MRI balance. If we can rule out shunt and tumor, meds at least might be correctable. The sunny Queen-of-bounceback might yet again.

We wait.

Meanwhile, I've been mindful that I don't get much solitude these days. When I'm home, even working, I stay close to Jeanie—round the clock in earshot. We ask so much of friends and family to cover for me when I'm on the road that asking for more so I could get a sabbath at the cabin seems too much. (I do know this is actually wrong, but feel we are straining people, and who knows what's to come?)

Anyway, several weeks back at the cabin, as I was headed off to work briefly on some paths, Jeanie followed me into the clearing with a question that never fully formed. At the far end, I turned her around, saying I'd watch her back to the cabin where her sister was waiting. As she turned, I said what suddenly dawned on me: "Hey, you never get any solitude either, do you?" "No," she replied wistfully over her shoulder, "I sure don't."

Then again. Last week the four of us were up to the cabin. Late afternoon, we stood at the window watching Lucy dance in a downpour, soaking it all in through her sundress, when suddenly lit, the sky changed. We hustled out to witness a double rainbow, noticing for the first time that the two mirror one another, reversing the order of colors. We stood agog and posed for each other framed beneath the covenant with all creation ...

Later: The news is good. The shunt is working (ventricles smaller), and there is no visible tumor growth. Essentially unchanged since May. (Actually one interpretation says there is some "linear enhancement," but no thickening, so still suspicious but indeterminate—this from folks I thought would have been wowed by the lengthening work of the chicken virus.) We meet Monday with the neurologist, who remains reluctant about a med change. We trust her, but we'll see what can be tried.

Last night, Jeanie rousing repeatedly, got me up at 4 a.m. The moon was down, but I noticed a subtle shimmering flash through the window. Northern lights! Out back the clearing was covered with this shifting luminous dome. Then, light upon light, a falling star. And another. And again, with a long orange tail.

Unbeknownst, we'd been waked to the Perseid meteor shower. Through wisps of light trailing up, they fell. We claimed it all for healing aura, to be soaked in though Jeanie's nightgown. Down and up they blessed. Dread scattered to the horizon or forgotten. A different hand, thanks be, upon my guts.

'Til the last morning star shall sing …

August was dominated by minor crises, medical and otherwise. Troubles with Jeanie's port and shunt. And, adding insult to injury, our computer's poor brain crashed or got fried, causing us to lose our entire address book. But we reached out, reconstructed, and persevered.

October 22, 2000: Horns of a Balance

So, a couple weeks back, across the restaurant table, eggs and hash browns between us, Jeanie suddenly sets down the front page and asks, "Should we go to the Middle East? To Palestine?"

I confess I laughed out loud. Partly for the matter-of-fact and slightly absurd logistics implied. Partly for her over-the-top bold and lucid nonviolent instinct. But above all with joy for her sense of justice equaled by her own sense of freedom, power, and self-possession to affect it. This is the Jeanie Wylie we love, and a measure of her health.

Another: she's been traveling with me. To New Haven, Cambridge, Elkhart/South Bend. Most recently to D.C., where the Sojourners (who have lit their candles from day one of this illness) laid eyes and hands and prayers upon her. More planned on the horizon.

Lydia breathes a sigh when I take Jeanie with me on a travel. No matter who is on hand to offer care, our moms or community friends, Lydia feels like she's really the one in charge when I go away. And point of fact, in a crisis, she would be the one with the cool head who knows the drill. It's truly a stress.

On two of those road trips Jeanie had seizures. One at our friend Chuck Matthei's place in Voluntown, Connecticut. He lives on the old CNVA (Community for Nonviolent Action) farm and makes his land-reform speaking and organizing forays from there. Chuck has cancer as well. In his throat. Here is a "voice," rare and singular, a voice rethinking ownership and equity—a voice now under attack. I think likewise of Jeanie's poor head, her mind so rich in editorial judgment, beneath the same assault.

These road seizures track one saga of recent months. We did wean Jeanie off the anti-seizure med that was damping her down and even issuing in mild hallucinations. She is, of course, effectively a permanent epileptic, subject to these things for the duration, and clearly needs something more than the primary baseline medication.

What's astonishing about ourselves in retrospect is that while we immediately sought out alternatives to radiation and chemo, when it came to seizures we've just been swallowing the pharmaceutical chemicals hand over fist. Our recent hope had been to use some alternatives (obvious things like quitting coffee/caffeine and additional ones like amino acid, vitamin and mineral supplements) in place of the second scripted medication.

But this string of continuing seizures has forced us into the good neurologist's hand and onto a second med, with consequences noticeable. More lost thoughts and dangling sentences. It seems like we're on the horns of this unhappy balance between seizures and fogginess. It's so maddening to have her in there bright and thoughtful, but then damp and doze her down.

The other saga concerns the delivery of the chicken virus ... We were on the brink of putting in a new port, but could not, as the left vein is now completely scarred and blocked ... We settled briefly for a PIC line (similar to a port, but even higher maintenance) in her arm. This device Jeanie subsequently pulled out, be it in a moment of erstwhile confusion or shrewd lucidity.

It seemed we were left with but one intravenous option: to risk the right vein connection. Then, pressed with some questions, the doctor mentioned that should that one become scarred and blocked, pressure would back up into Jeanie's head. This seemed like a bad idea on the face of it, so we pulled the plug on that procedure at the last minute. Now we're relying on a nebulizer (a glorified vaporizer) to deliver the virus. It's admittedly less efficient, and we've had more bumps getting unscripted parts, but that's the tack for now.

I get nervous about messing with the viral delivery, since the approach has been serving us so well. When we showed the last pictures to the original surgeon at Henry Ford, he and colleagues averred that they "did not recommend a change in therapy at this time." That, I suppose, is about as close to WOW as we're going to get from medicos for any non-AMA-approved treatment option.

It does seem to be working. We're two-plus years into an illness that offers an average life expectancy of six months. Jeanie is taking road trips with me, rendering fall trees in pastels, and being opinionated or feisty. I get overcome with joy and gratitude, every day a gift free and clear.

This day happens to be glorious in a string of such. Yesterday friends were here at the cabin for brunch, cidering, pumpkin picking, and late evening tabletalk over chili and beer. This afternoon the aspen leaves, green and yellow, flicker and quake against the crisp cloudless blue. When I fix on their shimmering, my body almost hums in tune ...

'Til those leaves heal the nations ...

Christmastide 2000: Walking in Dreamcatchers

"When the moon is full we wish for rabbit tracks."
—Jeanie

"Why lock your doors at night? Love is there. Trust is there. Justice and Peace are there. Don't lock them out."
—Advent window No. 9

Years ago at Cass United Methodist Church, a Liberian parishioner told me of his first U.S. Christmas. In his country, the custom on Christmas Day was to gather in the village center to share a common feast brought from all quarters. So when he saw the frenetic scale of preparations going on in this country, beginning as early as Thanksgiving, he said to himself, "This is going to be some feast!"

On Christmas morning, he loaded his family into the car, filled the trunk with good things and sweets to share, and drove to downtown Detroit. Only to find it empty, bereft, abandoned. A parable of sorts— warning against all empty preparation, marketing and hollow hype—without delivery day. These days of feasting in the Word, nevertheless, we think of you, dear friends, and honor the incarnation.

We had a very good MRI this month. Apart from some over- cautious equivocation in the radiologist's reading, these pictures show stable if not reduced tumor. I've seen it with my own eyes. My anxiety going in had stemmed not so much from Jeanie's estate as from the change in the delivery of the viral treatment.

But the seizures continue, the most recent on Christmas Day, surrounded on the floor by gifts and my family members. They go on, unabated by the multiple medications that get titrated up, making her lose track or nod off mid-sentence. Add to this a sinus infection these recent weeks that fogs her head yet the more.

So in these days of winter fog, I watch her gather things into piles, indiscriminately. Baptismal certificates, cardboard, coupons, letters from friends, junk mail, photos, and work faxes all get scooped and wrapped and carefully stashed by her lights. She is in effect holding it all together. Or packing for a cabin journey north. But I confess to spending inordinate time looking for things I've just put down. Then, of course, comes the occasion I've misplaced something myself, but am feverishly searching places I imagine Jeanie might have put it.

In one pile yesterday, I came upon a file of confidential email correspondence several years old, covering the Enneagram spiritual typology and her inner life. I read only far enough to understand what it was— and to let my heart ache a bit. It's the sort of work she couldn't do at present. But, then again, her distilled integration, her pure and straightforward Jeanie-ness, her sweet self-possession, even her fight against the fog, is the fruit of such work and prayer.

In Cambridge at a contributing editors' meeting this fall, the Witness staff stayed up late one night playing

Heresy, a biblical version of Fictionary, wherein one person selects an obscure verse and everyone tries to fabricate a line or two that others might guess to be authentic. It can be quite hilarious, and was. Jeanie held her own. And then as we reached the point of exhaustion, she scribbled this on her slip—purporting to be something from 2 Kings or maybe the Psalms: "When the moon is full we wish for rabbit tracks."

A couple weeks back, a homemade CD arrived in the mail from our friend Jay McDaniel. He'd turned her logion into a winsome song about the sufficient presence of God, an intercession and a hymn to the incarnation titled "I'll Be the Rabbit Tracks."

We had a lovely host of homemade gifts this year: photo collages, drawings, a hand-sewn travel pillow, shelves crafted to fit odd places, a St. Lucy crown bedecked with holly and candles for a doll. But the best was actually a birthday present for Jeanie in November (in truth for us both): an oversized Advent calendar, with pictures and personal poems for each day and a love letter on the back of Christmas Eve's door—destined to become an annual fixture of the season.

Lydia, the conceptual organizer of that project and author of the love letter, is a freshman at Mercy High School ... Jointly, she and Lucy—now a fifth grader at St. Thomas Aquinas—have become caretakers of a new kitten named Scatters. (I like the name because when you want him to come, you can say Scat!) I like the cat too, but keep my distance—for reasons allergic.

Last week Lucy and I went for a cabin walk in two feet of snow, using the gorgeous wood and leather snowshoes we recently inherited from Jeanie's parents. Pausing to catch our breath in a pine clearing, she captured the oddity and beauty in a single phrase: "It's like walking in dreamcatchers!" May we ever so ...

In all things we follow the Word. We wish for rabbit tracks. We walk in dreamcatchers. And in Love ...

Lucy with her parents after dancing and performing in "The Miracle Worker" at Mercy High School, fall 2005. Credit: Family collection

14

A Walking Miracle

April 26, 2001 (Stringfellow's birthday): Between the Loaf and the Alleluia

"When all due allowances have been made for doctors and for medicine, it is when these mysteries—healing and love—are joined that, in fact, a miracle happens … What is involved … is a love of self which, esteeming life itself as a gift, expects or demands no more than the life which is given, and which welcomes and embraces and affirms that much unconditionally. I mean self-love which emulates, and, in the end, participates in, the love of God for life … Or, one can be succinct: life is a gift which death does not vitiate or void: faith is the acceptance, honoring, rejoicing in that gift … It is freedom from moral bondage to death that enables a person to live humanly and to die at any moment without concern."
—William Stringfellow, *A Second Birthday*

Overheard soon after the Easter Vigil, to a friend around the campfire asking, "What is fire anyway?" Lucy: "Well, I know it's glowing gas, but you can start out with just a little bit and everyone touches candles, and before you know it the whole church is full of light."

To all wondering in their prayers: Jeanie is well. A recent MRI was finally interpreted for us yesterday. The neurologist declared her a walking miracle. I'm not sure there's a formal diagnostic code for that one, but the actuarial oddsmakers at an insurance company would surely find it incomprehensible anyway. The pictures are essentially unchanged for nearly a year now. (This is not permission to cease intercessions, mind you, merely a call to mingle them with thanks.)

She still has seizures, but even these have changed. They are shorter, less fierce, without extended paralysis, and seem to fall at liminal moments of transition ... Her most recent was at our community's Easter Vigil liturgy. Our family had led the renewal of baptismal vows, with Lucy putting the questions and Jeanie uttering a prayer as pure, simple, and clear as water itself.

Then, during communion, we gathered about the altar at St. Peter's Episcopal Church. Just as she was passing the bread to Lydia and trying to say "Body of Christ," she seized. We laid her down in the aisle and tended to her outstretched needs as people continued the service.

By the time the cup came round, she was sitting up and insisted on receiving. And speech returned to her as we sang the chorus of "Christ the Lord is Risen Today!" It hardly seemed a disruption. In an odd way, the whole thing felt like a blessing. Integral and somehow sacramental. Another healing moment.

This week the Witness office in the old pharmacy at the end of our block was finally closed. We had tried to find some other non-profit justice group with whom to share the space, but there's no parking lot and the prostitutes on the corner were a stopper ... End of an era.

I worried that Jeanie might have an emotional passage. She did, but not the one I had imagined. Walking up the street to a wine-and-cheese staff gathering, she sighed and confessed, "Well, it's going to be a relief not to be responsible for the magazine anymore." It's really more than a year since she's done any work, but Jeanie's been carrying it in her heart more than I knew.

This month we finally applied for Social Security Disability. Jeanie's been eligible for a year or more. But the Witness board and staff have been incredibly supportive, not the least of which financially. They indulged my procrastination while I suffered through an unfounded ambivalence. All this means Medicare and family insurance changes. These things, too, feel a momentous transition, although of a different order.

Easter week we were intending to visit dear friends in Lexington, Virginia, and drive the Shenandoah with a view to vacationing en route. The day before, however, our transmission gave up going backwards, so we spent some gorgeous days instead at the cabin. Lydia organized an egg hunt involving fourteen Peace Community kids, paths in the woods, two compasses, some riddles, and a large ball of string (not to mention piles of chocolate).

The girls have just completed their run in the community theater Paperbag Production of The Wizard of Oz, with Lucy playing Dorothy and Lydia the Wicked Witch. There were enough sibling dynamics bouncing around there to keep their psyches busy for weeks. They both stole the show, as far as their parents could tell …

We do go on. Fast and slow. With an odd joy between the body and the alleluia. And we count it that same joy to share our lives with you.

All freedoms and festivities of the resurrection …

October 7, 2001: Fistful of Beauty

Seems like every time Jeanie comes in the cabin door this weekend, she's bearing another fall bouquet of weeds and berries and pine. They blossom in jars and coffee cups all over the place, presenting themselves in unexpected corners. Chicory, high bush cranberries, scotch and cedar, burning bush. When we go for a walk I keep calling her to keep up, as the harvest of beauty goes on. She grabs it by the fistful.

Jeanie Wylie is doing terrific on all fronts, not the least her eye for beauty. She did have a small seizure night before last. That would be unremarkable, except that it was the first in three and a half months! Prior, I'd been despairing. If we had plotted her seizures and our counter efforts on a graph covering the last year and half, you'd have to conclude that no matter what we did, she was going to suffer an "event" every 10 to 14 days …

Me, I'm thinking let's take her off the meds. If she's going to seize, let her be clear-headed betwixt. So I'd been resisting the neurologist's urging to add just a tweak of yet a third medication. We finally acceded, following a really big seizure in July. And they stopped. Four weeks in, however, I was still debating the wisdom, since she seemed clouded further, nodding off at the dinner table.

Enter our friend Karl Meyer (not the famous Catholic Worker), who every Wednesday brings us brown rice or organic pasta dinners (heavy with garlic and kale and his homegrown urban vegetables). He's incredibly well-read in nutrition and alternative health matters. By and large, it's his regimen of advice we follow for Jeanie's non-scripted supplements. (He's also an amazing fiddle player. We are blessed to know such a bunch of really good human beings.)

Anyway, he takes a look at her bloodwork and notices an elevated ammonia level (a consequence of anti-seizure meds, and hallucinogenic at toxic levels). On the basis of a study, he suggests an amino acid called L-carnitine you only get in red meat. Hence, one we don't get. To make this long story short again, it seems to work! Quicker than anyone could expect, Jeanie is tracking, wakes knowing the day and its plan, remembers events the week prior, participates more fully in conversation, initiates projects, recalls names and lyrics when I'm stumped, and proofreads this letter for grammar. She still disorganizes piles and cooks strange meals (but, as a friend says of the latter, she's always done that.)

Granted, the improvements could also be the lack of being in perpetual recovery from seizures, or prayer, cumulative and exponential. Whatever it is, we're sticking with the third med and with the carnitine. Of course we're sticking with the prayers, too.

Meanwhile, midsummer, the neurologist read her last MRI, noted that the picture has been essentially unchanged for over a year, and said, "Don't stop what you are doing. We'll check it again in a year." A year? This is a glioblastoma! "OK," he says, "six months." This is to indicate that things are stable and we are staying our courses.

Last week, Jeanie joined me for a seminary recruiting trip. We showed her documentary, Poletown Lives!, now 20 years old, to a film class at the Mennonite seminary and Jeanie was on hand, a little road-weary but answering questions with me. That was a joy …

I was in the air to Chicago when the attack on the Trade Towers in New York hit. I saw the first smoke plume on a TV at Midway airport. By the time I trained downtown, the second had struck and the Loop began to empty out 'til it looked like a Sunday morning calm. A friend loaned me a car to drive home. When I walked in the door, Lucy broke into tears. We circled as a family to pray and cry. It echoed our experience of the last three years. This is to say, I'm mindful that we offer personal good news in a dark time.

As I prepare to send this, the bombing begins. We are warned to expect it to be long and protracted. Perpetual war, war without end, as it were. I fear the open-ended, blank-check war more than I fear the terrorism itself.

Trust us, they say. These are the same powers (the CIA through Pakistan) that trained and financed bin Laden and friends when their terror was aimed at the Soviets. These are the same powers that have pioneered violence against civilians: making and using weapons of mass destruction, anti-personnel weaponry, and the terrors of low-intensity war. From Dresden and Hiroshima to Vietnam to the Nicaraguan contra war and the infrastructure bombing (with a decade of sanctions) against Iraq.

We've already stopped noticing how the bombing of Iraq continues daily. How long before the anti-terrorist strikes cease to be news but the routine work of America's global economy? Cruise missile attacks targeting ideological commitments. Anywhere and anytime they say or want.

Still.

Miracles walk! So says Jeanie. God is in this history and our lives. So we are ruled neither by fear nor despair. We rejoice and hope and persevere. And grab beauty by the fistful.

'Til justice be the foundation of peace and death shall be no more ...

December 25, 2001: Christmastide: a rambling account of the season from Detroit

Advent is our favorite season in the Wylie-Kellermann household: prayers and song around the candlelit wreath; gifts hidden in the making; a small statue of erstwhile Roman prisoner Bishop Nicholas of Smyrna, standing witness on the piano, an oversized china Bible beneath his arm; and public vigils for peace.

I was fasting on juices for the first few weeks of Advent. Actually, it was a 30- day fast during Ramadan, in solidarity with the Muslim community so under attack these recent months. It was also in mindful intercession of refugees and war victims (now approaching the total of those killed in the Trade Tower collapse) and against that deadly bombing. It will be a long while before any truth of that horror on the ground is publicly known in this country.

Just to add: Ramadan is a very interesting season. Here in the Detroit area, with the largest Arab population outside the Middle East, it's difficult to tell if it's really a fast or a feast. During the day, the devout undertake this very rigorous and difficult fast. But come nightfall, families gather to break fast and party late into the evening. For the restaurants of nearby Dearborn, it is really a boom season. Like Advent, a sober joy.

For those eager for word on Jeanie, we had an MRI during Advent and received its report as Christmas good news in the flesh. The pictures are once again unchanged. At the very least: no new growth. Our various doctors who have all along urged us to continue "whatever it was that we were doing" are now asking for details about this Hungarian chicken virus, which appears to have some sort of miracle afoot.

Meanwhile, Jeanie is essentially seizure-free for nigh six months. This is an enormous change in our life. She can be left alone for short periods. We don't need to be constantly within earshot, on edge for the terrifying noise of collapse. She can even be the licensed adult when Lydia makes her permit driving forays.

Jeanie did most of her own Christmas preparations, wrapping gifts and hiding them away. (OK, she had to have a little help to find some of them—hey, me too.) She gave me a Christmas tree ornament: a tiny wooden outhouse, with a half moon cut in its hinged door. (Can someone explain this to me?) I like it.

We don't put up and decorate our tree until Christmas Eve (as is liturgically correct). Again this year, we drove up to a tree farm in The Thumb and cut it down ourselves. We always ask permission of the tree and give it thanks. And at least by our lights, they always seem gracious and happy to come along.

Our Christmas morning was in Detroit. Many of our gifts were handmade. Lydia was the champ in this regard. For Lucy: a rainbow knitted scarf and a T-shirt with all the parts from all the plays in which she'd ever acted, lettered in multicolor paints on front and back. (Lydia gave essentially the same thing to all her Paperbag theater buddies.) From both girls for Jeanie and me: a basket full of indulgent supplies for a romantic date—perhaps at the cabin.

I made dulcimers for the girls. Walnut and cherry. From kits. (OK, they still need finishing and hardware, but the smooth unfinished wood is so lovely to the smell and touch.) I suppose gifts are always an intercession of sorts, but with homemade ones, you get to think slowly and carefully on the recipient, virtually in a detailed prayer of nurture and thanks. I believe I've made the girls' main present every year since they were born. It keeps me praying, as it were.

By Christmas evening, we were at the cabin—Lydia pushing her skills at snow driving in the dark. As the licensed driver at her side, I even fell asleep—a measure of trust, or exhaustion? Once settled in with fires lit, water pump on, and Jeanie's childhood French creche set out, we went for a walk.

The moon, though not full, was high and bright. The dust of new-fallen snow reflected it in a luster of mid-day. Lucy declared its jeweled surface "enough to fool a greedy man!" Shadows from the trees were vivid, as were our own. It was like a crystal dream. We sang Cat Stevens' Moonshadows, and I recited Stopping by Woods on a Snowing Evening (though I must admit a certain solemn edge was taken off when Lucy imagined aloud the real reason he was compelled to stop with miles to go—and got a fit of the giggles).

Next morning we cut eight or 10 varieties of pine bough to decorate the cabin, in preparation for an overnight visit from godson Luke Wallis of Washington, D.C. He loved the tree house in the cedar cluster, and his Dad, Jim, even climbed to the second floor. His Mum Joy, a Londoner, explained Boxing Day to us: the working-class holiday for servants who had to work so hard all Christmas Day to make the gentlepeople's feast. (Unresolved: does the "box" stem from the boxed meals the gentry had to eat the next day, or from the church breaking open the filled "poor boxes" on the Feast of Stephen?) We were also blessed later in the week to have an overnight visit from the family of our Detroit goddaughters, Catherine and Theresa, who spent long hours skating on Lucy's labyrinth of paths through the marsh.

Two noteworthy prayer services. Feast of the Holy Innocents in Port Huron with the small and lively peace community there. It included an amazing meditation on September 11 by Zen master Thich Nhat Hahn (one by one identifying with each of the persons, and even creatures, structures, and elements, involved) and a street procession chanting and drumming to the four neighborhood directions: How shall we welcome the Prince of Peace in a time of terror?

Our favorite service of the year is New Year's Eve at Day House, the Detroit Catholic Worker (our own community). Before the intercessions, we go round, and people share their "highlights" and/or "lowlights" of the past year. The circle ripples with a rhythm of tears and laughter, of the ordinary and life's dire extremes.

Lucy's lowlight was the life-threatening surgery during Advent of our cat, Scatters, who had swallowed a knot of yarn that remained tangled around his tongue and so could not pass, accordion-ing forward his innards. Her highlight was that he survived and came home ... Typically, at midnight we are in the midst of the consecration when some move to seats on the floor, as our neighbors welcome the new year in a different fashion, by firing off their guns into the night.

I returned from my first Chicago trip this year just as Jeanie collapsed with pneumonia and spent several hospital days taking fluids and antibiotics through a tube. In a delirium early in that week, she asked me to make room so the angel could step out from behind the bed. Moments later she was reaching up behind her head to hold its hand. Questioned, she replied, "I'm being angelic." A sweet delirium suited to the times and the season. And one I'd trust more than all the random searches, checkpoints, and strikeforces of the present hour.

Guardian blessings and love, dear friends …

With the Kellermann clan, December 26, 2005. Credit: Family collection

15

'Dancing Will Encircle Them'

June 27, 2002: *The Garbed Stranger*

"I read them with a horrible pang, thinking of how none of us ever imagined what lay ahead for Jeanie and the kids and you. Getting left behind with your little sister, kidnaped by a black-garbed stranger, or victimized by divorce is small change compared to other realities. I think about all of you all the time, but am running out of cheery things to write. I love Jeanie. She is one of those rare people who actually do good things to help people, instead of talking about them. She is also the funniest, wittiest, most original lady I met in many a year."
—Dierdre Luzwick

> *Some context is in order to explain the above, from one of my favorite (OK, also darkly witty, brutally honest, and deftly funny) letter writers on this old planet. Witness readers from Jeanie's era would know Deirdre for her black-and-white prints, which may be studied for their load of cultural detail and dark irony. She reports that several years back, in response to an*

urging to do a book of prints on kids' fears, she put out a call to hear from the children.

Three responses (which recently turned up in an old porch cupboard) were from Lydia via Jeanie. Scrawled on Dairy Queen napkins are the following three scenarios of dread: "Father is nering and me and my sister trip and can not fint Dad. You are left aloan with your little sister"; "[A stranger] climbs up your window and caris you a way in a bag. He wares a mask and black cloase"; "Scared of parents divorsing or leaving you aloan." None of these is really small change, but I think how quickly that little girl has been forced to grow up, how wise she is beyond her years, and how, even now, she ministers to me.

This may be a tricky update letter to write. I will try to be deft and honest, if not witty. Jeanie is miraculously well on a certain level. The neurologist smiles and cries and hugs us once again in an assessment last week. She wonders if someone ought to recheck that original tumor—was it as deadly as they seem to have misunderstood?

Sometimes I figure JWK had more brains than us all and the Handicapper General has only brought her down to size. In social situations she has the unconstrained candor to cut through bullshit with a simple and straightforward word—and get away with it (she is ill, after all). I often come upon her singing hymns, including verses of obscure and artful Anglican tunes in minor keys. She woke this morning singing me a made-up love song, a blessing true.

As the girls are at camp this week, we are up at the cabin. Jeanie, per usual, is harvesting beauty by the vase—mostly daisies. She is incredibly sweet and, as

I asked her point-blank the other day, really as happy as she seems ...

Last week John Martinez, a union/community activist who works at the Poletown plant came by for a visit. He'd just discovered her book and was overflowing with enthusiasm and schemes to get the history in front of his union local and stir a few new people into action. We had lots of overlapping connections in the barrio of Southwest Detroit, and we're conspiring together to make something, even a participant reunion, happen.

He remarked on how beautiful Jeanie is (and this said even having seen the stunning photo on the book jacket of her when she was 29). And yet, the sad thing was the limit of her participation in that energetic exchange. She was clearly making the connections, trying to dive in, but couldn't get the details of the stories out. It's hard—and one of the things about her that I miss so much ...

So. These updates, notice, always end up being a summons to prayer. Get wise to it, dear friends, and see the pitch coming. Please pray, dearest of communities, for these folks and more.

In the long loneliness which is at once a blessed journey ...

Christmastide 2002: With a Litany of Saints

"... Nicholas knew that being poor in Lycia was so hard that it was like being locked up in prison. And Saint Nicholas knew about prison. The Roman Emperor, Diocletian, had put Nicholas in prison for following Jesus ... We smile to think of the saints of God in all times who have listened in the night and done whatever they could to show us the love of God. We delight in the saints even now who are listening outside our homes or in our hearts. We give thanks for the communion of saints who have died, but continue to care for

us. *They are listening and reaching to us with all their love, because God intends for all of us and for all things to be cared for and to be alive with the joy of creation."*
—from the text of a book on Saint Nicholas, which Jeanie wrote for the girls a dozen years ago.

Forgive the length of what this shall be. The actual news about Jeanie and the girls comes like winterlight at the end, but I have a litany of saints to walk through en route. Bear with me or run ahead. This has been a year of griefs and losses (and attendant joys of memory). Among the ones I can name, it strikes me that we're of the age that not only our parents and mentors, but also our companions, begin to die out from beside us.

In the spring we lost Jeanie's brother, Johnny (exactly my age) to a long intensive-care bout of pancreatitis. Right to the end, I kept expecting him to turn the corner and come out of it, but he never did. Johnny knew The Chronicles of Narnia in the sort of detail that provided text to life. I picture him on the last day following Aslan "further up and further in."

The whole family had visited him on Easter. In church that morning, when Widor's "Toccata" rose up from the organ, we all teared up at the happy coincidence, not realizing what it yet foretold. On the last day, his mother and sisters, nephew and nieces gathered round his bed in the ICU to sing him home with hymns in harmony (and descants, no less). Then they broke spontaneously into the old Jimmy Durante tune that has truck in our family as well: "Skinnamarinkydinkydink, Skinnamarinkydoo, I - Love - You!" It takes its place, ever since, side by side with Widor.

Next, on August 6, Feast of the Transfiguration, my mom suffered a cerebral hemorrhage while on her knees in the garden. She loved to tend and weed. Apart from a brief moment in the Emergency Room, she never came out of the coma. We moved her from intensive care to hospice space. Vigiling around her for several days, my three brothers and I had numinous conversations full of memory and tears and grace. We were all there breathing with her at the last.

Coming and going from her nearby apartment, we discovered Mom's prayer journals, a hidden ministry of intercession—including specific and even pointed prayers for ourselves. She was famous for her charism of hospitality, setting the table and appointing the feast. Advent was necessarily a season of (baking) preparation for her. So I should not have been taken by surprise (but was) when making her Christmas sugar cookie recipe with the girls a few days back, I stepped from the room and the moment I was alone, found myself awash in grief, tears and sobs breaking the heart's dam. I was knit together in her love, and I pray to make her ministries of hospitality and intercession my own anew.

As she lay dying in August, a friend was elsewhere crossing over: Ladon Sheats, who'd been in hospice for months at the L.A Catholic Worker, playing out the final throes of pancreatic cancer. Ladon was a mendicant discipler, himself called to life (and out of the corporate life at IBM) by Clarence Jordan of Cotton-Patch gospel fame. He lived a rhythm between the road, the monastery, and the prison—the latter for praying empty-handed in the forbidden places where weapons of mass destruction are made and stashed. Once, when I was struggling with ordination,

*he asked me with characteristic, if undue, sharpness,
"So, Bill, what's it going to be, Jesus or the church?" I
bear it even now in my flesh as a pointed and useful
query, holding me to the margins. And I sing him to
the communion.*

*In October, Chuck Matthei died. Formed at the New
York Worker and Tivoli farm under Dorothy Day,
he was instrumental in organizing the Clamshell
Alliance, the first massive campaign of nonviolence
against nuclear power, at the Seabrook plant in New
Hampshire. I met him in the early '70s on a courtroom
bench outside the trial of the Camden 28, a draft
board action group. The conversation we struck up
became life-long.*

*His gift was to comprehend economics, with a brilliant
and straightforward simplicity. He could make you
see the social mortgage on your property—the claims
of everyone from your neighbors to the earthworms
beneath. And where did that speculative increase come
from, anyway? He set out to do land reform in the
United States for God's sake! The American Vinoba
Bhave, as it were, he was a voice in the wilderness.
Since Chuck suffered a chronic case of writer's block
(though you couldn't stop him talking personalist
economics once he got wound), it was ironic, bitterly
so, that cancer attacked his throat, silencing him—
and, sweetly, that he thereby took to pad and laptop
and spoke unabated to the end. I loved him.*

*Then in November, Eddie Gersh passed. Unrepentant
hippie, urban street Jew with flyaway hair, Eddie was
famous for the outrageous among his friends. As a
prisoner at Danbury federal prison in the early '70s
(on a drug charge, as I recall), he fell in with a circle*

of draft resisters studying scripture with Dan Berrigan. Friendship became community, and soon action.

I've a vivid memory of doing a bannering action with him in Grand Rapids at a Reagan speech, early '80s. As we walked home, who should emerge from the Grand Hotel waving royally to the crowd but Henry Kissinger. Gersh, without so much as a second thought, leaps on top of a parked car, points his finger at Mr. K and shouts: "Murderer! Murderer!" (For all the tomes since and those which could be written, such remains true and concise.) Kissinger ducked for limousine cover and sped off. Today Eddie would have been shot, and may have been closer to it then than we knew. I didn't get to see him again. He died of colon cancer in Cambridge, with Jimmy Hendrix wailing him home.

Come December, Philip Berrigan joined that communion, going quick of liver cancer. Since I hadn't seen him in several years, I had hastened to arrange a visit, but not in time. I was blessed to be present for the wake and funeral and some aftermath visitations—all reunions and psychic roilings too rich to recount.

My first glimpse of Phil had been from the crowd of greeters when he walked out of Danbury prison in 1972, but my first conversation was a year or two later on the steps of the Capitol during the summer-long Tiger Cage Fast and Vigil against torture in Vietnam. Soon thereafter I found myself handcuffed to him, though the handcuffs were our own and they ran through a Pentagon door handle during a Holy Innocents lockout. (It is the anniversary of that as I write.)

Philip was a pioneer and perfecter of actions, from the draft board raid to Plowshares disarmament. He was an utterly single-minded nonviolent voice, latching onto the mind's ear in conscience and divine judgment. If he were a gospel character, he'd have been a disciple, a converted centurion now more tempted to guerilla zealotry.

I know he wasn't always easy to live with (hard enough perhaps to make you a saint), but at the wake, testimony after testimony was about his pastoral side. For 30 years he and Liz McAlister have been the anchor and sail for the Jonah House resistance community. At the funeral, their daughters Frida and Katie alternated a eulogy so full of hope you knew you were witnessing a torch being passed.

Amen and Alleluia all. I honestly hope you can't tell whether this is a litany of death or resurrection. Me? I'm thinking incarnation. Word made flesh and dwelling among us ...

We've just completed a truly amazing Word and World school in Tucson. Imagine Delores Huerta talking about Caesar Chavez against a backdrop of desert mountains. Or Hebrew Bible scholar Norman Gottwald in conversation with Native American theologian George Tinker, studying Judges with a class of eight in an open-air ramada. Or sabbath walks to petroglyphs in the Sonoran desert, surrounded by 200-year-old saguaro cacti. Picture late-night fires with music, poems, jokes, and tales, and public worship in the kiva-style sanctuary of Southside Presbyterian Church—spiritual home of the Sanctuary Movement—with a gospel choir that nobody could shut down. Lord! Now we turn toward Philadelphia in June.

As to the much-awaited news: Jeanie Wylie perseveres remarkably. They led us to believe she would enter that communion long ago, but she's now become the American poster child for Newcastles Disease Virus. Or prayer.

Medically, she's virtually seizure-free for over a year. We have an MRI scheduled for next month, but the tumor stays so unchanged that we are now a year out from her last. Jeanie was part of the Tucson school (and the inaugural Greensboro go-round before that). This fall she's taken two "solo" trips—one to visit her family in Princeton and another to the Upper Peninsula high school for reuniting with friends. She revels in the snow, loves to be at the cabin (from whence we write), and slows us all down to take in beauty. She never stops singing and now hums quietly in the next room while penning some Christmas notes.

On Lucy's 13th birthday earlier this month, still drowsing betimes in bed, I said to Jeanie, "Well, Lucy's now a teenager." Replies she, half-asleep, "Does that mean she's going to start yelling at me?" ...

Oh, the pending war. The cry heard in Rama. I have said nothing of the descending darkness in which the people sit, but trust I have at least hinted at the great light which we have seen and which the darkness has not overcome. You, dear friends, are the litany of living saints who testify to that light. Thank you for goodness too much to bear.

Summoned to the birth of hope ...

October 2003: Motown and Miracle

"An almost unbelievable goodness, helps us face the fierce unknown."

"Beloved, truly this is a time of sorrow and lamenting for Jeanie and Bill, but wait. Let there be no chagrin. for I am clearly planted in the center of their hearts and their children and their life scope. Nothing will fall within that center that I do not ordain. I will clear away the chaff and burn away the sordid, and I will bring in the cool, clear waters. Their sorrow will be lifted, and they will be nourished by the fruits of the earth, and dancing will encircle them."

> Labor Day weekend past marked five years since Jeanie Wylie collapsed on the bathroom floor with a seizure induced by the tumor on her brain. "We've got to have a party, Dad—a five-year survival celebration!" said Lydia Irene. She was right—and did we ever.
>
> Jeanie's last MRI, shot at the beginning of the year, shows things virtually unchanged now for a couple of years. A glioblastoma in remission is something of a non sequitur. No one knows quite what to call this medical state of affairs—except for those of us with a language for miracles.
>
> The pictures may be unchanged, but she actually improves—also against logic and over the remonstrations of our neurologist, who cautiously reminds us that Jeanie has taken the maximum hit of radiation, with its long-term permanent consequences. But Jeanie blithely breaks new mental paths the radiationists thought they had extinguished forever, improves her short-term memory, orients herself to the day, and speaks up cogently in group conversation. Plus remembers the words to an endless repertoire of songs constantly on her lips. (Some might actually

credit such music and prayers over the mysteries of chicken vaccine.)

As to the party report. It seemed itself somehow mystical and miraculous. We held it at Lucy's school, Our Lady of Guadalupe, close by in the neighborhood. Over a hundred friends and family appeared from near and far, bearing garlic dishes and desserts. We had a short program comprised of gifts, remembrances, and testimonies.

Ange Smith, Detroit jazz and gospel artist, brought down the house right off with her a cappella rendition of "His Eye Is on the Sparrow." Jim Perkinson, theologian and local hip hop poet, brought a poem for Jeanie (appended in entirety below). Julie Beutel, folk laureate of our community, sang—joined last-minute and unrehearsed by fiddler Karl Meyer, in from New York City, who transfigured the song with his backup beneath. These were the invited gifts.

Others came forward unbidden. Ron Dale with a "Song for Jeanie" performed by an impromptu choir. And perhaps most mystical of all, a Taizé-style chant, brought by Ande Gaines and Mike McCarthy, whose bass line of "an almost unbelievable goodness ... " was overarched with a descant of Thomas Merton's famous prayer from Thoughts in Solitude. Stunning.

One of the testimonies, moving and tearful, was from our friend Jane Slaughter, a labor activist, recounting Jeanie's words to her about the similarity of work in church and union, organizations both so good at heart but often losing their way in bureaucratic politics. She spoke of that work that summons both back to their true vocation, and noted Jeanie's contribution to the Detroit labor movement via Readers United during the newspaper strike.

Nancy Cannon, charismatic and ceramic artist, who figured decisively in our finding the Hungarians, sent the prophecy uttered above. Buried these five years in her journal, it now finally spoke its promise publicly—right down to the dancing—which promptly began as if on self-fulfilling cue.

Just a word of astonishment about the dancing. It was, of course, mostly to Motown, as Jeanie desired. And went 'til nearly midnight, when we had to pull the plug. But it was the high schoolers (of our own community now grown, and Lydia's friends) who held the floor. Here's the astonishment: these kids know not only the moves, but all the words to Stevie Wonder, Diana Ross, Marvin Gaye, and the Temptations. They sang while doing the Hustle! How? Like some weird cultural osmosis topping off the mysteries of the providential night.

Jeanie wrote later, "We danced and danced. And played. Everyone had a great time. I'll be ready for the 10th anniversary party!"

Oddly and inexplicably, she suffered a seizure two nights later, first this year and unrelated to any known medication screw-up. Almost as though the devil demanded his own jig time.

Who'd a thunk it? I could be writing about the dark and dangerous times we're all living through, but instead I'm enumerating miracles. And thinking of dancing. Another future is possible.

'Til the heart is parted …

P.S. Jim Perkinson's poem:

jeanie of the waters
8/29/03

dark branch against the wind
stark
as foreboding calm
full of ants and cracked bark
until the cloud breaks
and the rains run cold on
the ground

"there is gravity"
says simone weil

dorothy day
rejoins "and mercy
like a jail cell"

and gandhi grins gap-toothed
and sari-wrapped
before the bonfire of british weave

and francis appears barefoot laughing
in the snow his father's clothes given
away

aun sang su chi
briefly
haunts the door
eyeball against bullet

chico mendez chews his lip
a mere blip
in the rifle-sight

the night hides bonhoeffer's
fear, the bell soon to peel
morning and end
and beginning

and fannie lou hamer
fans the flies from her
head

and the clock strikes
and the hour comes
and the horns squawk coltrane
and the bongo beats a river
under the feet
and the nameless ones stand up
and the shameless ones kneel down
and the little ones leap
and the stupid ones answer
and the silly ones drool delight
and the corn grows as far as the eye can see
and the tabasco is poured
and the tongue tangos
and the tear falls
and the old woman rises like noon
full of brine and riddles
and the stars sing indigo rhyme
and underneath the sword
underneath the altar
underneath the breath
a word groans
and there is gladness

and there, there sits
one with head in hands
like john the baptist
returned from jordan
full of waters

and we all crave the sight
the family
torn flesh mended
in the dark
light

and i wonder what jeanie wylie
kellermann will command
as the true art of that hour
when the heart has parted
and the poor come home
to rest?

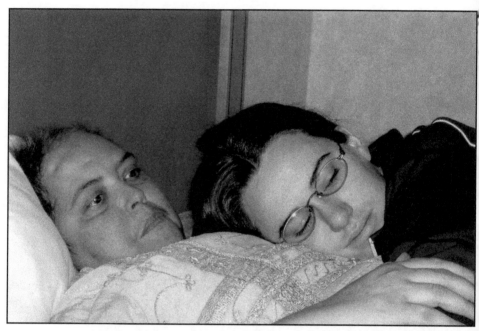

Jeanie and Lydia, Chicago, February 2005. Credit: Bill Wylie-Kellermann

16

A Tad Behind the Great Curve of Life

Advent 2004: You have a future

"Those first-century Christians, pursued and persecuted, scorned and beleaguered, as they were because of their insight, were right: the secret of the first advent is the consolation of the second advent. The message in both advents is political. It celebrates the assurance that in the coming of Jesus Christ the nations and the rulers of the nations are judged in the Word of God, which is, at the same time, to announce that in the Lordship of Christ they are rendered accountable to human life and to that of the whole of creation ...

"Christians rejoice, on behalf of all humanity and, indeed, all creation, at the prospect of the judgment because in that Last Day the destruction of political authority at once signals its consummation in the kingdom of God ... If some have put aside the expectation, it is not because Christ is tardy and not because God has postponed the next advent, but because the consciousness of imminence has been confused or lost.

"I regard the situation of contemporary Christians as much the same as that of our early predecessors in the faith so far as anticipation of the Second Coming matters. We expect the event at any moment. We hope for it in every moment. We live in the imminence of the Eschaton. That is the only way, for the time being, to live humanly."
—William Stringfellow

At the very outset of Jeanie's illness six years ago, that first Advent following the initial surgery, when we were casting about for alternatives to chemo and radiation, we had just finished a consultation with a doctor in Evanston and went out to a Chinese restaurant for dinner. I saved it for a while, and wish I could put my hands on it even now, but I swear her cookie fortune read: "You have a future in medical research."

We giggled for days. But over this last summer, she fixed her status as the American poster child for the "chicken vaccine"—MTH-68/Newcastles Disease Virus—by appearing as "Case 4" in an article in the Journal of Neuro-Oncology ...

Oh, she still insists on watching too much daytime TV, details page-long lists of intended purchases from mail-order catalogues, and would buy candy by the pound if she had the money in her pocket. Her judgment and emotional range can go thin, though last week she actually got angry back at me!—which, I might add, reflected good judgment as well. But above all, where the most she used to muster was an over-edited postcard note to friends, she now can now manage occasional letters by the page in longhand ...

Lydia graduated with some lovely honors from Mercy in June. She suffered a late-semester case of mono, missing a number of finals but rising from her sickbed to arrive at the prom with her circle of best friends by tugboat (therein lies a tale) ...

Over the summer she was angsting over her decision to attend Loyola University in Chicago. (Her inner debate concerned staying closer to home in Detroit— mostly for the sake of her Mom's care and her sister's psychic security.) She's flourishing in Chicago. Loves her studies, the city, the lake, and above all the good circle of activist companions with whom she's fallen in. They organize fasts, vigil in cardboard homeless boxes, and journey to the gates of the School of the Americas to protest war and torture.

Lucy, meanwhile, has proven Lydia's fears groundless. She loves Mercy High School, gets straight As, was cast in both the fall play and spring musical, takes five dance classes, has quickly made fast friends but seems to savor solitude as well, and drives everywhere on a permit—often with her Mom functioning as licensed adult. The two of them have a really lively and loving relationship, which I love to peek in upon.

With her Mom's med schedule or her homework assignments, Lucy's incredibly responsible and organized. Stepped up, as they say. She used to be the quiet one at the dinner table, with Lydia talking a mile a minute. Now she spiels away herself, rising to fill the space and make it her own.

Over the summer she hiked the White Mountains with her godfather and two best friends, and played Puck, dancing all the while, in A Midsummer Night's Dream (with Lydia as Helena, and me, lo and behold, as Theseus). That tale: I was at the end of a frustrated sabbatical (graciously funded by the Louisville Institute). The former Theseus in Lydia's community production had bailed at the last minute, and when she asked if I'd cover, I stepped up—doing four productions on the basis of two rehearsals.

At 55, my memorization synapses are a little bit pickled, but I couldn't have stumbled on a better spiritual discipline for distraction. Or one more fun. All the worry spaces of my brain filled with soliloquies, or preoccupied themselves with well-timed banter.

"The best in this kind are but shadows, and the worst no worse if imagination amend them." ...

The Stringfellow quotes at the head of this letter are from Conscience and Obedience, which along with An Ethic for Christians and Other Aliens in a Strange Land and Instead of Death, are being republished as an "ethics trilogy" just in time for the 20th anniversary of his death in March. He is so cunningly prescient. In a moment when empire couldn't be more openly embraced or its "theology" more publicly blasphemed around, he's like a gulp of biblical air.

I recently listened to a talk tape of his and began to cry—just to hear his voice, I suppose, but even more for the Word of hope in a dark, dark season. Hope that Advent itself remembers and brings round, right on time.

Live humanly, dear friends. For the time being. Hope. Yearn. Expect. Be. Our salvation is near at hand. Love and holy kisses ...

March 2, 2005 (20th Feast of Stringfellow):

"The decade locates me, at its outset, deeply in the midst of work as a white lawyer in Harlem, but it closes in fragile survival of prolonged, obstinate, desperate illness. It begins in social crisis, it ends in personal crisis.

"For me, these are equally profound because the aggression of death is the moral reality pervasive in both and, moreover, the grace to confront and transcend death is the same in each crisis. Indeed, I do not think the two episodes, which roughly mark personally the boundaries of the last decade, are essentially distinguishable.

"I doubt, in other words, that I could have had the capability to lately survive radical disease, unremitting pain and the shadow of death had I not spent those earlier years in the Harlem ghetto, discerned there something of the moral power of

death, and learned, from neighbors, clients and Harlem inhabitants at large, something of the triumph of life which human
beings can enter and celebrate despite death's ubiquity and
vitality. Harlem is the scene in which I first comprehended the
veracity of the resurrection—and that prepared me, more than
any other single thing, for devastating illness and ruthless pain."
—William Stringfellow, 1970

> *In her seventh year of personal crisis, Jeanie Wylie goes
> under the knife yet again. We're scheduled for surgery
> Monday, March 14th (Pray for us, Fannie Lou Hamer,
> on your feast day!). This will be an abrupt surprise to
> most of you (as it has been for us), since we've recently
> reported how well she's done this last year.*

> *The gadolinium of a routine MRI lights up a spot
> about the size of an egg. There is some small chance
> it's necrosis (dead tissue caused by radiation). Necrosis
> would actually be preferable to tumor, but both call
> for surgery. Several years ago, Jeanie announced she
> was done with cutting and probing, come what may,
> but she now declares herself up for this nevertheless.
> The surgeon, a great human being who's also brilliant
> at such things, doesn't anticipate any loss of function.
> And we trust him. Barring the usual risks, she ought
> to come through pretty much unfazed in the near term.*

> *We don't know what this means for the chicken vaccine
> treatment. The hospital tumor board recommends
> ceasing and desisting—their premise being that
> things work for a while, then tumors mutate or figure
> ways around them, so you quit and try something
> else: a standard chemo, as they would have it. The
> Hungarians, who have been dissatisfied for the last
> year with the strength and delivery method of the
> dosage, would rather see it increased in potency and*

injected directly. I'm inclined to hang in with them for the time being.

Lydia, who's at Jonah House this week on alternative spring break from Loyola, has had the hardest time, perhaps because of coping at a solitary distance. She's hauling in poems from her depths like netloads of fish. They leap to mind whole during Eucharist. All unflinching in honesty. I append one with permission.

Lucy seems fine, though she doesn't say much. May be working it out bodily, dancing her fears out on toepoint and tap. Pending the outcome and recovery, she still hopes to come to L.A. with me Easter week for a conference (and camping and surfing with our friends Ched Myers and Elaine Enns).

Apart from reorganizing my life in a pretty busy and even productive period, I'm doing alright. At the outset my emotions were near the surface, and I was perpetually exhausted. We met the other evening with our discernment group, or clearness committee, who put good questions and prayed over us. Nothing shifted decisionwise, but it's such a relief to share the burden and know we're going through this in community. Of course, this note multiplies and confirms that sense.

And Jeanie is, well, Jeanie. She's actually been having symptoms since Christmas (some she's only confessed since the MRI). For some reason she's shifted from humming to whistling—but perseveres with her musical self-treatment. I don't know if the news changes the way we look at her, but she's positively beatific. Her eyes dance and leap with sunniness. Go figure the mysteries. And give thanks.

We're at the cabin as I finish this. We venture through drifts into the clearing at midnight and look up at the winter sky. It's stunning. Everything is rearranged from what we know in summer. The Pleiades hang close in circle and are ready to set in the west. Lucy skates paths we've shoveled in the marsh. In front of the stove, Jeanie sits and reads the entire corpus of these update letters from beginning to end, in a packet compiled and bound by Lydia as a Christmas present. Rehearsing where we've been seems a shrewd preparation for Monday's next go-round.

In New York City, one Palm Sunday I told Bill Stringfellow I was going to marry Jeanie Wylie. As we crossed Ninth Avenue, he turned suddenly to us and said, "Never imagine that you couldn't live without one another." We tried to claim that very freedom from the first in our wedding vows.

Now, as above, he reminds us of the connection between struggles personal and political. With the two-year anniversary of ongoing war at hand this Palm Sunday, we solicit prayers both for ourselves and for the people of Iraq. Indistinguishable in our hearts …

PS. Lydia's poem:

Miracles
March 1

Something extraordinary
Beyond the power of any creation
Not of human power
Intended by God
Amazing occurrence
Wondrous
Divine mission
Contrary to the
Established constitution

All definitions
Of miracles
But I fear there
Is something missing

We pray for miracles
We celebrate miracles
Miracles are usually seen
As only good
As a gift
As an answer

But sometimes
It is not the answer
We are looking for
Sometimes it is not a gift
We want to accept

Miracles come in forms
Always unexpected
Always different from
What we had planned

No one would say
That they don't want a miracle
But there are those
Who are skeptical
Is there any truth
Is this possible

I think there is something
Missing in these definitions
Miracles do not come
And then go
Miracles are not an answer
Or an ending
Instead they are a beginning

Jesus performed miracles
He healed those who were sick

But those were healed
Did not walk away
Their life was forever changed
Their lives took a new path
These miracles called them to action

I want a miracle
Yes, I do.
But I know that a miracle
Is work
It is to be celebrated
And it is a gift from God
Beyond our wildest imagination
But it calls us into action

Right now, I don't know
If I have the strength to act
I don't know if I am ready
To accept a miracle
My heart wants it
So badly
But there is hesitation
Hesitation to say yes
Saying yes to God's miracle
Places us even closer
To the path of discipleship
To the path of faith
And belief
And complete surrender
To the power of God
I don't know
If I have the strength
To say yes
I need time—
The one thing
Which is also causing me the most pain

April 2005: Lost on Good Friday

Jeanie came through the surgery well. Thanks be for brilliant surgeons, medical mysteries, and communities of intercession. The news on the tumor (and it was a malignancy, not dead tissue) is that they were able to get 95 percent of the mass because, strange upon strange, this most aggressive tumor, normally diffuse in its boundaries, was surrounded or encased in a firmer, lower-grade tumor that made the borderland quite distinct. Much less of a judgment call on how much to take and how much to leave. Nobody has been able adequately to explain the pathology, but the strange circumstance was a welcome grace.

Her short-term memory has taken a bit of a hit—or at least is slow in being recovered. She did have a seizure in ICU (completely unnecessary, by my lights) so has been bouncing back from that, plus being weaned out from under the additional meds they piled on in consequence. So she's not been tracking as well as prior and suffers errors in judgment—some involving minor cooking disasters, others which send me into a panic—like getting separated for an hour in a monstrous big hospital (at noon, no less, on Good Friday, when we were headed for the Stations of the Cross walk). And some, more serious, risking the port they put in so we can up the dosage and delivery of the Hungarian vaccine. On the latter, we're pulling together the medical accoutrements to mix and shoot the more concentrated form of the virus.

Since the surgery, Jeanie has spent a lovely week with her sister Rene Beth, while Lucy and I went west for an Easter week of speaking and sun. Good days all. Tomorrow is tax day—so many reasons to refuse to ante up. I thought we were going to need to resist actively this year, but we came in under the limit again.

Meanwhile, the daffodils burst last week and are standing in a line of glory. Now the tulips are considering ...

April 24, 2005: A World Out of Sorts

It's snowing as I write. On the tulips. A winter storm warning is broadcast. The world feels out of sorts, large and small.

I'm writing this from Jeanie's hospital bedside. She collapsed on Wednesday and came in by way of EMS (the drivers and staff were great, but ER is a slow and exhausting way in, believe me). At first they worried us about the possibility of a stroke, but bloodwork and CT scan came back clear on that score.

She's sporadically absent and confused, even wandering off the floor into other units, leading them to suspect "low-grade sub-clinical sparking"—essentially constant seizing, but under the radar. They hold her while they monitor and get meds adjusted. Lydia is emotionally spent at her college distance and sending off more of her poetic copings. Lucy holds her own, cuddling and dozing with Jeanie in the hospital bed.

In the course of things, Jeanie had a couple lapses of "dysphasia"—like speaking in tongues. Inventing a language as she went or stringing together regular words in an incoherence. At first she was oblivious, spieling away, presuming she made sense. When she caught on, we giggled to the point of tears, she speaking for the fun of it—like someone breathing helium and talking in a falsetto voice. I do love this woman so.

But then frustrations set in—sentences ending with a face, or "Oh boy," or "Never mind." Happily, those episodes were brief and passing. MRI and EEGs have since all come back clear—which is to say, nothing definitive (no new tumor; no major seizing). All confusions slipping under the radar ...

As for myself, I manage. I hit a wall and crash in sleep when she finally comes home. I write on the laptop at her bedside, or on the plane, and get a few things accomplished, if a tad behind the great curve of life. Exhausted and eternally grateful ...

June 17, 2005: Abiding in the Shadow

"You will not fear the terror of the night, nor the arrow that flies by day, or the pestilence that stalks in darkness, or the destruction that wastes at noon."

The monks sing Psalm 91 in Gregorian at Compline (the last office of the day), laying themselves down to sleep in the freedom of trust. We've been reading it from the Book of Common Prayer at Jeanie's bedside in the Intensive Care Unit for over two weeks now. O Lord, come to our assistance. Make haste to help us.

This has been a difficult spring. Since we last wrote, there have been several hospitalizations and one all-night Emergency Room experience. Jeanie had been declining incrementally. Joining me, several weeks back, with Word and World folks on a planning retreat, she was needing to be lead round by the hand, all but ceased eating, was losing control of her functions. A trip to the hospital on my 56th birthday showed that the shunt had failed and she suffered hydrocephalus.

Just looking at my own journal, I'd been raising this each hospitalization going back five weeks! These symptoms were familiar from times past. Still, we rejoiced to know the cause, signed off for replacement surgery the next day, and went home to a happy window for birthday dinner (manicotti, salad, garlic bread, and brownies), all made by the girls and served by candlelight on our upstairs back porch inside the big pine.

They each presented me wondrous poems as gifts. And, grace upon grace, Lydia had the foresight to have Jeanie make me a card the Sunday prior, for which she necessarily needed to summon her inner resources to focus and write: "Hey love: You are my favorite!! Happy Birthday! I love you so much! Do you know that? Thanks for sharing the last 20 years with me. Love, Jeanie." Colored pencils and all. It uncorked my tears on the spot.

Then. The hospital called shortly to report that her cranial fluid had bacteria in it, and they needed permission to do an emergency bedside procedure (in effect a blind surgery, sans OR) to install an external shunt to drain fluid. Jeanie had gone completely non-responsive. The operation next morning would be to remove the infected device.

Our beloved surgeon warned soberly that she might not wake at all – and, if she did, the "meningitis" would severely compromise her. It was among the lowest points of the last seven years. Endgame seemed upon us, and we're told that won't be pretty.

But she woke. She smiled. She said Hi. She swallowed pills and fed herself meals. The infection, it turned out, had not yet inflamed the brain. It was only ventriculitis, and the remedy was to keep draining excess fluid and sterilize that remaining with big-time antibiotics.

She improved daily for a stretch. Then began to decline yet again. She stopped talking and had trouble swallowing. Graciously, for the sake of my heart, her eyes never stopped communicating. But the medicos had no explanation. The idea of "micro-tumors" was floated, too small to show up on MRIs.

Right, says Lydia, they don't know what's going on, so she must have invisible tumors! After several delays Jeanie had shunt replacement surgery yesterday— this time on the left. (Her skin on the right is just too stretched and scarred to cover another wound). It turns out, as per a CT scan two days prior, that her ventricles were once again enlarged. Even while fluid was measurably cumulating in that little plastic bag near her head. Don't ask me.

Last night she smiled and kissed and stroked our hands. This morning when the surgeon came round and asked how she felt, Jeanie replied, "Particularly well." God knows. Or so we trust. We ourselves don't know what's to come.

The medical prognosticators are playing it close to the chest. They purse their lips and warn of expectations too high. For having said no more cutting, we've now had four surgeries in as many months. Each what the neurologists call an "insult" to her brain. She'll certainly need physical therapy and more to get herself back home. But I know of no one with a stronger will. And the woman has one helluva resilient brain.

It's been a long stretch. My emotions have been blessedly near the surface. Tears get triggered by things turned up in a pile—or reading Psalms at her bedside. The girls do well, though their tears have yet to find their tap. They worry about me, locating knots in my back and rubbing them into quiet submission.

I worry about them, but they've thrown themselves into a project: spring cleaning our flat, as organized by dear friends on the block. I come home from the hospital to rooms transformed. And I'm forced to sort papers one step ahead of them, lest my known disorder dissemble before my eyes. But the place feels stripped and simplified …

"When she calls to me I will answer. Protect her for she knows my name." Abiding in the shadow of the Almighty …

July 2, 2005: Eyes on the Prize

"Paul and Silas bound in jail, had no money for to go the bail; Keep your eyes on the prize, hold on!"

Before Jeanie Wylie's first meal home today, a modest Lebanese feast, the four of us went round the circle with intercessions and thanksgivings. When it came to her, Jeanie began to sing as above. We all joined in and knew it to be a prayer of both grace and will, of freedom and intent.

After lunch, we spent some time re-laying Jeanie's altar. Now that the apartment is stripped and cleaned and rearranged, the mahogany library table inherited from her family home has taken that function and overflows gorgeously. It includes her smudge kit of hawk feathers and the huge clamshell we found on the Indian Ocean side of South Africa. We prayed again, and she smudged us all with California sage to mark this amazing homecoming, one we more than once doubted.

It's exactly a month since Jeanie went into the hospital. More than two weeks in the ICU draining fluid from her brain and strength from her body. It took 10 days of rehab with the good folks at Cottage Hospital to get her climbing stairs—the minimum for getting home to our second-floor flat. She did three hours of therapy each day—physical (muscle strength, walking, and eventually those stairs), occupational (relearning and practicing daily tasks), and speech (which covers most of cognition).

Her short-term memory was pretty shot and she was "perseverating," which means getting stuck in a repetition. For example, she wrote a page-long note to her mom, which started perfectly with declarations of love and then abruptly fixed on an endless repetition of "I have to have to have to … "

That's now eased, though it has its behavioral equivalents. She still has some trouble "scanning" her environment, which can be a safety issue. At the outset of her stay, they suggested we have a back-up plan to getting her home, but she put her mind to it and, well, here we are.

Jeanie's mom and sister Rene Beth were here for five days during rehab. They sent me up north a couple days to where our community was camping for the week. I needed it—basketball and sailing and, above all, time with Lydia and Lucy sitting on the dock or at tabletalk. With her mom and sister we had communion at bedside one Sunday, Jeanie reading the Psalm and breaking the bread. Writing this letter makes me realize what a sacramental presence she exercises among us.

Late in her time at rehab, believe it or not, she went fishing on a field trip and reeled in a 14-inch smallmouth bass. If they'd have had a camera, I bet she'd have appeared on the front page of some local paper, hoisting it up from her wheelchair. Jeanie let the great creature go and by supper time couldn't even remember it, but she was the talk of the hospital for days.

We have to be cautious not to fall back into old care patterns now that she's home—Jeanie needs more constant attention, at least for now. We're convening the discernment group to think some of this through, though it looks like Lydia will quit her summer job and take on a substantial portion of the caregiving. She's lots of energy and ideas for continuing therapy.

Two days before Jeanie came home, I got hit one evening with chest pains that wouldn't quit. The girls were at rehearsal (Godspell and Love's Labors Lost), so I drove myself to the ER. My blood enzymes and an EKG both showed fine, but they kept me overnight to do a stress test the next morning (which I passed handily, I might add).

It was apparently gastro pain, which yet needs to be diagnosed—not that I've been under stress, mind you—but what a relief to have cardio ruled out. And it was a sweet irony, a simple twist of grace, to be heart-wired to a monitor and stuck to a saline drip, not to mention poked and pricked all night, just like Jeanie has been more or less constantly for weeks. It engendered not only thanks, but that sympathy of experience we call intercession.

SCUPE, meanwhile, has been incredibly generous to me, as my work responsibilities have gotten short shrift these last few weeks—well, these several months, for that matter. Likewise with my voluntary Word and World commitments. Other hopes for the remainder of the summer include getting back in the work saddle, finding some family vacation time (we're slated for Block Island later this month, but that's up in the air—a poor location to have a medical crisis, but a splendid place for body and spirit. The girls are irrepressibly eager, and the ferry reservations are holding firm). Who knows if life can return to normal? And who knows what's baseline normal for us all anyway?

With eyes on the prize ...

Lydia MCing the 49th birthday gathering at the Waldorf School, November 2005.
Credit: Bill Wylie-Kellermann

17

Turning Toward Home

A retrospective reflection from Lydia:

Summer 2005: Scrabbling Exotic Dreamscapes

The past summer I spent with my mom. She had been in ICU for two weeks with several scares that this was the end. We had been called in the middle of the night to come immediately for emergency surgery that was unclear if she would come out. We didn't make it to the hospital in time to say goodbye before the surgery began. But somehow she did come through.

Then she spent two weeks in rehab re-learning to speak, walk, eat, go to the bathroom, get into the shower, etc. Her days were filled with intensive speech, physical, and occupational therapy. They finally let her go home, but really urged us to keep up with the therapy because she still wasn't back to where she was before she entered the hospital, but they thought she still had potential to keep improving.

At the time I was working at an ice cream place where we sang for tips. It had the potential to be my all-time favorite job, but instead turned out to be quite miserable on numerous accounts—and was minimum-wage to boot. It was clear we were going to need to hire someone to be with my mom because she could no longer be alone at all. I suggested the possibility of making my summer job being with my mother. I would do the care 9 to 5 so my dad could keep working, and I'd stop working at the shop.

We decided this would be a good idea, and I began spending my summer with my mom. The time commitment became much more than I had bargained. Suddenly, I was getting her up in the morning and being with her until I would tuck her in at night. However, it turned out to be the most meaningful and life-giving time in my life. I am so grateful that I made this decision, and it is time I cherish.

More than anything, I spent that summer learning. Learning patience. Learning to be still. Learning to enjoy the little things. Learning to pay attention. Learning how to love. Learning how I want to live. My mom and I didn't do anything big, but the little things became big. Much of our time was spent getting dressed or sitting in the bathroom. But those are exactly what I miss the most.

She began to really trust me. I learned how to talk to her. I could convince her to do things when she wouldn't listen to others. I could get her to swallow pills, leave the house without stopping on the way, even up until the final days. I would often be awakened in the middle of the night by my dad asking me to come help get mom into bed.

In the morning, I would continue her therapy by having her choose between two shirts that she wanted to wear. She couldn't make a plan of what she wanted to wear, but she could choose between two things. She would let me sit with her while she went to the bathroom. She would let me take her clothes off. In many ways she had lost all her privacy.

She was generous to me in how close she allowed me to become. We developed a relationship that was closer than I had ever been. When I cry over my mom these days, I think about what I would do if I had just one more day with her: I would put on her socks, I would run my hand over her head, and I would just sit. It is those little things that I miss the most.

When my dad was packing up her clothes, he was throwing away socks that had holes in them. I took one of them with me, and it is now in my sock drawer. Ruffling through that drawer and laying my hand upon it brings me to tears faster than most other things. I can remember her leg and her toes so well.

I began to see my mom as truly beautiful, in a way I hadn't noticed before. My sister has since painted these wonderful pictures of my mom naked from the back sitting on her bed. She has learned the outline of my mom with all the indentions and lines. Changing my mother became ritual and showed me a new kind of beauty altogether. (In many respects, I think this summer and experience helped me read deeper into the understanding of my sexuality and its beauty.)

All summer we played Scrabble; she got better and better each day—though it was difficult to get through it without her trying to make fly some nonexistent word. However, Lucy's and my vocabulary was so much smaller than hers, so we never really knew when she was fibbing. But all three of us got pretty good and would play several times a day.

Our routine consisted of meals together, exercise, art projects, games to work her brain as rehab had showed us, naps, reading out loud to each other, walking around the block and stopping to enjoy the flowers. It was simple, but it was suddenly the only thing that mattered.

At night I would help her into her pajamas and cover her up. Every night I would pull the blankets over her head. Sometimes she would laugh. Sometimes she would wait patiently for me to remove them. Sometimes she would say "Excuse me," "Hello, I'm in here." Then we would kiss each other each goodnight, on each cheek, forehead, and nose.

Then I would ask her what she was going to dream about. At first, I did this to push her imagination during rehab. I would say, "Mom, what are you going to dream about?"

"You," she would answer automatically. And sometimes my sister, too. Then I would ask, "And where are we going to go?" This part would be much more difficult. Most of the time she would end up saying "someplace exotic."

Even up into her final days, I could ask her what she would dream about and immediately she would respond "You." I loved believing that we would meet each other in our dreams. I remember what a relief I felt when I realized that I could meet my mother in my dreams after she died. I hope that she will pass through my dreams throughout my life and that we can always go someplace exotic.

In my love for her ...

I picked up the thread again, as the inevitable became clear:

October 11, 2005: The Turning Time

"Holy God, holy and strong, holy and immortal, have mercy upon Jeanie, strengthen her with all your saving help. Restore her when and how it pleases you, that, as a living member of your faithful, she may give thanks and praise you, now, and for all eternity."

> *We are summoning prayers yet again, though of a new and different sort. It is the turning time, and we are making a momentous turn. Today we did not begin chemotherapy as offered us. We have in effect ceased treatments for Jeanie and are beginning the careful walk of homegoing.*
>
> *In September, Jeanie was in the hospital for a low-grade fever that was affecting her functions. The fever was traced and treated and her port (the most likely source) was pulled. But in the course of searches, they also did an MRI and found large-scale tumor growth not only filling the cavity left by the March surgery, but even lighting up spots on the left side as well.*
>
> *We knew of a certainty that we were done with cutting (it wasn't even being pressed upon us), but the four of us—with a little help from our friends, the discernment and support group—had to sort through the odds and costs of a new chemo option. Getting on the same page always entails exercising a family charism of forbearance. The four of us each deal with all these things, including the conversation and discernment, differently.*
>
> *Lydia wants to know everything, asks incisive questions, needs to be party to decisions, and likes to have matters clearly settled. She herself quickly made decisions, dropping a class and reorganizing her*

work-study job to enable homestays four days a week as needed or desired. Lucy ducked the conversation with the neurologist passing us the hard news and generally absents herself from such tables. But once the story is known, she hurries to the hospital to crawl into bed with her mom and cuddles a nap. A body person, she's not vocal at the decision sessions, and probably processes more in dance and theater.

I'm inclined to stay open to the possibilities, listen longer than others in the family, weighing and balancing alternatives. I was the one most urgent to pull the discernment circle into shared decision-making. Jeanie is alert and mindful and participates in the conversation, but can't cope with an either/or. These days she'll generally choose both. So having her on board means painting a scenario and reading how she sits with it. And perhaps doing so repeatedly.

With her at hand, I was telling someone our recent decisions, whereupon she turns to Lydia and says, "Do I know about this?" Short-term memory loss has its advantages when it comes to any obsessive brooding.

This morning she was an image of presence and grace at our opening conversation with the hospice nurse. She wanted to be there and didn't flinch in the least, even when it came to the tougher questions. Like how we might handle the body at the time of death. The woman, accustomed as she said to an ordinary level of denial, was taken back and "blessed" by Jeanie's visage and our exchange.

This weekend was the Word and World mini-school on William Stringfellow, marking the 20th anniversary of his death. Since I was point-person for the event, there was an earlier debate about the wisdom of going forward with Jeanie's crisis hovering. We persevered. I hadn't imagined how providentially the two things would become one, but in fact, our turning time coincided precisely with the weekend, gave incarnational substance to so many of Stringfellow's themes (think: biography as theology, the ethics of vocation, and resurrection as freedom from bondage to the power of death), and our health was in turn addressed and nourished by his wisdom and the love of friends gathered.

I'd turned up a video interview that Word and World friend Uncas McThenia had done with Jeanie about Stringfellow 10 years ago, so she was (in all the wondrous, articulate, excruciating fullness of her beauty and power) part of the panel concerning his life. In it she was characteristically candid about his sexual ambiguities and the undue male ambiance of his theological circle, all while loving and appreciating him. She told of his constant pain in the failing months, picturing him ceremoniously carrying a huge bowl of chowder to table for a group of us—a costly grace of hospitality.

But notably, she spoke of his blessing our marriage ("May the one who raised Christ Jesus from the dead quicken your mortal bodies also"), read cryptically from the Book of Common Prayer "Service for the Burial of the Dead"! And his admonition that she and I never imagine that we couldn't live without the other. Thus, she simultaneously opened up his humanity, while coincidentally bringing our own moment as content to Stringfellownian reflection.

A stunning event of the weekend was a presentation prepared by Kate Foran of our Word and World staff, which lifted up Stringfellow's theology of the circus. He beheld it as an emblem of the eschaton, the regathering of all creation in the consummation of the "kindom"—all sorts and creatures convened in the circle where death is defied (not deified), all the while living in tents, in the eschatological alienation of exiles, sojourners, and nomads. His theological essay was quoted, along with the poetry of Robert Lax and the wisdom of "priestly fool" Ken Feit (whom Stringfellow counseled and sent off to clown school), all under the gorgeous circus serigraphs of John August Swanson, along with commentary on those from Joan Prefontaine. It was lush and lovely.

AND THEN, by what prodigious providence should the Cirque du Soleil be in town! So after all was said and done, and a long Sunday nap, Jeanie and Lydia and I went. And how more could it be that the "plot thread" of the show concerned the death of a clown, or the dream of his death? He ascends from his sickbed, beset by a procession of rambunctious comforters, up to the heights to learn his wings (more like swimming than flying, should you wonder). And thereafter he wanders, the ordinary human, through the extraordinary acrobatic feats of all that follows, or sometime floats high above riding his bicycle through the skies. Angels likewise drift through the performances, perhaps assisting the tightwire artist, or even serving as "catchers," lest she strike her foot.

Stringfellow surely smiled from the great cloud. The prayer above is taken from a little service of exorcism that belonged to him. It's the one he employed to exorcize Richard Nixon, and also the house on Block Island after Anthony's death in 1980. Rose Berger, whose vocation as priestly poet among us is long since confirmed, read it in the closing service of anointing, where tears ran even more freely than oil.

Elaine and Ched had brought from the L.A. Catholic Worker a quilt that first covered Kieran Prather— spirited writer, notorious out gay man in the Worker movement, who died beneath its cover of AIDS. Beneath it Ladon Sheats also crossed over into memory and glory. It has wrapped Philip Berrigan and countless others in the hospice and healing ministrations of the Worker.

It wrapped Jeanie, Lydia, and myself for the anointing, through which sweet pastoral hands and even sweeter tears blessed us in our turn toward hospice. And then it came home with us. We are grateful beyond words. Love abounds. And we couldn't be more peaceful in our decisions or the everlasting arms.

We are thinking through (Lydia ahead of all curves) how to organize our lives for this next phase. The medicos are, as always, fain to utter timelines, but it's likely that by late November we will begin to see substantial change in Jeanie. Eventually, we anticipate that she will fade and slip quietly into a coma. But, meanwhile, we are seizing these days for family time and for friends to share their love and prayers. Hence this.

Julian of Norwich's words ring true: "But all shall be well and all shall be well and all manner of thing shall be well."

Message in a plastic bag

Sometime during this stretch, as I was cleaning the house for the pending hospitality, I came upon something in a stack of papers I might easily have tossed—several hand-written post-it notes in a little plastic bag. The pages were carefully numbered, and the penciled instructions were in Jeanie's hand. They had been written the year prior, and she must have carried them on her person, or maybe in the medical bag, with an eye toward final contingencies:

> *To anyone who finds this:*
>
> *Lucy just started h.s. She's vibrant (taking 5 dance classes on M & W), sings in plays—nice pitch—and gets straight A's Cell #[Lucy's cell number here].*
>
> *Lydia has a cell phone too and because she's extremely responsible, she's—of the 3 W-K's—most likely to have it on and she's a good sleuth. (She'd be most able to track Lucy down—unless she went home with a new friend from school.) She'd also apply herself to finding Bill. (In finding people, she's as capable as me.) Her cell # is [Lydia's number here]. I was planning on having all our cell #s end in 1967, Year of Detroit's big rebellion. But Bill got Lucy's phone and they assigned her the first available number.*
>
> *At present, I'm the only one without a cell phone and without a computer of my own. Bill promised me one as a birthday gift (contingent on my clearing space for it. Never mind that he has a study upstairs you can't even move in without stepping on something of value.) His cell # is [my number here].*
>
> *Like Lydia his first response would be to come home. I'd be really glad to see all 3 (as long as I can recognize them). The last thing my kids need is for me to smile and say "and who are these lovely girls." (Your Mom is practically required to know you.) So make sure someone is present to interpret. 1) Any time you notice that I have more context than they've been provided—point it out. 2) Any time you see that I care for them—point it out. 3) If it seems I have a sense of who is living with me point that out too.*

I laughed and I cried. I am so busted by that.

The cell phones, which I had long resisted, were a concession to medical emergency and the persistence of my road work. The birthday thing is true; she couldn't be trusted alone on my laptop without navigating her curiosity into software settings or somesuch damage, and I never delivered on my intent to arrange her something else. A true regret. (After the note surfaced and I addressed it, she did forgive me that.) And my attic study truly is an untraversable mess, to which I forbid guided tours.

I wept for the love and care she was taking with the girls, even me. And for her imagining an end she would need to self-manage among strangers in a hospital or nursing home. I'm so glad we all conspired to make that end different, even sacred and beautiful, though God knows she self-managed a good bit of it anyway.

Hospice: Institution or community?

When it came to the hospice time, Lydia knew it immediately and without reserve. She was holding Jeanie's hand when we were discharged from the hospital after getting the tumor news. Prepared to live into the new reality, Lydia turned to her and said, "Mom, look back at the place. This might be the last time you are ever here." Jeanie smiled and sighed, "Oh that would be so nice."

You'll recall that we made, in effect, at the time of the radiation, an earlier decision for hospice on which I reneged—wisely, as it now seems, but not without complication. This second, for-real hospice decision had its own interior travail. At least for me. I suspect for us all.

Here the collective inner effort was the big shift from the act of will in fighting our way forward, to the graceful yielding that is involved in letting go. I know there is gut and grace, perhaps in equal measure, both in healing and in dying, but the decision to quit treatment and die well is still an extraordinary event of inner turning. Or so it was for us.

It was only complicated by the emotional contradictions that accompany the traversing of such terrain. In the long-haul fight, I confess a weary inner voice, largely secret and suppressed, that periodically whispered, Couldn't it just be over? Or, like Lydia, How many more miracles can we bear?

Suddenly that voice seemed to have been given its reign in the dying time. But now, with its wish all but fulfilled, I grasped at precious moments and might have clung to life by my fingernails if I could but hold it—all the while letting go. Grace upon grace means being granted (and granting ourselves) the permission to be in the turmoils of such contradiction.

Hospice was waiting for us in the wings, but to get there meant setting aside certain medical options. One was an oral chemo, generally well-tolerated and with side effects easy to control, which might have granted some additional time. Sounds good, no?

Yes, but … The odds were short that it would work, and even those were based on test subjects who were fresh cases, not folks like Jeanie at the end of the long haul. But above all, it would tie us to a rigid outpatient regimen of weekly blood tests and scans to monitor the dosage, and then submission to hospitalization if adjustments were needed. With the discernment circle at the dining room table, I remember my inner sigh when we decided to forego it.

The tandem implication was that we would also cease the NDV chicken vaccine. Sadly, this was beyond the comprehension of the Hungarians. They had been so wonderful—compassionate and accommodating. They were among the good doctors who not only cared for, but seemed personally to care about, Jeanie.

Yet, don't forget, she was their American success story for the vaccine, written up in medical journals, so there was some self-interest at play. And they passionately believed in the miraculous power of their discovery. If only we would increase the dosage and frequency, or improve the delivery method, surely she would bounce back yet again.

I wrote them a long letter explaining our medical logics, filling in some blanks in a history they generated. I granted them access to Jeanie's records for research purposes, but also spoke frankly about the spiritual issues—including the sort of freedom in which we had been able to find and choose NDV in the first place, and how it was the same freedom with which we now set it aside.

Let me slip in an odd note here about the desperate proffering of last-ditch alternatives. When it became known that we had ceased treatment, suddenly new alternatives were pressed upon us. They came out of the woodwork. I'm uncertain of the logic.

Perhaps the assumption was that we'd lost faith in our current treatments, and now we'd be open to something new. Maybe it was a sense that if we were ready to face death, what could be the harm? Generally those who came forward were true believers, being helpful and generous, though sometimes a pyramided financial interest was involved. Anyway, as a rule, these seemed to be folks who themselves didn't quite get the spirit of hospice, the freedom to die. These things had to be explained, sometimes in detail.

Hospice, and perhaps especially the hospice care movement in North America, stakes a claim for dying well—which is not to say that they are synonymous. Jesus, as I've suggested, died well in excruciating torture. An assassin's bullet, an absurd car wreck, a frantic hospital effort to save and survive—none of these preclude dying well in my understanding. I try to imagine the latter, scrambling mightily in a heroic fight with all the medical resources in hand and watching a life slip away. That would surely make for a different variety of grief, at least initially.

The movement for hospice, however, conscientiously reclaims the intent of carefully dying well.

By conventional definition, hospice involves non-interventive palliative care: simply making the person as comfortable, and aware, as possible while she dies. She is treated as a person approaching death rather than as a patient.

Hospice reclaims space for dying, takes it back from the more exposed and invasive locations of American medical care. It opens the possibility, at home or in a comfortable facility, of making beauty, of re-creating sacred space. It involves an act of freedom, reasserting personal control of decision-making, unhooking from the grip of the medical regime. It opens the way for family and community and friendship to become primary. Relationships and the inner life of the dying take pride of place over any of the ordinary distractions.

And yet hospice, to be made more widely accessible, becomes less community or movement than institution. It is these days supported, if not encouraged and funded, by the insurance industry—because people in hospice effectively opt out of expensive procedures and last-ditch heroics. Commercial necessities have their sway. From the perspective of Jeanie's deathbed, I would say that a hospice program best supports and enables a real hospice community to gather round.

Peeking in on her own funeral

When we made the decision for hospice, Lucy declared, in a moment of counterintuitive brilliance, that we needed a party. Jeanie's 49th birthday was at hand—which marked the beginning of her Jubilee Year. We figured to make it a big one.

Jubilee is a Jewish festival celebrated every 50th year in the Hebrew Bible. It is the "year of the Lord's favor," which Jesus proclaimed in connection with the "kindom" of God. It takes its name from the *jubal,* the horn that was blown to announce its start, and it was marked by the freeing of slaves, the redistribution of capital, and the restoration of property. I like that.

In an interesting coincidence, it is said that our bodies change entirely every seven years—each molecule being replaced by another in the great Hereclitean fire of creation. By the time of Jeanie's party, her body had passed through seven such sevenly exhalations. She was one with creation, but couldn't have been more herself.

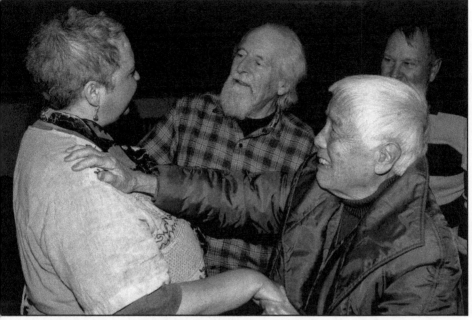

Jeanie at her 49th birthday party, 2005, with Grace Lee Boggs, C. Peter Dougherty, and Jasiu Milanowski. Credit: Bill Wylie-Kellermann

So the date was set and the organizing begun for a real celebration. In a certain sense, it was akin to Huck Finn peeking in on his own funeral—like Jeanie got to be present for her memorial celebration. Indeed, both had the same atmosphere of thanksgiving and resurrection joy. And everyone was in on it. Many people who came from a distance knew they were making a choice between the party (where they could give Jeanie a last face-to-face hug) or the funeral. For most, it was an easy call.

November 20, 2005: Jeanie's Jubilee

"Sometimes I'm so full of life I don't know what to do with it."
—Jeanie to her friend Maureen calling from Brisbane, Australia.

> *Thanks to so many of you for kind notes, greetings, and prayers. This just to send a quick report of Jeanie's Jubilee party.*

The evening was really wonderful. Lydia transparently herself as emcee. Julie Beutel sang of life and hope. My brother Jimmy played piano accompaniment for hymns, and a couple Peace Community kids (Rachel and Catherine) did a piano/cello duet.

Poetry happened. Dan Berrigan sent one on resurrection, and I had the nerve to follow his with several of my own for Jeanie, written in the last couple of weeks. Connie Supan offered one about Jeanie's transfiguration into a right-brained artist. And Jim Perkinson made the trek from Denver, plus overcame belating misdirections, to deliver a new one for her during a break in the dancing.

Folks came from afar and out of the past. Jeanie's best friend from kindergarten and her partner appeared early in the day for lunch, likewise some from high school days in Menominee, and college roommates from the University of Michigan. Also among the celebrants were Gene Stilp, one of the Nader Raiders during the Poletown struggle, Mel and Leda Hall (and other former Cass Church folk), newspaper strikers, nonviolent activists, Word and World compatriots, bishop friends, editors and journalists, and our own wide Detroit community. I invited several of Jeanie's beloved doctors, but I suppose they can't begin doing events like this or it would never end for them.

Folks testified that they'd never been to a party like this one. And I believe it. We danced 'til midnight. Jeanie loved it. Even when she pooped out, she just lay down on a bench at the edge of the dance floor. People took turns holding her hand and swaying to the music or surrounding her with a dance circle.

More visitors are to come. This week we'll have a Wylie reunion over Thanksgiving dinner—her mom remaining for the week thereafter. Michael Moore and Kathleen Glynn plan a visit. At this point it seems we've declined hospital, but we're organizing ourselves for hospice and hospitality.

Jeanie is slowing down and fading a bit. She's in minimal pain, thanks be; has had no further seizures (though I suspect one of the increased meds is making her weaker—noticed in her trying to rise from a chair or climb stairs). She becomes a woman of few words, and fewer completed sentences, but does really interesting art.

Maybe a word about that. Friends provide water colors, pens, crayons, colored pencils and markers in abundance. I'm trying to think of her assorted artistic companions. Among them: Susan, Ange, Maryanne, DeeDee, Nancy, the girls, of course, and her sister Mary. Every sitting is different.

She does perseverate. In writing that means repeating the same sentence over and over; in art, it comes out as large images with very detailed repetition of lines. So things like rainbows, mountain ranges, ocean waves, desertscapes, or sunrises start with a single line and proliferate. She does these meandering river and tunnel segments in which figures line up in the passage like mummies or cocoons, each a little more transmorphed.

A self-portrait has long hair and rosy cheeks, with a sun-moon pendant, but the whole thing is composed of finely waved pen lines—even the sprouted rainbow wings. Makes me wonder about those guys devising pointillism. She sees in waves.

Jeanie writes notes with sufficient prompting questions, and still reads aloud to caregivers. The first words out her mouth in the morning and before sleep at night are "I love you." In one form or another, that is the constant topic among us all. With her we go one day at a time, rejoicing in gratitude for each.

That very love and thanks to each of you ...

The scandalous drawing, December, 2005. Credit: Jeanie Wylie-Kellermann

18

All Good and All Gift

When we alerted the wider circle of support to our hospice decision, we received one of the strangest responses from friends in Wisconsin: They had made Jeanie a coffin. Jacob was a former Franciscan brother and a carpenter. He and his wife, Jeannie, had met, as I recall it, in the cruise missile action days at Williams International and had been in and out of jail with us back then.

They had begun the casket when Jeanie Wylie had first taken ill and her prognosis was so dire. Then, when she surprised us all with her longevity, they had set it aside, nearly completed, in the basement. There it became an oddity for their children's school friends, who would venture excursions into the spooky depths to view it.

At the time, they had touched base with another friend about the propriety of the gesture, but had never checked in with us. So their announcement, utterly gracious, was a surprise, to say the least.

Since I had already begun to envision such a contemplative project for myself, perhaps an Advent task, I had to pause and swallow hard. I didn't answer right away. But soon the idea began to warm in me. It was a gift. It was made with love and prayer. What else but to say yes! To say: Bless you! And thank you!

Some issues, however, remained. As a side effect of several drugs, Jeanie had put on a good bit of weight since Jacob and Jeannie had seen her face-to-face. Put crassly, would she fit? And, conversely, since we were expecting to lay her in state in our home, would a coffin that fit Jeanie also fit out the door? We planned to keep her body on dry ice; would there be access to spaces beneath her torso once she was in? Could all these contingencies be taken into account, in this case, after the fact?

As it turned out, the size was right—both for holding her and for sliding out the front room window. As to the dry ice question, Jacob ended up designing a collapsible little prop on which Jeanie could lie, granting the needed access, and Jeannie threw in an insulated "blanket," yet another clever and lovely design. Both fed their thoughts of a vocational enterprise in home-making coffins.

The crafted oak one they sent was more gorgeous by far than the plain pine box I had conceived. As for me? My Advent projects turned out to be crafting a container for the ashes and putting together a video of Jeanie's life. It was all good and all gift.

On Onion's Eve

The Wylie family reunion on Jeanie's birthday at Thanksgiving was another gift. We sang rounds, a Wylie tradition. But most amazing was an afternoon in a circle telling Jeanie Wylie stories. Her nieces and nephews had never heard tell of most. We laughed and cried. Both hard. The very thing our souls required.

And then Jeanie, the girls, and I turned our attention to pastoral care for our family. In this home stretch, to whom did we want to be turning? From our worshiping communities, we had two obvious choices, both much beloved. One was a thorough extrovert, thinking aloud, filling a room, aggressive and inventive in a crisis, diving in with both feet to move institutions or remedy situations. The other was a complete introvert, the epitome of contemplative nonattachment, but fully present in a kind of Zen silence. Hmmm. The girls shook their heads and thought. Long. And nothing was resolved just then.

Present at the October Word and World Stringfellow school in Minneapolis had been a number of dear friends from around the country who'd been sharing the journey with us from the beginning. Several, let it be noted, had long talks there with Lydia and surmised her—and our—need. We took counsel together and first tried to organize a single gathering at our place, which complex schedules in the short run simply did not allow.

In lieu of that, we calendared in a series of weekend visitations from those in the circle, and others as well. We didn't realize it at the time, but we were in effect stumbling upon a new pastoral model. Let me christen it: serial intensive pastoral care.

First in the serial came a longstanding social justice activist and writer and, more to the point, a longstanding friend, Joyce Hollyday, who co-pastors a congregation she helped birth in Asheville, North Carolina. She joined us for Onion Day weekend.

Better step back and explain this little Feast Day, invented by Lucy when Jeanie first took sick. It falls on October 25th, if you want to mark your calendar and join the festive rites. There are, of course, Onion Day foods (onion rings and French onion soup atop the list). Also an Onion Day song (a quirky radio ditty from the '60s called "I Love Onions"), a film (*Holes*), a poem (Neruda, no less), a Scripture text (Numbers 11:5, ambiguous to be sure), an onion Christmas tree ornament (one holiday calling to another), and even an Onion Day icon (a potholder crocheted in its layered likeness by our friend Michelle who was visiting when the feast arrived—which hangs even now above Jeanie's altar).

But the Onion Day ritual is the centerpiece. The family gathers on Onion's Eve and passes around the circle a large onion, each person peeling off one layer at a time. Now, before the peeling begins, everyone guesses how many layers will enfold. You'd think after seven years we'd have the numbers generally ball parked, but no, we always forget and guess wildly, many times wide of the mark.

The person who gets the smallest inner layer, the undividable center, has to make everyone else laugh. Of course, tears are already running down our faces from the onion itself, so the reversal of emotional extremes is enhanced. And the person who came closest to guessing the number of layers gets to open the first present on Onion Day morning. Oh, I forgot to mention the presents. Remember, this is a festival invented by an eight-year-old.

Anyway, we must have alerted Joyce to the festivities, because she arrived with her presents already wrapped and packed. Her most notable gift, however, was her care pastorally. She made time to get a walk and a talk with everyone, including Jeanie, probing with questions the state of each heart. Then, her last evening, we gathered around for a family conversation, which she facilitated. We talked freely, but she knew where all the hidden cards were waiting and needing to be laid on the table. It was good.

Organizing the way home

Next, Ched Myers and Elaine Enns flew themselves in from California. A few years prior, they had been primaries in the hospice community that had surrounded our friend Ladon in his crossing over. So they brought tested wisdom about ways to order such a community. While tending our hearts, they effectively offered a short course in pastoral administration for the dying time.

Moreover, in connection with Ladon's passing, they had researched and experimented with the ways of keeping the body and with what's sometimes called "green burial"—in Ladon's case, beneath the reds and browns of the late-summer desert. So they knew about ducking the mortuary system, about homemade coffins, how to get dry ice and what parts of the body required it most. They had resources to share. They brought a wealth of community wisdom, a common store for which we yearned without even knowing.

Without their counsel, we would surely not have organized ourselves so carefully. As the days intensified, I felt myself center and open. I was at my best, fully alert, mindful of my own heart, but attentive to others and the dynamics of the scene. Getting organized and organizational assistance meant I could consult, and to an extent help direct the process without being whelmed over by the logistics. It was a rare gift, one not to be presumed.

Carpentry would happen around us, widening door space. Prayer groups arrived with psalms and instruments in hand. Airport runs were coordinated and meals rewarmed in casserole dishes. We were being borne in community.

Although they weren't part of the original design, I'll mention our friends Will O'Brien and Dee Dee Risher in the pastoral sequence. Journalists, activists among the homeless, directors of an alternative seminary in Philadelphia that fed Word and World (Will led the Bible study on Rizpah that so transformed me), they brought gifts that you'll see, as I let Dee Dee's poem recount their visit:

The Way Home
For Jeanie

> All night we drove the icy backs of the mountains,
> following the slick black ribbon through
> rock passes where beautiful waterfalls of frozen water
> waited
> to be released, over bridges spanning chasms of white
> silk.
> The stripped, dark bones of the trees strode up, down
> every gorge,
> still upright against the smooth grip of the snow.

Sometimes we topped a ridge to see a valley spread below
smooth as a cotton sheet, blue and glowing.
In the center, there might be a house lit, gold spilling out onto the yard,
Touching the barn, remembering for us that these were the waiting weeks before Christmas,
that blue-silver dark time
in which we await the advent of the
we know not what.

In the end, these lights led us through the spare landscape
and the unknown route.
Every few miles we would see in the distance
a homestead lit against the night,
Inside every one of them is someone who
knows something of what it means to love in this world.
And this carried us when we at last reached the wilderness of turnpikes
and detours and the sleeping city.
Still there the bold lights called,
waved us on from block to block
until at last we reached your window,
you looking out
for us, waiting against the night,
A flame, burning.

When morning came, we lit all the candles in the house,
from both ends. It was advent.
It was the last days.

We sat with oil lamps, waiting for the bridegroom, the
we know not what. Call that the day I learned
that waiting is sacred. I remember
her beautiful, quiet face bent over all the colors,
changing them completely as she painted,
and you at your journal. I remember how we did not
talk
for long periods. How we broke rules,
just this once, let carols take wing from the piano
and soar through the house
though it was barely mid-December.
We were awaiting some different and more difficult
birth—
the time would give.

Around us is the holy sanctuary
you have built from your shared lives—
altar spread with drawings, sculpture,
photos of daughters and others beloved.
Walls hung with a world of images
that speak your passion for this earth
and one another. There is room here for the silent tears
that slip from her lids when you go out
and she thinks no one is looking. Place for
the glad "Hey, you!" when you return;
For the tremor in our hands, voices.
Everywhere here the touch of intimacy and welcome,
a space into which no true stranger can come.
Even death has been prepared for with intention,
which becomes its utter defeat.

In the old story, they say the travelers
Who followed the starlight
Went home by a different way.
That's what I want to do.
When I am not sure of the path
I think of her,
Who gave to us both boldness
And the practice of resurrection.
Her clear voice reminds me: What is resurrection
If not the conviction that there is always
Another path to travel home,
Always a way to arrive,
Wholehearted and intact—
No matter how shadowed the pass,
How cold the night,
How distant the star
Riding the dark and unknown sky.

Even placing it in here pastors me again, releases my tears.

Liz McAlister of Jonah House signed up for a week that turned out to coincide with Jeanie's passing. She offered us the option of her presence at the memorial service or a week of pastoral care afterward. We opted for the pastoral care.

The Jonah House community has reclaimed an old cemetery in Baltimore, where they built a simple home and offer care to the place, with the help of some sheep, goats, llamas, and a few well-oiled machines—a kind of retreat center for resistance spirituality and action against the relentless encroachment of death. Liz's life partner, Philip Berrigan, was buried there in Advent of 2002. That burial also affected my thoughts about Jeanie's.

I was blessed to be part of the funeral procession that began at the cemetery and headed to St. Peter Claver Church. Phil's body was in a coffin made by his son Jerry, carried in the back of a flatbed truck. Bagpipes droned and wailed the grace notes as the entourage swung onto West Baltimore's neighborhood streets, flowing by homes and housing projects with gigantic peace puppets and banners bearing words of justice and nonviolence. It was funeral as political action: Philip Berrigan leading one last march.

Liz bears the lessons of community and relationship accessibly in her heart and bones. She's seen it and lived it in joy and in grief. She has the authority to call to account and utter a word of grace in the same move. She can sort the complicated dynamics that living together brings on and cut through them with light and wisdom. She encourages and nurtures and summons. And pledges a prayer—a promise I know she keeps with rare fidelity.

With sacramentals overflowing

Dee Dee's hauntingly beautiful poem makes reference to Jeanie's altar, a topic I've put off far too long, perhaps because beginning a description is so daunting. If I were to tell the story of each item that crowds the table, it would be another book, or at least a complete reframing of this one. An interesting thought, that.

The altar stands behind me as I write. It has had several platforms and locations since Jeanie began setting it early in her illness. The current one is a gorgeously carved, narrow mahogany library table from the Wylie household, which runs the length of the dining room wall. It looks like a Mexican *ofrenda* created for a *Día de los Muertos* celebration, dense with sacramentals spilling over it so thick I'm fain to begin naming them.

But here a glimpse. In the middle, a ceramic finger labyrinth with the braids of some "women's hoop" project flowing out from beneath it. Jeanie's ashes would rest there between Epiphany and Easter, but it was often the place of an intercession list, naming certain people for whom we were praying.

There is a thrown-pot oil lamp and assorted candles, freestanding or in braces or holders. A clamshell we found on the coast of South Africa was Jeanie's smudge bowl, and it bears

a small bundle of dry California sage. There is a basket where
she ritually deposited her hospital wrist bands each time she
returned home. A scattering of family photos, variously framed,
her mom most prominent.

A late addition was Jeanie's last drawing, a Christmas present
for me, also framed. It's a provocative intrigue: We are facing
one another, me unaccountably skinny and naked, she in a dress
with her back to view—possibly bowing shyly, but more likely
lifting her skirt and strutting her stuff.

Lucy's original painting of Jeanie naked from the back is at
the far end. Other icons include a Madonna hand painted by a
priest friend, a Greek triptych, and Bill McNichol's iconic rendering of Stringfellow. Jeanie's effigies of herself fabricated from
natural and found materials are there. A dinosaur Lucy formed
from dug Cedar Spirit clay that we had insisted would never last.

Other sculptures and carved figures: a Guatemalan storyteller
woman surrounded with children, a candleholder with a circle
of community sitting round its flame, scores of angels (one
crocheted by death-row prisoner Wiley Dobbs), assorted other
creatures, plus a woman in meditation carved from Nicaraguan
soapstone, and an African family standing entwined on one
another's shoulders. Crosses of woven palm frond and teak.

There is the clockwork of a music box that plays a Carol King
tune (wish I could recall its history, if I ever knew) and a big
conch shell ornately carved with images of three young women,
which was Jeanie's childhood lamp. A few handmade cards, and
handmade books (like my poems for her, and another with the
Stations of the Cross).

But most elements are natural finds: great rocks, rough or
smooth-worn or painted, some with words (one tells me I was
a good husband). There is a big wooden bowl brimming with
collected stones, another of shells. Jars of seacoast. Feathers and
pine cones. Dried flowers, even gilded ones.

I have not yet exhausted the altar's inhabitants, and you are
lucky I don't begin working my way up the walls of that corner
and naming the photos and art that fit together around it like a

rich puzzle—not to mention the flotsam mobile drifting above. Nor have I exhausted its prayer and its praise. Thank you, Jeanie.

All mortal flesh

The Christmas drawing of me, skinny and naked, calls to mind our lovemaking—as it seems verily designed to do. I wish I could recall in specificity the last time Jeanie and I made love. It is best, I imagine, to make love always as though it would be the last.

An ethic of sorts lies in that approach. The simplest way to frame it is to ask: Would I be content for this to be my last act? Would I be willing to be transported suddenly to the presence of God, while I am engaged in this word or deed? It clarifies the mind in a very concrete way.

Of course there are heroic doings and grand gestures that appeal readily to this ethic. But there are also simple and ordinary ones. My mom collapsed, recall, while gardening. She'd have been content.

Notice, the question is not, Would I choose this way, but, Would I be content? I might not want to die in a car crash, but where was I headed and on behalf of whom? Routes or actions that give us pause might want to be rethought on general principles. One could call this an "eschatological ethic"—the moral content of "last things." Or, just as well, the ethics of dying well.

Anyway, as to lovemaking, it must have been around the time of her Jubilee party, but I'm saddened not to have a precise memory. At a certain point she just began declining my bedroom advances, though never my tender affections. That ought to have made an impression, since it was so rare—in fact, she with equal ardor would as often initiate. But then, her demure became persistent.

It could certainly have been a simple body thing, the gradual shutting down of the drive along with other systems. Each reluctance seemed fair at the time, or natural, since she had a right to feel weary or even in pain. But now I wonder if it weren't a kind of decision unannounced. Was she beginning a deliberate process of disconnecting from her own body of desires? Slowly trimming the lamp. Banking the inner coals.

Was she saving the two of us the great final wrench from each other's arms? Was she protecting me in some sense? I don't know. The Christmas drawing is a playful tease. Perhaps not having, in memory, the one "last time," makes all the times equally penultimate in a wild and vivid joy. Even now in bodily memory I conform myself in the night to where she's not, and smile or cry.

I will put here the poem I rose to write for her on Christmas morning:

Let All Mortal

> *Because the Word takes flesh*
> *we wreathe winterlight with candles,*
> *make feast and sing*
> *to story the stable*
> *where end and beginning*
> *flesh from flesh*
> *are one frail body, even divine.*
>
> *Once in a jail cell*
> *waiting out another Advent*
> *I harbored arcane joys*
> *by summoning in memory and anticipation*
> *every inch of your sweet flesh*
> *by candlelight kissed and caressed;*
> *such enough is an ache*
> *on which a body may thrive or survive.*
>
> *How many times before and since*
> *have I breathed your breath*
> *or fit dreaming beside you?*
> *Even now I rise from a dream's breath*
> *to write.*

Your belly is marked
with the rivulet stretches of child born spending
flesh of your flesh of our flesh
pushed and pulled 'til
breaking the light of this world,
those two.

I think of others unmet
flesh still too soon
witnessed in roots or branches of
this or that apple tree's grief.

Now your flesh is marked
with the surgeon's knife
chasing the intruder
whose death grip
pretends dominion in you.
But no.
Not in your wounded head
let alone your great heart.
Not today. Not ever. Not in the end.
That nor this.

God you were strong
though by muscle or pure will
I could never be certain,
but to be the one in your grip
squeezed as never to let go—
I could hurt with that joy
forever.

What among the griefs
to watch the ebbing of that power,
grace supplanting will
by necessity and choice

I do know the weight of your flesh,
hefting it upright
these days again and again
overriding my own back's focused complaint.
How many more times will you resist the pull of earth
to walk your will upon the stairs?

And still this morning
I kiss your hands and lips
surrogate for everywhere and always,
this body of earth
filled with the glory of God
and the dwelling of the straw strewn Word

All flesh
with your sweet body
shall see it together.

Bill with transition manager, Simone Sagovac, fall 2005.

19

'May the Lord Bless and Keep You'

Godson and the musical moan

What a wondrous Festival of Incarnation we had as a family, almost as though Jeanie had been waiting out Advent in her own way. We made it to the cabin just prior to Christmas, to bake cookies and cut a tree. Jeanie made the last entry on the last page of our family cabin journal, drawing a strange creature with her notation.

Her last trip out of the house was to Christmas Eve Eucharist at Day House. After pushing herself valiantly for weeks, she collapsed on the stairs coming home, and we surmised we were finally housebound. Her gifts to us next morning were all paintings she had done, including one matted and framed by friends: a striking watercolor of a pine-studded hillside, with a burning riverbed or an underground sunset beneath.

Among other things Lydia presented was a year's worth of poetry, all pertinent and artfully bound. Lucy's gifts were molded snow scenes and wood-burned framings of photos. In addition to a Block Island driftwood work for the family collective, and the poem that came to me that morning, I gave Jeanie an edited video of the footage we have of her (so little, and so remarkable), expanded with a short life story in stills over gospel music. Jeanie liked it, clearly getting its double purpose as both gift and liturgic to come, a tribute that would be played at her memorial service. What a visibly blessed life together we have had. I must say that viewing, culling, and sequencing photos from our albums was itself an effort and occasion of tears, an exercise in preliminary grieving. But in a certain sense, we've been grieving for years—so we know how to do it.

The following day my brothers and their families came for dinner and gifts. I don't recall that they had ever all come to our place at once, but now around table and tree we squeezed into our upstairs flat. It was a day akin to the Wylie reunion. The last photograph we have of Jeanie shows her face peeking through a Kellermann family hug completely encircling her.

Jeanie had her final meal with my godchild Luke Wallis and his family. Luke was born the weekend Jeanie collapsed, so we've always known his age from the span of her illness, and vice versa. He's spiritually precocious and knew what was up, paying close attention to everything.

Jeanie ate a Mexican *botana*—a Detroit invention, as far as I know—sort of like nachos loaded with everything wonderful. It was her favorite, though unplanned in any sense of a "last meal." She was very present to the conversation, but eventually wearied and headed for bed.

When she'd gone, Luke spoke up: "It must be hard to lose your wife after so many years." It was. I generally thought of this visit as an opportunity for godfatherly responsibility, a tutoring in the faith in the face of death. Jeanie's death would lay ground for our conversations in the months to come around his grandpa's passing, but now, unaccountably, Luke was comforting me. It was an unexpected pastoral touch.

What took me by surprise was how quickly Jeanie moved from housebound to bedridden. When she took to bed that afternoon, it was for the last time. Without spreading any sense of urgency, the hospice nurse allowed that it was time for the delivery of the hospital bed, which seemed to appear with an unobtrusive quiet, almost immediately. But I clung to Jeanie for one last night in our own bed, dampening her flannel gown with tears in the dark.

In the dining room, above the altar and tacked into every available wall space, art and photos had proliferated over time, partly on the premise that this would be the sacred dying space. Now another logic prevailed. If we used the back door as entrance, the living room could be calmer, unlike the dining room, which would necessarily be the intersection traversed en route to the kitchen or gathering spaces. It could be quiet and subdued, with lights from the tree sufficing.

Things moved more quickly than we foresaw. We had out-of-town visitors and vigilers scheduled well into the new year. On the 27th, Jeanie's head pain ramped up suddenly, and we were treating with morphine, progressing quickly from tabs to patches and an oral liquid. By Holy Innocents Day, she had quit eating and was unable to walk.

The hospice community gathered round in earnest, folks vigiling with her through those days and nights. Daily prayer times ranged from drumming chants to recited liturgies of antiphonal psalms. We sang to her more or less constantly—singly, and in groups. Jeanie did her dying in community.

When earlier we had put out word inviting this intentional community process, 60 folks showed up for a planning potluck. We were further graced to have Simone Sagovac, a friend with organizational skills grown in environmental and labor work, suddenly available to coordinate. So we came away from that meeting with lists (and eventually spreadsheets) of friends prepared to cook, drive, vigil, caregive, paint, offer hospitality space, do access carpentry, lead prayer, run for dry ice, assist at the point of death, and more.

Jeanie had too many wonderful visitors in the closing days for me to mention them all. Let me name just one here. Vincent Harding was in Detroit to celebrate Grace Lee Boggs' 92nd birthday and came to see Jeanie. His beloved Rosemarie had passed the year previous.

Jeanie was by that point much slowed, resting in the hospital bed by the Christmas tree. In other parts of the house, a certain bustling ensued, as preparations of various sorts were undertaken. Vincent sat with Jeanie for a long time, holding her hand and touching her face. I could see her respond, subtly and calmly.

He spoke low to her in a kind of hum. It wasn't exactly singing. Something akin to a musical moan. Or a groaning meditation. It seemed to anchor the whole place with a sacred center. It tended my own heart wordlessly.

Going with freedom

On December 29th, Lydia decided to make an overnight visit to a beloved friend in Indiana. Her soul needed it, and I trusted the wisdom of her need. Though things were progressing faster than we knew, the trip didn't seem reckless, just a little dicey. I sent her off with the urging that she needed to be free from guilt or regret if her mom died while she was away. It was an admonition that proved unnecessary in that instance, but came into play later on the dying day.

As this account narrows and intensifies in vividness, here's Lydia's recollection of departure and return for Jeanie's final night:

> *I hugged my dad before I left and again he repeated to me, "Go with freedom. You need to go freely, knowing that she may die. That needs to be ok." This was hard to hear, but just hearing it from him, I did feel a sense of freedom, though I didn't believe there was much reality in it. But I breathed that all in.*
>
> *I went into my mom's room and climbed into her bed. I snuggled up under the covers right next to her. She didn't even stir when I came in, which is unusual, because no matter how much she's sleeping, if you say anything like "I love you" she says it right back usually. I looked at her face deeply, taking it all in. I held her*

hand and rubbed it in the way I usually do. I touched her face, memorizing every part of her face and head. I stroked her hair. And I told her I loved her. And then I just lay there for a few minutes.

Then I sang "You Are My Sunshine." I'm not sure why. I don't think it is a really important song to me. But it is a children's song. It made me feel like a kid again. And her like a mother. It was simple. And honest. "You are my sunshine, my only sunshine. You make me happy, when skies are grey. You'll never know, dear, how much I love you. Please don't take my sunshine away."

It is the last line that stopped me. It was perhaps the first time I said out loud near my mom that I didn't want her to go. Of course she knew that I loved her and that I wanted her in my life. But I was always afraid of saying that I didn't want her to go, because I wanted her to have complete freedom. I didn't want her to worry about me.

But I sang that song and I cried through it all, barely getting through it. Although I didn't think of it as a real goodbye, and it was just a few minutes long, it felt rich and real and could suffice as a goodbye, if it must . . .

I got home around 9:30 p.m. I came in the back door, which was to be the entrance while my mom was in the living room. I came up and hugged my dad. He took me into the living room to see her. It was weird to see a hospital bed, which was so familiar, but in our living room and next to our Christmas tree.

There was quiet music playing. Her breathing was different and a little scarier. There seemed to be more phlegm or spit built up in her throat that she was trying *to breathe through. It was more even, but seemed labored. I went up to her and said "Hey, beautiful mommy." I grabbed her hand and kissed her forehead.*

She smiled and turned her head so she was closer to me. My dad said she knew I was here and that was for me. It was more movement and acknowledgement than she had given that day. It was the last acknowledgement I had from her.

My dad said we needed to turn her and change her diaper and give her some pain medication. But first he said he would give me some time with her. He went into the dining room and closed the curtain between the rooms.

I climbed into bed with her and just loved her deeply. I held her hands, kissed everywhere on her face that she would kiss me: cheeks, chin, nose, forehead. I ran my hands through what little hair she had. Feeling each groove and wound where the shunt was and where the bones had shifted after surgeries. What a beautiful, beautiful head she had. She was so incredibly beautiful, it was unimaginable.

I talked to her and said some things that I'd been meaning to say. They were words that could be, and were, like goodbye, though I didn't expect them to be. I told her how much I loved her, how I wanted her to have freedom. I told her how this struggle in the past seven years allowed me to find myself and find my own spirituality. I told her that she had been such a gift for me learning to pay attention to life and take it slower and enjoy it.

I told her how much her spirituality and politics previous to her illness meant to me. How it was clear that I had learned so much from her and how that was the direction I wanted my life to go. How I planned to continue to learn from her. How very much I loved her.

How she would always be in me and I would know myself through her. How she had loved me and molded me and how I came from her body and always will. How much life would be different and how much I would miss her. How much I loved her. I lay there cuddled up with her for a few minutes. Shed a few tears. And eventually went back to the dining room to see my dad.

Lucy was in her bedroom working on her monologue for Forensics. She performed what she had already memorized for me. Then I went back to my dad, and we were going to change Mom. I needed to learn all of the medical things from my dad, for these would most likely become some of my tasks.

I always knew what everything was and how to do it all. Though the last few days I had stayed away from some of that. I didn't know how to do everything. Which felt good. Weird, but good. Not the place I would usually want to be, but clearly where I needed to be at that point.

We rolled her over and she opened her eyes a little, her eyes were way rolled back and foggy and distant looking. She moaned out of some pain. I just wanted to leave her alone and not touch her so she wouldn't be in any pain. We changed her diaper (which is really what it was), and it was wet, which was a good sign that her systems had not yet shut down. She peed right to the end. My dad gave her pain medication and washed her mouth and got it wet with these little tube sponge things.

My dad left do something and Lucy crawled in at the top of the bed on my mom's left side. I squeezed in on her, right next to the Christmas tree and on a stool. I lay my head down next to hers. I never stopped touching her and holding her. I wanted to so much to never let go of those hands. Ever ever.

Of course we knew that this was a moment for song. For every moment of every day is a moment of song. We decided to sing "May the Lord Bless and Keep You" which is an Irish round that we learned from doing theater at Mercy High School. However, once Lucy and I learned it together, it became much more a family song than a theater song. Lucy always starts and I follow second.

We sang it over and over again, holding our mommy. "May the Lord bless and keep you; may she let her face shine upon you, and be gracious to you, and give you her peace." Over and over. I marked a cross sign on her forehead, as I did so often these days. And as she'd done to us every night just before we fell asleep.

When we finished, I asked Lucy if she could remember the tune to the song Mom and Dad would sing to us when we fell asleep. It was the way they ended each night after story or song or backrub. It had almost the same words, but a different tune. It was funny though. because both Lucy and I remember being scared of it. Neither of us nor my dad could come up with the tune. We knew my mom would have been able to.

My dad wanted to finish reading "The Last Battle" from The Chronicles of Narnia to my mom. It was the final chapter. Lucy and I stayed where we were, and my dad sat in a chair to read. The lights were off and the Christmas tree was lit. It was, one could say, a perfect moment.

My dad read and we showered my mom with love. Holding her and letting our love sink through our fingers and lips onto her hands, face, head. One could do nothing less than feel completely loved. The last chapter is about the end of Narnia, about heaven, and dying, about the shadow lands. The book ends like this:

"And as [Aslan] spoke he no longer looked to them like a lion, but the things that began to happen after that were so great and beautiful that I cannot write them. And for us this is the end of all the stories, and we can most truly say that they all lived happily ever after. But for them it was only the beginning of the real story. All their life in this world and all their adventures in Narnia had only been the cover and the title page: now at last they were beginning Chapter One of the Great Story, which no one on earth has read: which goes on forever: in which every chapter is better than the one before."

What a beautiful idea. Filled with hope and perhaps some relief. This is where she was going. Reading the final chapter was just another one of those perfect-timing things. One of those moments that made it seem like the heavens and earth were in perfect alignment for those 24 hours ...

Time of alignments

Nor did the timings cease. Some were pure providence, like the overnight snowfall Jeanie would have loved. In the Peace Community, she was always blamed for winter weather, as though she'd conjured it by pure will—and I'm willing to suppose that she had summoned even this snow shower. Other timings, however, required the prodding discernment of beloved Simone. She was doggedly organizing the point-of-death team— folks who had volunteered to hurry to the scene when Jeanie passed.

Ordinarily, at the moment of death, families and their grief communities are immediately separated from the body of their beloved, disempowered in their decision making, and alienated from the traditional community rites of passage. The sacred body of the dead is legally regulated, and by those regulations assaulted, physically and chemically. Burial is controlled more by commercial forces than by health concerns and is, in fact, counter to real organic cycles. The process of grieving is likewise commodified. Pastoral care is limited and reframed by social and economic forces not of the faith community's making. But it would not be so among us.

We could avoid the undertaker, but not rigor mortis, so we needed a disciplined readiness to act quickly, moving Jeanie to the downstairs flat where the wake would take place, preparing her body, and positioning it in the coffin. Simone came prepared with handouts, lists of responsibilities, also details of changes a body goes through, quite frank about the untoward messiness that was possible.

On the morning of December 31st, Jeanie's breathing was labored, with a rattle of congestion. We still didn't guess how close things had come. And yet, by coordination, plus the orchestration of the Spirit (I even suspect Jeanie's own behind-the-scenes ministrations), everything came together right on time.

Tom Lumpkin, our priest of 25 years, came by and anointed Jeanie, giving her last rites, which was right and good and served our souls. My brother Steve and his wife, Carol, were dispatched to fetch the coffin from Milwaukee. Stevie loves to drive and dropped everything to accommodate, delighting to have found his perfect role and niche in the doings.

When it arrived, we found inside the gorgeous coffin a poem from the makers, written in the prayer of their work. We gathered round while Lydia read it aloud, holding back tears. So its arrival was in time for practice runs, but even more, it served to ritualize this practical communion of necessity and grace. We were ready.

What seemed like the lone glitch of grace or miscalculation was that Lydia and Lucy went off that afternoon to be tended by friends and receive massages arranged by the community. My brothers and in-law sisters vigiled with me at bedside. The real glitch was less the girl's absence than the miscommunication that ensued.

Jeanie's breathing grew more belabored as the fluid in her chest increased. My concern was growing, and I felt that the girls ought to have been done and on their way back. I called Lydia's cell phone and got her voicemail. I left a careful message, urging them to hurry home, that Mom's time seemed to be upon us, and that I loved them both so much.

The time was indeed upon us. Jeanie began those long lapses of breath. I held her and spoke love to her. My brothers were close. We were one in hands and tears. Oh, Jeanie. Oh, heart of my heart. Oh, love of my life. Sweet partner in all things real.

With the gentlest of easing, her breath held and did not resume. When she took her final breath and crossed over, I prayed for us all. Thanks be to God. Jeanie is. One long journey was complete—and another, as she had no doubt, only begun.

We prayed and wept and let her go. We sat in silence for a bit. Then I called Jeanie's mom. I also called Simone, who activated the phone tree, calling the community to come.

Now the hard thing. Lydia called in from the ice cream shop where she and Lydia had gone with friends after the massages. Without thinking, I assumed she was responding to my urgent phone message. She wasn't.

The exchange remains sharp in both our memories. I want to make allowance for my still reeling from Jeanie's passing, but it wasn't a time for the luxury of shock. My pronouncement, "Mom's dead," came to Lydia without benefit of the message of preparation.

The countering grace is that this transpired as she and Lucy stood among their closest friends in community, kids they had known since the birth of each. And further, that they were driven home in shared tears by these very friends.

Dead weight

Meanwhile, I surely was a bit beclouded. Although the point-of-death team was on the way, a number of them from homes right on the block, I felt a great urgency to move Jeanie's body. We had worked out to use our oak Amish armchair to carry her down the front hall stairs, as it was much easier to navigate around corner landings than any sort of stretcher we had available.

The chair was there by the bed, and in my state, it seemed to me a simple maneuver that my brother Paul and I could hoist her into it. I'm thinking, heck, I'm accustomed even to getting her up off the floor when required. If we sat her up, swung her feet round, and then lifted her in one smooth motion, it ought to work.

You know, there really is a thing called dead weight. And Jeanie had become it. She was not in a position to help us in the least. As we made the one smooth motion, that reality suddenly dawned on us, as she began to slip toward the floor. Near at hand, my sister-in-law Pat, who is small but athletic (a high school phys. ed. teacher), stepped into the breach. She was not about to let Jeanie suffer this indignity.

Paul and I were practically forced to stand back as she wrapped her arms around the torso, all the while breathing, "No, baby, no. You are *not* going down." And with a single irresistible lift, she set Jeanie in the chair. In the memorial service program, we thanked Pat for "the dead lift," and I do so again here.

Keening like Eucharistic prayers

Slumped, but upright, Jeanie sat enthroned in the Amish chair with firm wooden arms, which we had bought for the latter living days so she could help lift herself up and out. Now they held her in. We fixed her eyes closed and jaw shut, as well advised, and tied the jaw in place with a scarf. The point-of-death team, and others on the block who'd gotten word, were trickling in and gathering round, beginning to think logistics for the move downstairs, for which we knew we had a certain narrow window in time.

But everything—including, it seemed, time itself—stopped when Lydia and Lucy arrived. They fell on their mother, wailing and sobbing. It was as though they knew keening in their souls.

Each of their godmothers was present and close. But everyone else stood back, reaching out only with tears, letting the girls voice their pain, and in it the lament of the community. The whole group was fully focused, completely present, almost as though we were transfixed in a common mystical experience. Looking back, I wonder if the depth of that shared moment came because something similar was rehearsed among us each week at the Worker Eucharist in the body lifted—another mystery beheld in common.

I stood back myself and allowed my daughters' cries to be my own. And then, when I knew it to be right, I came close and whispered in their ears, calling them back into the room, back to themselves. Lucy was the harder pull, finally having to be lifted and commended to other arms, so that logistics could again assert themselves.

Herein, the glitch that was a grace. Lydia later confessed that if she had been present at Jeanie's passing, she would have kicked into organizational mode, holding off her tears with tasks and calls. Instead, both girls were granted this disconsolate release. And I suspect that Jeanie, who might have found it unbearable to take her leave with her beloved daughters at her side, knew just what she was doing, protecting them to the end.

Extreme smudge and the bounce

As we prepared again to move, I had the presence of mind to mark the moment with a smudge, igniting in a bowl a bundle of California sage borne east by Elaine and Ched. A big bundle. Immediately left unattended, it would burn potently of its own accord.

Meanwhile, the scarf was proving inadequate to hold Jeanie's jaw shut. The Amish chair worked perfectly, but as we carried her body down the winding stairwell I noticed that her mouth was opening. Her lips formed a perfect "O," as if she were some belated caroler echoing the angels' "Gloria." I thought: This bodes ill for a casket pose; is this the first sign of being in over our heads in handling the body ourselves?

In the downstairs dining room, things were coming together. The cooling board, an unused door from the basement, was leveled with Bible commentaries. We positioned the chair and discussed the maneuver of hefting Jeanie's body to board. Beneath my locked fingers, I cradled her head lovingly and felt the ache in my chest.

On a count we lifted and swung her over to the board, but as we reached the spot our coordination went out of sync. I felt her sweet head slip from my hands. As I uttered "Oh, no!" her head took a small bounce on the table; her jaw snapped shut as if by design, forming her lips into a subtle smile worthy of da Vinci's brush.

Meanwhile, the group joining prayer for the evening's bedside vigil began to arrive. A big group. And the smudge unattended was making its purifying presence densely known. When the hospice nurse arrived to arrange the death certificate and reclaim by count any remaining morphine patches, her eyes reflected a degree of panic: there were 60 people in the house; it seemed to be full of smoke and Latin chants. This was not your ordinary hospice situation.

The deep knowing of women

The chants were on a tape brought along impulsively by one of the attendees. They were lyrical prayersongs from the Taizé Community of France and infused the candlelit atmosphere. When MaryAnn, who lived in the downstairs flat, returned from an errand, she felt like she'd been transported into some ancient rite of preparation. She may have been right.

A company of women moved together with the ritual assurance of some deep memory recovered in the doing. Lydia had the opportunity literally to feel the warmth go out of her mom's body, to wash Jeanie's face with her own tears, to anoint her in a company of holy women, who didn't even know they knew how to do this. But did. It was like a collective memory in all our bones, only lately stolen or suppressed, but a generation or two fresh.

Among this number were a couple of nurses who brought a certain experience, but this was a first for both of them. An IHM sister who had been privy to deaths at the motherhouse had brought cotton balls and knew the places they were needed. And certainly Simone's frank instructions about what to expect cleared the air of some anxieties.

But it seemed these women just knew in their hands and their bones what it meant to treat these practicalities with love, with a sacred deliberation. Lydia wrote a poem, shared in the context of the memorial service, about the inner shift that occurred in her while washing Jeanie's face with her tears, portraying what it meant for her to be surrounded by these remarkable women.

Being the only man with access to these intimacies, I witnessed it all. I didn't do the washing, but it also affected a shift in me. As if I myself were being loved and tended in the process. I came and went freely, sometimes coping with the hospice nurse's paperwork or medicine recovery; or fetching to the scene Jeanie's goddaughter, Theresa, who hadn't realized there were other young women being mentored in these rituals; or setting in motion a task of phone notification to a handful of high school young men eager to somehow assist.

I also pulled Lucy into the process by asking her to choose her mom's burial clothes. A simple earth-green dress Jeanie often wore, a black velveteen scarf with silver stars, and a macramé necklace were prominent. But Lucy's striking choice was the hat: a felt red bowler with a black band the girls had given Jeanie for Christmas the year before. She did love it.

Meanwhile, the men took to instinctive helps as well. They dismantled the hospital bed and medical accoutrements and carried them off to the basement, returning the living space immediately to its more regular, hospitable use. They rehung doors that had been removed for wheelchair and medical access. While the downstairs flat was being sanctified, the upstairs was normalized.

When it came time to move Jeanie's body to the casket, the intuitive gender division dissolved and the lift was shared. The casket was a perfect fit. The dry ice, timely at hand, was packed with ease into the special compartment along with the deft "blanket." Jeanie was in state.

Josie Winterfeld had arrived earlier that day from Waterloo, Ontario, where she and her family had moved the previous year so that her sons could be immersed in their Canadian Mennonite roots and culture. We knew her from a variety of connections, but substantially of late from Word and World. She had been a pastoral leader at Jubilee Partners in Georgia, a spin-off of Clarence Jordon's Koinonia Community, with a hospitality ministry to political refugees and death row prisoners. In the latter connection, the community members had designated a space on their land as a cemetery in which a number of victims of state execution had been buried, and in that sense, they had pioneered a ministry of burial.

Josie had arrived expecting to do a New Year's weekend of intensive pastoral care with us. She came prepared to lead prayer that evening at Jeanie's bedside, but now the ground had shifted beneath her feet. We called upon her to lead us as we gathered instead, for the first time, around the body. This included all those called in to move and prepare the body, and also the crew that had arrived for the evening prayers as planned, plus any number of others who just began to appear.

Josie's touch was simple, poetic, deep—just what the moment required. In fact, she managed from resources at hand to find a poem about all being in order and this being a good day—a very good day—to die. Throughout the long night that followed, in a tradition taken from her own Russian Orthodox roots, our neighbor Martha sat down by candlelight to read in its entirety the Psalter over Jeanie's estated body.

Grace upon grace.

Lucy dancing to "Breathe on Me, Breath of God" at memorial service, January 8, 2006. Credit: Family collection

20

Was There Ever Such a One?

A body of story and a glitch of grace

In those three days of holding Jeanie's body in the downstairs flat, I got a lesson in sacraments. Everything necessary and practical and essential was simultaneously sacred and ceremonial. A holy rite. Like eating and Eucharist, if you will.

And like true sacrament, it was also a body politics of cultural resistance. A deep remembering and reclaiming and reinventing. It was Jeanie teaching us one more truth.

Another gathering was conjured on New Year's night, this one announced and more formal. It was the official "wake." When the liturgical moment arrived, the house was packed wall to wall, with folks on the floor or standing tip-toed, craning their necks for a glimpse from the front porch and back kitchen. Here, our pastors Ed Rowe and Tom Lumpkin, the extrovert organizer and the Catholic Zen master, presided.

I helped as well, and must have told some stories. Our friend Tom, who has the casually polished knack of an M.C., facilitated the time of storytelling. Herb snapped a photo of me touching Jeanie's face with tenderness. Tears are running down my cheeks, but my face is slightly contorted with a chortle of laughter. It was exactly that sort of evening.

I'm moved to think of all of the stories gathered and shared, beginning with the family Thanksgiving weekend right through the memorial service. Hey, this book itself. A life, as they say, is re-membered. Membered again. A body is waked in memory and word.

During that service, our friends the casket-makers called from Wisconsin to see how Jeanie was doing. Their shock was palpable upon getting news that the wake was even then in progress. In the improvised notification arrangements, they had been missed.

Now, in the background I could hear a wail taken up, one inconsolable. It was certainly for Jeanie passing, but I know it was as well for missing the event where their casket-work was fully and beautifully serving. Jacob said they would figure it out and then called back to say they were packing up on the spot and driving all night to Detroit.

To honor their arrival, we planned another gathering for prayer around the body in its beautiful oak casket and a small brunch, next morning with friends. More stories, of course, around the table. Plus several guitars, and songs offered, including Jacob's own version of *The Lord's Prayer* ("Heavenly Mother, Heavenly Father … "), which Jeanie so loved, but which neither of us had heard in years. It was a lovely moment in which our friends and their work were duly honored, before they departed for the Franciscan monastery (Jacob's erstwhile order) to crash before leaving for home the next morning.

Jeanie's firm desire was to be cremated, and arrangements had been made. But that morning, due to a scheduling change at the crematorium, we got a call saying we were expected to deliver the body by 11 a.m. Fortunately, our builder friend Ed Bobinchak had constructed a makeshift ramp of two-by-six boards on the front lawn, so that we could slide the casket straight out the front window. (What must the neighbors have thought?)

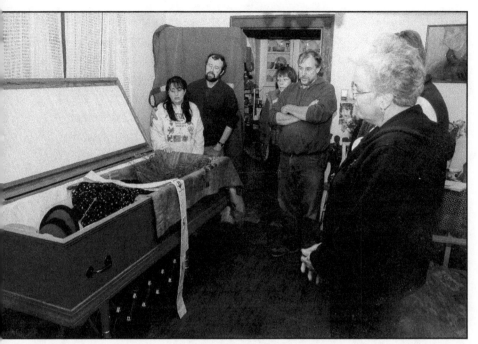

Gathering before closing the casket, made by Jacob Mersberger, second from left, and the sending to cremation, January 3, 2006. Credit: Herb Gunn

We called my brothers and a few friends, previously designated to help. This time I remembered Jacob and Jeannie of the casket and called the monastery, only to find that I had missed them by but a few minutes in their departure for Wisconsin. Drats! The glitches were prevailing.

My brother Stevie's van (whose capacity for holding the oaken box had already been tested in that long drive on the dying day) was backed up to the ramp, and we gathered in the downstairs flat for the closing. Thereupon a knock at the door. The Wisconsiners, driving past on the expressway, had decided to double back for a goodbye hug and arrived unawares for final ceremonies. One might venture that love makes its own providence.

I believe I presided for this event myself, putting on the embroidered stole that was a gift from Jeanie. Lydia placed in her mother's hand Jeanie's original paperback of *The Lion, The*

Witch, and the Wardrobe—the one she'd first read as a child before the Bishop of Lincoln's fire. After silence and song, we removed the ice and collapsed the hinges of the brilliant little platform, sealed the box, then rolled it to the window and out.

Jeanie was wearing on her left ring finger a ring that I had given her on her birthday. In early fall, during the very last of the hospital hectics, I had noticed that her wedding ring was gone. "Oh Billy, I remember taking it off, but I don't remember where," she lamented. Thereupon a search of plastic admitting bags and MRI lockers, with messages left at clinic desks and nursing stations—to no avail.

So I gave her a new wedding ring, repeating for her our vows as I placed it on her finger. And it was that which she wore when the casket endured its final push. Then, two days before the memorial service, searching for something in the bedroom, I looked down by the dresser to see her ring, the original family heirloom. A mingling of tears and joy.

The journey to the crematorium was a family thing: my brothers and their spouses along with Deb Choly and John Zettner. Once again we saw what's conventionally hidden. In that, we must have seemed an oddity. I'm sure the workers were unaccustomed to people pulling up to deliver bodies themselves, though they were awkwardly gracious. One of them sketched for me the dimensions of the ashes container we would receive, on the back of a yellow order form.

The place was a small industrial operation. We backed round to a roll-up docking door and, like thoroughly functional pallbearers, bore our burden inside to the furnaces, hoisting Jeanie's sweet remains into the mouth of the great gray iron device.

It seemed our ceremonialism was exhausted. No circle. No prayer aloud. The final push into the burner was its own spare and complete act. The simplest of lettings-go. And the door rolled down without a glitch.

'An almost Unbelievable Goodness (helps us face the fierce unknown)'

Does it even make sense to try a description of the memorial service in all its luminescence? Yet another amazement. From drumming chants to the final organ notes of Widor's "Toccata," it was just shy of four hours, but no one, I swear, noticed. It was as though in worship and remembrance, time was transcended.

Central United Methodist Church was filled to overflowing. Lydia, Lucy, and I processed in as a family to the "Unbelievable Goodness" chant. We set the altar with the Worker's hospice quilt, assorted emblems of memory, the communion elements, and Jeanie's ashes.

I must say a word here about my extraordinary daughters. Lydia offered reflections framed by a reading from *The Lion, the Witch, and the Wardrobe*. And, with a stunning and steady grace, she shared this poem that she wrote for the moment:

I never knew death

> *I never knew death to be so cruel*
> *The mantra sounds through my head*
> *As the days slip faster than I knew*
> *She moans out in pain*
> *She struggles to say "I love you"*
> *She tells me she's unhappy*
>
> *Why must one leave this world in pain*
> *Leaving is hard enough*
> *But why must she struggle so*
> *I want to be inside her head*
> *Calm her pain*
> *Let her know she is not alone*
> *And hold her heart in my hand*

In the end,
Or what I know to be the end,
She slipped through that door
Peacefully and gracefully
The hour sooner than we had planned
But precisely the moment she planned
Taking care of each of us
To the final moment

A phone call
Tells me she is dead
Shocked and filled with immediate
Guilt and anger
I rush home
Run the stairs three at a time
And collapse on top of her dead body

I hold her tight
Not wanting to ever let go
Her body is still warm
I hold her hands
Trace her face
Take her warmth as my own
I begin to wail
I am no longer conscious of anything
My body, my heart
I let it all go
Covering her in my love and pain

Surrounded by women, light, and music
I cleanse every inch of her face and her head
My tears pour down my face
As if they are endless

They fall upon her cheeks and her eyes
Washing her with my tears
I wash her hair
Deeply feeling her head
Misshaped from the wounds
Of her battle

The room was filled with tears, prayer, and laughter
I fall into the arms of friends
They rock me back and forth
I weep
Knowing my deep love of my mother
Knowing that I did indeed show her how deeply I
loved her
Knowing that she loved me more deeply than I can
ever know
Knowing that at that moment
She was falling into the arms of her
Father
Brother
And all the saints
And indeed into the arms of God
I knew that she was laughing
And dancing
And at home
And at the same time
Here with me
Being the arms that hold me

It was at that moment
That a new mantra began
I never knew death to be so beautiful

Lucy's dance to "Breathe on Me, Breath of God" is just plain beyond recounting. People were amazed that she'd even attempt it, never mind pull it off with such full-bodied presence of spirit. I recall asking her in advance if she really thought she could do it. Her response was quick and unmediated by thought: "I can do it for Mommy."

Later, still in amazement, I asked again. I could see a shadow cross her face, as if the question pressed were offering a contagious doubt. I ceased to inquire and only encouraged thereafter. The dance was pure grace, in its several meanings.

Jeanie spoke to us through the video, enlightening us with her thoughts on marriage, resurrection, and the communion of saints. I included in my reflections a recitation of our wedding vows—a description of the life she strove with me to live.

I'll mention a couple other highlights. Pio Celestino, Lydia's godfather and much beloved of Lucy as well, is a Peruvian Indian who founded a refugee center in Texas. He was pronounced brain dead some years ago after a pick-up truck in the bed of which he was riding flipped on a mountain road in Nicaragua. A penniless mendicant to this day, he was cared for by friends who mortgaged their house and helicoptered him to a hospital in Denver, which brought him back around. The slow recovery from his head injury always made him sympathetic to Jeanie's ailments and deficits.

In the memorial service, Pio read in English a poem of the Uruguayan poet Mario Benedetti, which had become a fixture at Word and World gatherings, a celebration of hope amidst the harsh truths of reality:

Porque cantamos (Why We Sing)

> *if each hour brings death*
> *if time is a den of thieves*
> *the breezes carry a scent of evil*
> *and life is just a moving target*
>
> *you will ask why we sing*

if our finest people are shunned
our homeland is dying of sorrow
and the human heart is shattered
even before shame explodes

you will ask why we sing

if the trees and sky remain
as far off as the horizon
some absence hovers over the evening
and disappointment colors the morning

you will ask why we sing

we sing because the river is humming
and when the river hums the river hums
we sing because cruelty has no name
but we can name its destiny
we sing because the child because everything
because the future because the people
we sing because the survivors
and our dead want us to sing

we sing because shouting is not enough
nor is sorrow or anger
we sing because we believe in people
and we shall overcome these defeats

we sing because the sun recognizes us
and the fields smell of spring
and because in this stem and that fruit
every question has its answer

we sing because it is raining on the furrow
and we are the militants of life
and because we cannot and will not
allow our song to become ashes

Several other highlights are present in this book, incorporated elsewhere. Ched Myers' homily can be found whole cloth in the Appendix. Joyce Hollyday shared a story that is in her epilogue, which you've yet to read.

I wish I had at my fingertips Maureen Taylor's tribute to Jeanie. She is a welfare rights activist, an un-intimidate-able warrior from the trenches of the poor. With a grace unmerited, she told of her last encounter with Jeanie in the church parking lot—"You go, girl" being the refrain.

I'd love a text, were there one, of Tom Lumpkin's homily on Isaiah 42, delivered with classic Catholic Worker simplicity. Isaiah's Suffering Servant moved him to tears, and he took us along with him. And how could I begin the hopeless task of conveying the riches of gospel music laid down by Ange Smith and Bobby Thompson, or the chants and songs of all our friends? Just imagine the ways our joy was made complete.

'May be the last time'

I wrote what felt like the conclusion of this seven-and-a-half-year journey in a letter on Martin Luther King Jr. Day in mid-January 2006. I opened it with these words from an African-American spiritual:

May be the last time, May be the last time, children;

May be the last time, May be the last time, I don't know.

This was the lament drenched with uncertainty that enslaved mothers and fathers sang on the last night of the year—what became known as Watchnight. Plantation masters bought and sold their slaves on New Year's Day, and no parent could be assured that beloved daughters and sons would still be with them for another year. With Jeanie's passing on New Year's Eve, the hymn touched a new and poignant resonance in me.

I closed that letter with these words:

> *I have no clear idea how the grieving time will go. We feel our way along the path. Lydia is back to Loyola, but coming home regular for family solace. Lucy and I are the new household, and she my deepest partner in tears at present. She goes off to school having been granted reprieve from last semester's finals. I return to SCUPE work, to teaching, and hopefully to writing projects long put off.*

> *But not too fast. Mourning our beloved will take its own sweet time. Lord, was there ever such a one? Not in my life or experience. Amen, dear friends. Amen and Alleluia.*

Lamp post which marks her grave in Port Sanilac woods, Easter, 2006.
Credit: Family collection

21

Love in All Directions

June 2006: Through Tears and the Rail

Dear Friends:

It's coming on the six-month anniversary of Jeanie Wylie's death. If you've had enough of this eight-year saga, feel free to utter a prayer of closure and hit Delete. Know our love and thanks for attentive companionship complete. I'm trusting, however, it's not self-indulgent to think that griefwork goes with the communal territory as well, and that some portion of you will be curious for news about our mourning rituals and the changes we now undergo. I promise not to write in perpetuity, but our own work is still in process.

I set this down at a retreat center connected with St. John's Monastery in Minnesota, where I'm participating in a "writers' asylum" (you can figure out exactly what they might mean by that). I find myself thinking about this very chronicle of letters. Any number of you (including the other asylum attendants) have urged that there is a book to be unearthed and compiled here.

I'm taking those injunctions seriously, even guessing that rereading, editing, and filling in certain blanks with introduction, poetry, journal rants, and epilogue, will itself be a grieving ritual. I surmise as much from my own tears spent just this morning.

We buried Jeanie's ashes Easter Day at the cabin, with a small circle of friends and family. A lamppost—a nod to Narnia—now marks the place in a pine grove, her favorite beauty spot.

The night before, we had carried the little wooden box forward with the gifts at our community's Easter Vigil liturgy, held again this year at St. Peter's Episcopal. I was mindful that Jeanie and I (and eventually the girls) have renewed our baptismal vows there on Holy Saturday for 20 years or more. I'm grateful that in our renewal promises, when we renounce Satan and all his works, we name those works: militarism, consumerism, environmental contempt, racism, sexism, homophobia among them.

Lucy danced to Vivaldi's "Gloria" as the altar was reset, and Lydia was homilist. No doubt their roles in Jeanie's memorial service commended them to consideration. Suffice it to say that Lucy leapt with free exuberance and that Lydia did indeed have a Word for our community, pulling no resurrection punches, personal or political.

I'd only been back to the cabin for the first time Holy Week to clean and prepare for the burial gathering. The trip had been postponed as the girls repeatedly declined my overtures to make a visit. Since Jeanie loved it and made it happen, since it everywhere holds and hides her touches, since it was in fact the place we were when news of her illness first struck, they weren't yet willing. It remains layered and freighted with meanings. And, well, presence.

So I went alone. There my noisiest grief. I had no idea how ready I was to cry out with total abandon, sobbing Jeanie's name aloud un-selfconsciously, without fear that someone would feel the need to comfort, tend, or otherwise fix me. I tidied, but the main work was exhausting. Having read C.S Lewis' observations of his own grief, I suspect he'd find me self-indulgent. I don't care. I hope never to lose the taste of those tears.

As to further transitions. Lucy and I are now a two-person household, she with two more years of high school remaining—years in which I want to share and delight. So I've taken a two-year leave from SCUPE and, as of Pentecost, am half-time pastor of a church kitty-corner from old Tiger Stadium in Detroit: St. Peter's Episcopal. Yes, one and the same. I'm grateful to my (now two) bishops for allowing it to happen. Pleased to be rooted in a place so rich in common history. And happy to be trading the plane for the bike, reducing my ecological footprint so substantially in one easy step.

St. Peter's provides a home for Young Detroit Builders, teaching construction trades to young people by rehabbing houses. (Last week they had a devastating setback when pissed-off drug dealers torched a nearly completed project.) The church basement is home to Manna Meal, our Worker soup kitchen. It occurs to me that the church actually functions much like a parish for the Day House community. Witness the Easter Vigil, or the fact that we begin and end the Stations of the Cross walk at its red door. We've gathered for weddings there, even book parties.

The little congregation includes people I've known and loved for a quarter century, not to mention soup kitchen regulars and homeless folk stashing their plastic possession bags in the back pew for church. Sadly, as a Methodist, I don't bear the sacramental umph to make Anglican Eucharist, or forgive sins, for that matter (though as of this writing, the denominations are taking timely steps toward one another at the table). So for now we are doing a version of Morning Prayer, which recesses at its conclusion to the back of the sanctuary, where we complete the service with the thanksgiving prayer around tables spread with an agape potluck. A veiled communion. Anyway, we're improvising liturgically, resting in the knowledge that our life together is itself sacramental.

Also on Pentecost Day, we began a two-day retreat on Dietrich Bonhoeffer at the cabin. The Word and World interns provoked it, and Joyce Hollyday of the faculty joined us, leading a session. It also included St. Peter's vestry members and former SCUPE students, so all these main parts of my life conspired ("together breathed") a transitional moment. It was a demanding gift to read The Cost of Discipleship and Life Together in the context of Bonhoeffer's imperial moment, and so hence our own (which seems way more like Germany in the '30s than I'm usually willing to admit). Ripe times for new or renewed community.

Lucy, who after all is the main point, couldn't be happier with the re-rooting. My spring travel stayed heavy, but she endured it gladly with the changing winds of Pentecost promised. She's actually flourishing in this period. Lots of theater and dance, which seems genuinely integral—neither distraction nor busy denial (though either would be fair enough).

She qualified for the national forensics tournament (single-handedly performing the spat between Helen and Hermia from the wooded love-crossings of A Midsummer Night's Dream) and was in the spring musical (Liza, as in Run Liza, Run from the stylized play within the play, if you know The King and I— now there's a meditation on cultural imperialism!).

Here's a weird thing: I had found myself worrying that since Lucy was only 8 when Jeanie was struck down, she might not have memories of Jeanie in her fullness and power. Whereas Lydia, being 12, I trusted would. It is exactly the reverse. Lydia, whose spiritual life began like an alarmed door the day of Jeanie's collapse, has opined of having no real memory of Jeanie before the illness. She has memories, but Jeanie is not in them. I'll return to this.

Lucy meanwhile remembers everything. Actually, she remembers the day she was born if you can believe it, and I do. When she heard of Lydia's version of amnesia, she began making memory lists in her journal, lists headed "The way she … ": " twirled her hair between her fingers when driving" … "let you crawl into her long skirts and hide" … "could do anything she wanted to." Now, there's a vivid memory of power.

Lucy remains my closest partner in mourning. Tears can still swamp us in the same moment, and we cling to one another in the wave's surge. She's devised another striking tactic in her own grief process: drawing pictures of Jeanie. It started with a sketch of her naked back, which Lucy clearly knows in studied detail from helping her dress, even while deferring to her modesty. She rendered it dead on, reproducing it initially in several media. The watercolor version rests upon our dining room altar.

That set in motion a sketch book, an image journal, now half-filled—some images from memory and others drawn from favorite photos—her own face, often as not, in shared if partial view. I will occasionally track her down, alone in her room with pencil in hand and tears wet upon her cheeks. Here's a seed sprout: she's suddenly interested in art classes.

Lydia is also flourishing. Same with the grades, though more activism than acting for her these days. She remains the summer in Chicago, having moved with a circle of friends from Loyola's Agape House into their own off-campus apartment. Perhaps in direct response to her own memory issues, she's begun collecting and reading Jeanie's essays, articles, and editorials.

The impulse, another good instinct in the grieving process, is precisely to know, reconstruct even, her mom in that fullness of Jeanie's thought and power. She has a Women's Studies faculty member potentially lined up to let her read it all as an independent study. Add that Liz McAlister wondered aloud to us if we oughtn't edit Jeanie's work into a volume, and there may be yet another little book afoot. Perhaps a daddy-daughter project, which would serve my grief and complete my joy—in equal parts.

Before her own father's abrupt and unexpected death, when Jeanie was herself in high school, Sam and Bea used say to each other that if one of them went first, they would always meet at the communion rail. Jeanie recited that promise often enough that I knew we pledged it, too.

Propped above the table at the Detroit Worker is a gorgeous photo of Jeanie before her illness, fulsome in white beneath the luminous tent of a wedding reception. Each Sunday at Eucharist I see her face and hear her voice, one with the entire company of heaven.

I meet her and miss her so, ache with love and loss, grieving and rejoicing—all at once.

Intercede for me, Jeanie Wylie, as for your girls, and for us all.

Through tears and the rail ...

One form of faith

I suppose it's only fitting that I've attempted to start this section several times, gotten swamped in my tears, and saved it as a document with but a single sentence. I'll press through now. But, God, I miss Jeanie Wylie. Going on a year, and my heart still aches.

I miss her in the fullness of her power, and I miss her in the sweet graciousness of her self-possessed weakness. I miss her mind quick and her mind quieted, but attentive. I miss her body, strong and supple, and her body spread and heavied by assorted medical side effects or the self-indulgence of comfort foods. I miss being loved by her from beginning to end. This, actually, I still cling to and enjoy even in the ache.

In one of the late letters I mention that our closure is not yet. As a pastor, I've often counseled bereaved folks to think in terms of a year for the work of mourning, but that's mostly to urge the long view and encourage ritualization. I don't really believe in "closure" as such. Or that my tears will ever fully cease.

I certainly expect to make transitions (I have already), to move forward, to live fully in my changed estate and enter new commitments. But I doubt my heart will ever stop crying out "Jeanie" and "Thank you" nearly as one. Even now, I can't tell if that utterance is the introit of a conversation or a prayer.

Jeanie was such an undeserved grace in my life, and I know it. Does my gratitude go to her, or to the God of all providence? With her gone to God, it seems hard for me to distinguish.

As I think about it, that doubled cry actually captures my grief. Some might say too readily, but my ache is inseparable from gratitude. That's been so from the first.

The girls like to recall a family meal (I'm not sure whether it preceded or followed the first surgery), where for grace the four of us began to sing an African-American church refrain: "Thank you, Lord." It is sweetly moaning and repetitious. As we sang, we began to weep together, singing on through our tears.

By Lydia's lights, we were grateful for the fact that Jeanie was alive. Yes, true, but more: Within that we were grateful for all that had been, and even all that was now set before us. We were thankful for every gift that the loss and threat of loss now made so utterly clear. We were thankful that we could hold one another's hands in prayer, and for a community to lean utterly upon.

I don't quite know how to put this, but in the midst of all this, I think I was thankful to be thankful. We were just so aware of the gift beneath everything. Thanks is one form of faith, I suppose. Giver implied.

Infinite patterns of grief

I think of poor C.S. Lewis in his *Grief Observed*, so frankly disabused, experiencing God's absence, the big silence, the great heavenly door slammed shut in his face. But, honestly, from the beginning of this thing I've never felt God's absence, at least any more than usual. And as I say, the whack of events woke me to paying attention in such a way that I've noticed the graces that have borne us in loss.

I suppose that's partly to underscore that everyone's pattern and experience of grief varies, among other things, by context, personality, community or its lack, pace and abruptness of the catastrophe, ailment, forces involved, tradition and spiritual disposition, even theology. Though I attend to them, my grief is not Stringfellow's, or Lewis', or Ken Wilber's. And yours will not be mine. Of course, they are all connected. And, needless to say, I've put all this out there in the hope that it would be somehow

not merely interesting, but helpful; though I've never intended
it, and you've not read it, as a guide to be followed or replicated.

There is a notorious pattern of grief into which a couple
generations of seminarians and helping professionals have been
tutored. It's the famous sequence identified by Elizabeth Kubler-
Ross in her 1969 book, *On Death and Dying*. The sequence
goes like this: denial, anger, bargaining, depression, and acceptance. Originally identified in connection with a dying person's
encounter with the catastrophic news, it's been applied to loss in
general, and specifically to bereavement. (I guess acceptance is as
close to gratitude as that sequence is gonna get.) Even the author
would say it is not actually a sequence, and that everyone takes
it on differently or partially, but that doesn't keep people from
imposing on themselves or others its pattern in rigidity.

I don't intend to use it as a frame, but I do want to say
something about denial. I understand how healthy a survival
mechanism denial can be in certain circumstances, a sane way
to cope in the short term. So let me affirm it up front and in
passing, but add that as a long-run tactic it is dysfunctional.
As already stated, I also believe it is politically endemic to the
culture. On societal scale, it hides the body bags, renders the
tortured or the prisoners or mistreated workers invisible, obfus-
cates privilege, distances us technologically from the explosion,
misdirects our gaze with media, deadens us to suffering (of
others), and outsources the necessary violence of empire. Among
other things.

Catalogs of rage

As an Enneagram Nine (who tends to swallow anger in great
gulps), it behooves me to say something about that in particular—and even about anger at God. There were generic flashes of
the latter at the beginning. By "the beginning," I mean collapse
and first news of the tumor. Our grieving process—coping with
the change in our life, and suffering (howsoever gracefully she
endured it) the incremental and erratic swings of losing Jeanie
piecemeal—has been ongoing. So, some of what I offer here will

concern not just mourning her death, but grieving her illness as well.

I do remember that first autumn, alone in the bedroom, throwing things against the wall and beating the mattress in angry lament verging on despair. I swore in tears I couldn't bear it. Insofar as those were prayers, God did take a hit of anger.

I was going to say that pretty much exhausted any expression of my anger, but that would have been a Nine-ish lie, a self-deception unconsidered. More than once, doctors drew my ire. Not God, but those who imagine they are. We were, on occasion, not just pressured, but deceived. Impugned.

In one instance, I was so furious that I wrote the physician a long and detailed letter, copying it to the patient advocate, the ombudsman, and the hospital executive. Can you believe I never heard a single word back from anyone? That will make you fume the more. I presume the lawyers advised against apology, or even deference, lest it appear self-incriminating.

The girls remind me, and I recall it, that I had long stretches of low-grade pissiness, waiting to snap. Let's say I was capable of quietly seething. I recall writing another long letter to the head of a local oil company, after a gas station attendant short-changed me and then treated my correction with contempt. OK, it may have been a contemptuous correction, even a profane one. This was during Jeanie's radiation treatment, and I offer it to confess that I am capable of misdirected rage, or that my reactions could sometimes get out of proportion. (Not with the doctors, though.)

The worst thing—not uncommon, I know—is that the targets and recipients of my anger were, often as not, those truly least deserving: the girls, and even Jeanie. They were close at hand. Such little things could draw my ire.

One example, late in the game, would be Jeanie's slowness of movement, especially at departure times. O, sweet woman, how I regret that. Through most of our marriage, Jeanie lived by a phrase she had coined: "Anything worth doing is worth doing quickly." As a rule, we could dash out the door in tandem and off to events, gathering things, even kids and their paraphernalia, on the run.

In the time of illness, I never fully shifted gears on this. I would be managing all the details and assembling all the necessities single-handedly at speed, expecting of her only that she come at the moment of departure. But no. She would futz. Picking up mail or throwing out some bit of trash, casually checking windows or snugging the shades.

I swear there was a level of willfulness in the foot-dragging, leaning back against my anxious rush. She was in no hurry to depart anywhere (fair enough, I suppose). She no longer had the drive, and even apart from the constraints of body, her pace was one area of life over which she had a modicum of control.

As I think about it, we were still able to fight, even in the later times. I hardly ever recall winning a quarrel with her, but during her illness she would prevail less by quickness of mind and clarity of argument than pure, stubborn will. I would be beside myself.

Ever the sensible mediator, Lydia more than once intervened. She was capable of sending me to my study, then talking me back into my center and some measure of common sense. "Angry at Mom? Think about it, Dad."

The maddening thing was that, even if I quietly harbored any bit of the disagreement, for Jeanie it was immediately dissipated. Whether it was the short-term memory deficit, the simple forgiving graciousness with which she lived, or some overriding sense of real priorities, our tiffs would just roll off her back. I pray she forgives me so easily even yet.

Since Jeanie's death (I may be stuffing more unbeknownst), I recall only one specific bout of the low-grade seethe. It was after the first month and, while my anger was displaced at the girls, it had a more complicated source. Too soon after the memorial doings, I accepted a request from SCUPE to take on a position of substantially more responsibility.

I had discerned against some version of this job change more than once in the course of Jeanie's illness, which itself was a prominent factor. Now my debt and gratitude for their long support was in my mind, and the change made sense for the organization's life and need. I was, however, way too emotionally vulnerable to make such a commitment, and I did it quick on a phone call without even consulting the girls. (Good Lord, they heard about it secondhand!)

So when we were together for a weekend that ought to have been full of family comfort, we were totally out of sorts with one another, me in a pool of quiet anger, dragging them in. Now, I'm prepared to grant, as in the other just told, that beneath it in the depths was the anger of the five-step grief process. Yet, when I saw and named it in connection with my work decision, when I asked the girls' forgiveness and reversed myself by requesting instead a two-year leave, that anger departed, not to return.

The undoing of theodicy

There were indeed other angers, which come to the point I was originally intending to make: that in the course of Jeanie's illness and death, I've not really found myself angry with God. I never really raged against the locked doors of heaven, or demanded to know why the Divine should permit such bad things happening to one so good as she. I suspect a reason for this that is theological. I wager it has to do with our shared biblical view of the powers.

Getting the principalities, the fallen authorities and structures of power, onto the map of social ethics changes ones political view, as with the strike or nonviolent resistance. Getting them onto the pastoral map likewise modifies the formula for everything from prayer to, yes, grief. In prayer, it means that while God may hear the groans and yearnings of the heart, and wills to meet and answer those needs, there are other forces, powerful ones on the scene. As William Stringfellow says, the drama of history and our lives is played out not just between God and human beings, but also amidst the institutions and ideologies, authorities and structures which are the "powers that be."

God may hear the cry of Iraqi innocents, and also our intercessions on their behalf, but that does not immediately halt the aggressions of empire, of the military technocratic complex, of oil companies and an array of corporate interests, of religious and political parties, just to begin a list. On behalf of children and civilians in Iraq (255,000 and counting, killed at this writing), I am indeed angry. My rage, however, goes not to God whose heart breaks, but to those persons and powers who sponsor wars of aggression, shred international law, and employ the terrors of administrative torture.

A similar inner alignment prevails with illness, death, and grief. Think of the hospital. More prayer per square foot is probably uttered there than anywhere else. But how many ailments are treated as personal tragic happenstances, rather than the work of the principalities?

Cancers and birth defects, allergies and immune deficiencies, which are the assault of toxins loosed upon our bodies and earth by industry and government. Addictions fostered in cold calculation by the powers of commercial greed. Corporate stress rupturing hearts. The hurry-up indifference to hazards of the workplace. All the grinding and chronic ailments of poverty. The epidemic of gunshot wounds pouring in the Emergency Room door, which can be traced back to the shipping docks of the domestic armaments industry. Hell, the economics of the insurance industry and government policy turning certain people away, gradually or finally, at those hospital doors. And this is just to name a few. Tribulation, distress, persecution, famine and sword—we are led, as St. Paul puts it, like lambs to be slaughtered.

Did I mention cancer? There's no single cause, or generally not. I consider it the great imperial disease. The blowback of Hiroshima and nuclearism. The fruit of industrialized food with additives, pesticides, genetic modifications, and elaborate processing. A culture of the chemical solution.

Of course I'm talking about Jeanie's tumor. The psalmist speaks of a moment "when evildoers came to eat my flesh." Who? The disease, or the disease-makers?

The doctors waved off suggestions of environmental causes. But they do the same downwind of the Nevada nuclear test site, or adjacent to chemical facilities leaching the groundwater, and I've heard the testimonies and even know some of the families with multiple cancers drinking or breathing under such influences. In Southwest Detroit, where we live, just north of a surreal industrial landscape that includes the Ford Rouge Plant, assorted refineries, and steel mills, the rain dries in grey streaks on clapboard houses, or polkadots the backyard picnic table with the same gritty distillate. I can only wonder what breathing it does to us. Did to Jeanie.

This is say, it does make me angry, but targeting God strikes me as a theological displacement. I'm angry at the powers in the dehumanizing assault of their blithe indifference. This sort of anger is not something to "work through" or "get over" in moving on to the next step in the grieving process. It's a political energy to draw upon in the work of social transformation.

My journal shows that this first dawned on me in a conversation with Lydia in which she was making first medical, then theological, inquiries. From her perspective, God had sent the tumor and could take it away with the snap of a divine finger, so must have some purpose in it. I thought this problematic and replied I didn't believe God intended or desired this, but that it came from the toxics of corporation and culture. I said that God was with us in the struggle, that miracles were possible with God working through people and creation, and, yes, that God could use pretty much anything for good. The zinger came back my way when Lydia concluded that all this was fine, as long as I spoke more hopefully when discussing Mom's situation.

When Jeanie was first diagnosed, we went as a family to Eucharist. The gospel reading must have concerned a healing, though it kindly escapes me now. The homilist, mindful of Jeanie's news, attempted to address the spirituality involved (without blaming God, but also without the benefit of seeing the principalities in the mix).

The preacher's take was that cancer expressed some inner dis-ease, and he actually employed the example of a tight-assed business executive coming down with colon cancer. Jeanie, by implication, presumably had over-exercised her brain or otherwise thought just a little too hard, or some such. Blame the victim? Talk about anger. Jeanie was furious and unforgiving. Ironically, the homilist probably functioned as lightning rod for her own Kubler-Ross anger awaiting a ready target on which to focus.

Now, just to run this theological conundrum to its den, the preacher's point is not entirely vacuous. I say that by no means to affirm a "blame the victim" syndrome, but to allow for taking our share of personal responsibility. Recognizing the role of the powers may keep us from displacing anger at God, but it doesn't let us off the hook personally. We are more than victims.

Much like an addict is not merely the victim of a chemical substance, or an aggressive street-marketing apparatus, or a dysfunctional family system, or even the social mechanisms of addiction—but a person making choices for his or her own bondage—so we have some complicity in the assaults of the powers. We can't seal ourselves off hermetically from a toxic culture of death, but neither do we have to indulge it. We don't have to consume it or passively endure it.

Our lives and our appetites can choose against it. People of privilege may have more freedom than the poor in this regard, but often end up in the deepest bondage. Anyway, the theological footnote here is that an appreciation of the powers may accurately redirect our anger, but it doesn't obviate our sin.

Love's other year

The church community lives its story in a yearly liturgical cycle. I'm blessed that for me, it functions as a pattern for grief. As you know, we decided to bury Jeanie's ashes on Easter morning. I have a friend, actually one wise as a counselor, who said,

"Don't do it. You'd be better off not confusing Easter with that memory." This was one time I just flat out disagreed with him.

I have myself preached funeral sermons in which the day or the death fell upon one of the high days of Christian celebration. And I've always proclaimed the good news that death casts no shadow on the feast day, but that the feast day sheds its light upon the death and the life.

But this was even more than that. If I've been redundant about nothing else in this chronicle, it is that Jeanie lived in the freedom of the resurrection. Free from bondage to death. What could be more right, more in accord with the day, than to commend her to earth and to God on the feast of resurrection?

People infer the same about Advent and Christmas. "It must be hard this year," they say. I'm not quite sure how to respond. Do I cry often, prompted by the touching sacramentals of the season? Yes. Does that mean it's hard? It means the season is rich in memory and meaning—it's full of Jeanieness.

Because last year the Christmas tree vigiled beside her dying-room bed, is the tree this year less, or is it more? There is pain, yes, but it's the pain of love. I'm not conveying this very well. Grief is love, a form of love, or a stage of love. So it's Christmastide and I'm loving Jeanie. I love her so much it hurts.

To mark the Feast of St. Nicholas, Lucy and I lit the Advent wreath, put the ceramic statue of the red-mitered bishop in the middle of the candled circle, and curled into one another's arms to read the little book Jeanie made for the girls, with the gold-painted illustrations by our friend Virginia Macsymowicz. We read her motherly advice to parents about the advantages of teaching the roots and mystery of St. Nicholas, over against the fat elf of naughty-and-niceness into which he's morphed, who now presides over the feast of consumerism. We read the sweet legend of his helps to the sisters, and when we came upon those concluding words about the communion of saints already cited in the letters, we heard them differently, now suddenly about none other than herself:

We smile to think of the saints of God in all times who have listened in the night and done whatever they could to show us the love of God. We delight in the saints even now who are listening outside our homes or in our hearts. We give thanks for the communion of saints who have died, but continue to care for us. They are listening and reaching to us with all their love, because God intends for all of us and for all things to be cared for and to be alive with the joy of creation.

Lucy and I held one another and wept. It was so good. Love in all the directions.

Epiphany 2007: With Friends for the Feast

I begin this hoping to get it out and round before Twelfth Night, in the remains of Christmastide. Many of you have been mindful that it was in this liturgical season of birth that Jeanie Wylie crossed over into light a year ago. Just this week, in a retreat of the hospice community that gathered around her, several people commented on the similarity of that dying time to the process of a home birth. Yes, I think so as well.

It is such a gift that Advent and Christmas, which she so loved, are now forever marked in our hearts as the season of her dying. For us the festivals are not made poorer but deeper. Tears by candlelight are full of memory and hope. A season of watching finds us, more or less, alert and awake. Delight is not diminished, but edged. Glorias have an ache that renders them the more real. It dawns upon us yet again how Word made Flesh is about life—hers and ours and God's. Thanks be.

A year really is a cycle of mourning. And grief has been among our works this last one. Each New Year's Eve (now become Jeanie Wylie's holy anniversary), we go around the circle at Day House and share our highlights and/or lowlights of the year past. For the girls and me those were all tied to Jeanie.

Lydia found her highlight in the ordinariness of life (a relief from the relentless and exhausting extraordinary). As I say that, to be clear, I should convey that she did find Advent this year different from Advents recent. Somehow the patient waiting (for life or death), which had long been mingled with the season, was gone, yielding a time more spare and ordinary.

At Loyola she is in the process of forming an intentional community with some students for next year. A group of eight or ten will move into a big house together. It will become base as well for the "Food not Bombs" project she and her dear friend have been running out of their apartment—a portable weekly soup meal for street folk made from dumpster-dived food and served with conversation about the times. More directly on the grief front, Lydia has been reading through and sorting Jeanie's correspondence in a Women's Studies independent course that moves toward archiving her writing and papers.

Lucy has thrown herself with untold discipline into school work, theater, and friends, all overlapping. She's still in dance classes, but they seem to get short shrift if the others demand. Actually, the high school spring musical, for which she has been in some level of rehearsal since long before Christmas, is Forty-second Street, in which there is lots of tap and she plays the role of choreographer. She's quite computer adept (this should be some sort of news, you say?) and is in constant touch with friends by such means. I love having time with her to eat meals, or ice skate, or go to the Eastern market. She moved my heart when, at the Worker, her highlight for the year was me moving my job back to Detroit to be with her. It was true.

That new work is more than a job. St. Peter's has been good for my soul, a simple joy of the year—though in a way I feel like I'm still trying to get my pastoral feet under me. Preaching every week to the same circle? Regular involvement again at the soup kitchen has been an unexpected gift of the relocation. Replanting also includes things like sitting on the board of Centro Obrero, the labor center largely for undocumented folks. It brings with it friends who are a delight to my soul and may bode connections yet unknown.

Another joy is a conversation that will get carried forward this week, about connecting the 40th anniversaries of Dr. King's "Beyond Vietnam" speech and the 1967 Detroit uprising in a summer-long project, which will link local community-building struggles in a vision of Detroit as a City of Hope. It is even possible that Word and World will connect with that in a sort of Theological Freedom School. I continue teaching, now "adjunct" for SCUPE, but also at Ecumenical Theological Seminary here in town. I've had more freedom for direct action—a trial come February for a D.C. witness against the war. And we plan a local action against torture this month, marking five years for the Guantanamo prison. Close it down.

As to my own grieving of Jeanie Wylie, I know it will ease but never cease. Following the lead of a friend, I'm fasting at present. It has something to do with a cleansing, another marking of mourning's full year.

We did the latter communally as a hospice group in retreat last week—days full of remembrance and story-telling, but also opening on a new stage of our community's life. So good. The young people among us were fully engaged. Conversation rare in this culture happened freely. Joyce Hollyday and Josie Winterfeld, two of our long-distance pastors, facilitated.

Also, the book on Jeanie's death and life about which I wrote last summer has certainly proven key to my own process, and it now comes to completion. I almost began this letter "Dear friends and readers," a salutation signaling a certain strangeness in the writing, an odd double awareness I have. If the book is indeed published, this Epiphany letter will serve as a kind of final entry. A number of things come toward completeness together.

The retreat and the writing have made me conscious of how connected the personal grief for Jeanie is to more public griefs current—for a planet whose caps are melting and species endangered, for the assault on international law in illegal invasions, occupations and the open embrace of torture, for another assault on constitutional law in surveillance and the denial of habeas corpus. For 3,000 U.S. soldier deaths at present and 100, or more likely 200, times that in Iraqi civilian victims, for a wall that imprisons the Palestinians and a similar fence being constructed across our own southern border that will not bring security either but only more death in the desert, for a global and national economies so inequitous and predatory as to be deadly ...

In none of this do we despair. I see that the passage from denial through grief yields hope. I don't believe there's any way around it. Only through. It breaks the heart and moves the body. Tears prove a truly moving gift. Between you and me, they are among the fruits of

Love,

Bill

Perseverated self-portrait, October, 2005. Credit: Jeanie Wylie-Kellermann

A Homiletic
Afterword:
"In the Baptism
of Jesus"

by Ched Myers

*Do you not know that all of us who have been baptized
into Christ Jesus were baptized into his death?*

Romans 6:3

Just a year before Jeanie Wylie-Kellermann collapsed in
the bathroom of their home with the first seizure of what
would become the long journey that ended on New Year's Eve,
2005, she was the keynote speaker at the 1997 Finger Lakes
Conference in Geneva, NY. The theme of that gathering was
"The Politics of Baptism."

Jeanie spoke about how she had struggled with whether to
baptize her daughter Lydia when she was an infant. In an article
she wrote for the Detroit Catholic Worker paper some years
before concerning this issue, Jeanie reflected on her protective
impulses:

> *Water, words, community. Offering our child back to
> God. We would stand with Abraham at the sacrifice.
> We would give her to a God who models the cross. We
> would invite her to listen for a voice calling in the
> night, to vigil, to put herself at risk, to leave family
> and friends, to speak clearly a truth for which one*

*can be executed. We would thereby invite her into the
risks we have already elected and, by God's grace, still
will elect to take with our own lives. In the act of
baptism we would wash away the possibility that our
concern for her might justify a diminishing of our own
obedience to our Lord's perverse ethic of vulnerability
and gain through loss.*

These concerns reflect not only Jeanie's well-known charism
for fierce honesty, but also how seriously she took the Baptismal
Covenant, which she believed demanded an active commitment
to justice, to solidarity with marginalized people, and to personal integrity. She also knew these things are marks of costly
discipleship.

I suspect she inherited these convictions from her family, her
church, and her political work. She also knew their roots in
the gospel itself. Today's reading (the first Sunday in Epiphany)
offers us the story of Jesus' baptism by John in the river Jordan
(Mk 1:4-11), a famous scene that our tradition has overly senti-
mentalized and under appreciated. I want to note four strands in
Mark's version of the story that I imagine might have informed
Jeanie's conundrum.

First, of all the mentors Jesus of Nazareth might have chosen,
he makes his way to a politically notorious prophet whose own
days are numbered because of his vocation of speaking truth
to power. Mark portrays John the Baptist as a re-embodiment
of the great prophet Elijah (Mk 1:6). He wants us to be clear
that Jesus is opting to follow in the footsteps of this tradition
of prophecy, which animates public conscience (however
inconvenient that may be to the nation's leadership) and which
relentlessly advocates on behalf of the least. John's message is
one of "repentance," which is a call to a whole people to change
their historic direction, not just their hearts. Jesus will take up
this same proclamation after John is thrown into Herod's prison.

Clearly Jeanie understood and embraced this aspect of the
baptismal tradition. She chronicled the struggle of Poletown

residents resisting General Motor's destruction of their neighborhood, organized solidarity with striking Detroit Free Press newspaper workers, insisted upon gender justice in all venues, and vigiled fiercely for peace. In this she was a follower of John and Jesus.

A second notable strand in Mark's story is its wilderness location. We are told that everyone comes from the center of society to meet John at the margins (Mk 1:5). This means to remind us of the origins of Exodus Israel's faith. The biblical God stands outside civilization, undomesticated and wild, and is most reliably encountered not in the vortex of power, but in the void. John himself is a feral figure in dress and diet, and Jesus will, immediately after baptism, be driven deeper into the wilderness on his own vision quest (Mk 1:12f). Their common experiment in prophetic renewal understood the need to retrace the footsteps of the ancestors to find out what went wrong: only a radical diagnosis of root-causes could bring the possibility of healing.

Later in her life Jeanie was increasingly drawn to earth spirituality and a deeper relationship with the land and with the ancestors, a passionate exploration that she and I shared. So she also understood this part of the baptism story: that we are called out of conventional social constructs of conforming religion and spiritualized or intellectualized theologies toward a wilder discipleship more grounded in the Creation.

A third noteworthy detail in Mark's depiction is the fact that while everyone else is being baptized in the Jordan, Jesus is baptized into the river (Mk 1:9). Herman Waetjen contends that this signifies Jesus' more thoroughgoing defection from the dominant culture, his dive deeper into the depths of the older, wiser tradition, his complete immersion in the alternative vision of God's Kingdom.

Jeanie understood this, too. She didn't do anything halfway, and it seemed like she interrogated everything, often in the pages of *The Witness* magazine she edited. Indeed, she was at her best when she was challenging conventions—those of the dominant society and church as well as of the social movements we all are part of—even as she struggled to imagine alternatives. As Ed Rowe said today, Jeanie, like Epiphany's Magi, went home by a different way.

So Jeanie correctly grasped the conundrum of the gospel tradition of baptism. On one hand she worried about how to prevent her daughter's baptism from being a mere ritual of nominal church membership. On the other, she feared for Lydia because of the consequences of baptism's true claim and cost. A fourth aspect of Mark's story, however, gives us a clue how we might bear this formidable contradiction.

Jesus rises from Jordan's waters to a vision of the "heavens rent asunder" (1:10). This alludes to Isaiah's poignant lament:

> *Oh, that you would tear the heavens open and come down to make known your name to your enemies and make the nations tremble at your presence, working unexpected miracles (Is 64:1f).*

Indeed, from the prophetic perspective which is firmly located among the marginalized, there is much to lament, then and now. The racist treatment of Hurricane Katrina victims; a Federal budget that shamelessly subsidizes the rich and squeezes the poor; the plight of prisoners at Guantanamo; the continuing silence surrounding our kidnapped Christian Peacemaker Team brothers in Iraq. Our most visceral sense of justice longs for the truth to come out, for the violence to end, for reconciliation at last.

Yet in the moment of Jesus' baptism as narrated by Mark, this prophetic longing is realized: the heavens *are* rent asunder, the Spirit descends, and the long-silent Voice is heard. Modernists cringe at such tales of "supernatural intervention," but I believe this moment holds the key to a true understanding of baptism. Down Jesus goes, getting to the bottom of things, fully absorbed into the waters. Up he arises in a mystical trance: He is staring into heaven, up Jacob's ancient Ladder, into the *axis mundi*, through a cosmic wormhole opened up right there in the streambed. It's a pillar of Fire, the eye of the Storm.

What does he see? More than a dove, I'm guessing. I think he sees it *all*. He sees how *good* the world is, ecstatically experiencing the untamed, juicy Power woven into all of Creation. He sees how *bad* it is: alienated and degraded, hostage to the Powers of greed and objectification and domination. And he sees a vision of the redemption of *everything*. Then Jesus hears the Voice (Mk 1:11), which both affirms his filial identity and demands a rupture with business as usual. It is his commissioning by the One who refuses to give up on us, refuses to compromise with us, and refuses to leave us stranded.

This moment could not be more incredible. Yet it doesn't beam Jesus up out of the weary world into blissful, Docetic communion with the Divine, as our modern eschatological fantasies of salvation-as-escape would script it. No, he remains right there in Jordan's muddy flow, still a member of a subject people in a land occupied by an imperial army, surrounded by grinding poverty and refugees and illness. Jesus is stuck with us in our murderous history, and this apocalyptic vision doesn't rescue him from it, as if it were some cosmic lottery ticket or get out of jail card. Rather, Jesus' vision at the Jordan compels him to struggle in and with that history, even unto death, but with a liberated sense of both his own humanity and that of others, even his enemies. As Audrey Lourdes famously put it, "We will never dismantle the Master's House by using the Master's tools."

It is *this* wild baptism into discipleship, John reminds us, that Jesus offers us ("I have baptized you with water; but he will baptize you with the Holy Spirit," Mk 1:8). Jeanie apprehended and embraced it with eyes wide open, not only in health, but in so many mysterious ways even after her cancer and the innumerable surgeries, when her countenance was transformed from the warrior we knew into an inscrutable angel smiling so sweetly. I wonder whether in these last years she somehow already had a foot in that Jordan wormhole, which has now swallowed her wholly into transfiguration.

And it was this baptism from which her protective maternal instincts also wanted to spare her daughters. After all, in Mark's story, the rending of the heavens at the Jordan becomes, at the end, the rending of the Temple's veil as Jesus expires on Calvary (Mk 15:38)—a reminder of the essential connection between baptism and Cross.

We can never know what shape this Cross will take in our lives. Lydia and Lucy were indeed baptized as infants. Yet have not the past seven difficult years represented their true immersion, as they watched their beloved Jeanie fade, caretaking their caretaker? No ritual of water, this long and wearying journey. Rather, a baptism of excruciating fire, and of exhilarating Spirit.

Now, dear ones—Bill, Lydia, Lucy—we are gathered at the River for a different ritual, sending dear Jeanie upstream to the great Headwaters. "And the River is *humming.*" You have lived up to your baptisms, as did Jeanie. I dare say that with you God is *also* well-pleased. We are here because of your faithfulness, and "that is why we sing." I know it is the desire of everyone here today, and the hundreds of others around the country who we represent, and the ancestors who hover here, that you would feel our love, our deep respect, our solidarity, and our accompaniment surrounding you like a healing quilt, holding you and keeping you. It is all we have together—and it is an *almost unbelievable goodness.* This is how we navigate this passage: we sing Jeanie over, and she prays us forward.

So, as the contemporary hymn by Bob Franke puts it:

> *Sweetness in the air, and justice on the wind, laughter in the house where the mourners had been ... the standards of death taken down by surprise. Alleluia, the great storm is over, lift up your wings and fly!*

Now, may the One who commissions us through baptism grant you a season of recuperation and renewal, that you might continue in the Way in which your beloved wife and mother walked, until you are reunited on the other side of that magical Jordan. Amen.

Camp Chick, June 20, 2003

The Detroit Peace Community at Camp Chickagami, Presque Isle, MI, 1983.
Credit: Family collection

Epilogue

By Joyce Hollyday

I suppose it's fitting that we walked into the beautiful retreat center on the edge of Michigan's Lake Huron and decided immediately to rearrange things. The meeting room with straight-backed chairs and buzzing fluorescent lights seemed less than amenable to the sharing and worship we hoped to experience on this retreat marking the first anniversary of Jeanie Wylie's passing. So we moved downstairs—to a warm, open room with a brick fireplace and an expansive view of the lake.

Bill, Lydia, Josie Winterfeld, and I pulled out couches and end tables. Lucy, Jeanie's sister Rene Beth Rogers, and niece Misty Carter scattered random chairs behind the couches and big pillows in front. Perfect. Jeanie would have done it this way.

Then we read the rules and regulations. Rule Number Three: No moving of furniture allowed. Even before our subversive room rearrangement, we had broken Rule Number One: No eating in the rooms. The complete lack of utensils in the place should have given us a clue. But we managed to scoop take-out Chinese food into our mouths using coffee stirrers and stalks of celery—dinner in a hurry while we waited for the imminent arrival of the 40-or-so other participants.

I looked at Bill and quoted the ever-popular proverb of peace activists everywhere: "Better to apologize than ask for permission."

I've taken the same approach to writing this Epilogue. Bill has asked me to reflect on the late-December 2006 retreat that brought together family and friends who had formed a hospice community around Jeanie. And I intend to. But I want to indulge my memories for just a bit, as context, and also to take up a little space paying tribute to Bill, Lydia, and Lucy. Because somebody has to.

Accompaniment

In June 1999, I received a letter from Bill, which contained the achingly sad news that Jeanie had a new tumor and needed another surgery. I had just moved from Atlanta to the mountains of western North Carolina and bought my first house. It was a cozy cottage in Pisgah Forest, within earshot of a small waterfall and nestled in an acre of pines and rhododendrons. I was just settling in when I got this word from Bill about Jeanie's turn for the worse—one of many plunges on the physical and emotional roller coaster she rode for more than seven years.

A sunny spot on the slope by my front door begged for a tree. Something to celebrate my decision to "put down roots" in this lovely corner of the world. I bought a crepe myrtle that harbored a promise of rising to 50 feet over time. Late on a Saturday afternoon in September, with a brisk breeze blowing and the sky erupting in sunset hues, I gave the tree to the earth. With every shovelful of soil I dug, I prayed a blessing for Jeanie: strength, hope, courage, faith. My falling tears gave that planted tree its first watering.

Since then, I have been blessed to be among those who received Bill's regular updates on Jeanie's changing situation. His letters brimmed with such eloquence and devotion that I voiced to him many times my hope that he would gather them up into a book some day. Hallelujah and amen that that day has arrived! I am immensely honored and grateful that I can contribute in some small measure to this moving tribute to Jeanie, so lovingly penned by Bill.

My tree thrived. And so did Jeanie. In the years that followed, I saw her regularly. She often accompanied Bill to weekend planning retreats and weeklong schools that we convened around the country as part of Word and World, an experiment in theological education that Bill and I and a couple dozen friends launched in January 2001. As my crepe myrtle displayed an increasing bounty of bright fuchsia blossoms summer after summer—and as Jeanie defied all predictions of her demise, recovering from every setback—I was lulled into believing that she would be around as long as that tree.

In October of 2005, I knew that I could no longer cling to the hope of a long life for Jeanie. The Word and World community was gathered in Minneapolis for a school focused on the legacy of William Stringfellow, a lay theologian noted for his musings on the pervasiveness of death in our culture. Indeed, death hovered at the edges and lurked in the shadows that week. The ravages of Jeanie's cancer had so altered her in appearance and capacity that we all knew that she wouldn't be with us much longer. Bill reported that the doctors didn't think she would last until the end of the year. They were right, but only by a margin of hours.

During our closing worship service, we wrapped Jeanie in a quilt that had been carried from Los Angeles by Word and World board members Elaine Enns and Ched Myers. It first enfolded a Catholic Worker dying of AIDS and had embraced several other dear ones in their final days as it was passed among friends around the country. Bill and Lydia joined Jeanie in the folds of the quilt, clinging tightly to one another, as we all gathered around and offered a tearful blessing for their journey through Jeanie's last days.

After the service, Lydia and I took a long walk in Minneapolis' autumn chill, ending up at a café and sharing more tears over mugs of hot chocolate. I heard a plea behind her words, "Everybody comes to help take care of Mom, but nobody comes just to listen to us." Two weeks later, I went to Detroit just to listen.

Laughter

My visit to the Wylie-Kellermann home coincided with Onion Day, an annual tradition invented by young Lucy when she first heard her mother's diagnosis—based on the premise that amid all the sadness, there should be *something* to celebrate. We all sat expectantly around the dining room table for the 2005 Onion Day ritual, knowing that the winner would be the person who came closest to guessing the number of layers in the onion we passed around, and that the one left holding the last piece of onion was obligated to make everyone else laugh.

Her daughters encouraged Jeanie to guess first. Though the exact numbers have slipped my mind, I remember that it went something like this. Jeanie guessed that the onion had three layers. (An average onion—well attested by copious data collected from seven years of Wylie-Kellermann Onion Day celebrations—contains 20 to 25 layers.) Lydia smiled sweetly at her Mom and guessed that the onion had 274 layers. Lucy went next, guessing 526. We continued around the table, with Bill's guess coming in at 832 and mine at about 1,287. Then we passed the onion around, each peeling away a layer—22 in all—until we were all weeping and laughing at the same time. Jeanie—the winner by far—was triumphant on her last Onion Day.

Then came the presents. I've always been impressed by how the Wylie-Kellermanns lavish thoughtful and stunning home-made gifts on one another. An elaborate dollhouse that Bill created back when his daughters were very young still stands in the living room. I was touched by Lucy's gift to me that Onion Day of a plaque, lovingly and beautifully crafted with a wood-burning tool. Lydia gave each of us a jar filled with small stones, on which she had written words—the very same words that I had voiced years before as I prayed over my crepe myrtle tree: faith, hope, strength, courage. She offered them to fill the void "when we have run out of words."

Jeanie was indeed running out of words—and time. As we all sat at breakfast the next morning eating our oatmeal, she started a sentence and then lost her train of thought—a common occurrence in those last weeks. In frustration, she declared, "I'm having trouble finishing my ..." We all waited expectantly ... patiently ... for her to say "sentences." Long pause. And then she said "cereal." She laughed. We all laughed. Heartily.

That weekend slice of life in the Wylie-Kellermann home spoke volumes about this rare family. About their extravagant devotion to one another and their extraordinary care for Jeanie. And about a precious insight that sustained them in tragedy: Laughter has great capacity to bring healing and hope. They were always able to laugh. Even on the worst days, they were able to laugh.

Resurrection

The Wylie-Kellermanns were honest and real right to the very end. As with Jeanie's dying, there was no effort in her memorializing to sanitize the truth, to make it all palatable and pretty. The moving video tribute to Jeanie that was shown at her memorial service exposed all the beauty—and all the loss. It included clips from the days when her hair was long and flowing and her words articulate and clear; and, at the end, pictures of her poor, wounded skull with its sparse patches of hair—which, despite it all, still surrounded a smile that never quit. Lucy, Lydia, and Bill clung closely through it all, lavishing on Jeanie their loving words and embraces.

We'd come to expect passion and eloquence from Bill. But those of us gathered for the memorial service were done in by Lucy's elegant and grace-filled dance to "Breathe on Me, Breath of God." By the pine box holding Jeanie's ashes that Lucy had decorated using her wood-burning skill, and by all the other thoughtful and intimate touches of a devoted family.

Lydia moved everyone present with her recollections of Jeanie reading her *The Lion, the Witch, and the Wardrobe*—a favorite book from C. S. Lewis' *Chronicles of Narnia*—when Lydia was a child. With a poise and strength I've rarely witnessed—even in people twice her age—Lydia read the saddest part of that book to the packed church, describing two sisters coming across beloved Aslan the lion after he gave himself over to death: "And down they both knelt in the wet grass and kissed his cold face and stroked his beautiful fur—what was left of it—and cried till they could cry no more. And then they looked at each other and held each other's hands for mere loneliness and cried again … And it was all more lonely and hopeless and horrid than I know how to describe."

Then, Lydia closed the book. She gazed out at us, and smiled. A smile I had seen on Onion Day, and many days before. A smile I had seen on her mother. And then Lydia declared brightly, "But that's not the end of the story! There's resurrection!" There was a hush in the church. And I thought—as I've thought several times in the year since—that if Lydia Wylie-Kellermann, in that moment, could claim the truth and the power of resurrection, how could I ever doubt it? How could I ever be tempted to live as if it isn't true? As if death really does have the last word.

Remembrance

A year after Jeanie's passing, her community gathered on the edge of Lake Huron for a retreat to remember her, to share what her dying had taught us, and to celebrate the truth that her spirit and legacy live on. Julie Beutel provided the rhythmic heartbeat of the weekend, drumming as she led us in chants and songs that have become a mainstay at protests and other gatherings of the Detroit Peace Community. Josie Winterfeld called us together with this assurance: "Suffering produces endurance, and endurance produces character, and character produces hope, and hope does not disappoint us, because God's love has been poured into our hearts through the Holy Spirit that has been given to us" (Romans 5:3-5).

Together, we created an altar in Jeanie's memory in front of the fireplace. Proclaiming the exhortation from 1 Peter 3: 15—"Always be ready to make your defense to anyone who demands from you an accounting for the hope that is in you"—I invited those gathered to bring their gifts and stories. Lydia provided the centerpiece for our altar: a candle she crafted, bearing the image of the lamppost under which her mother is buried—a replica of the one marking the entrance to mythical Narnia. Bill placed on the altar his journal of poems to Jeanie and the stole she had made for him. Lucy brought a portrait that she had painted of her mother, reflecting both Jeanie's vulnerability and strength.

Pictures and gifts from others followed: a pencil holder Jeanie had made, a self-portrait she had drawn of herself with wings, an onion, a roll of toilet paper. That last offering was explained by her dear friend Deb Choly, who told us that, many years ago, she and Jeanie had determined to survive a year of living together without buying toilet paper. (They stole it from public restrooms when they needed it.) The stories evoked warm tears and hearty laughter.

After a couple of hours of sharing, we still had energy to spare. And the youngest among us had an appetite for more than leftover Chinese food. So we piled into cars and headed to The Oasis, a biker-bar-turned-Christian-coffeehouse. We arrived minutes before the scheduled closing time and rather overwhelmed the locals there enjoying karaoke night. The energetic, under-21 set of our group offered several rousing numbers, showcasing an amazing amount of talent. The coffeehouse's owner, a friend of Bill, graciously extended the hours so that everybody who wanted a moment of glory (or embarrassment) at the microphone got a chance.

I had the great joy of spending Saturday morning with the young people, who ranged in age from 12 to 20. Most of them had grown up together on the same block in inner-city Detroit—daughters and sons of members of the Detroit Peace Community, who have spent decades offering hospitality to homeless people and witnessing against war and violence in many forms. They understand that they've been raised differently from most of their peers; that the unusual practices they witnessed and participated in around Jeanie's illness and passing were a natural outgrowth of their parents' long-held countercultural assumptions regarding faith, simplicity, community, and death. As a group, they expressed a remarkable commitment to the values of their parents and to one another—and a deep appreciation for the community in which they were raised.

Nathan Bobinchak shared about how alone his grandparents seemed when they were dying, hooked up to tubes and machinery in a hospital, and how they finally simply "vanished." Gabe Angelini-Knolls, who lived below the Wylie-Kellermanns in the apartment where Jeanie's body was kept on dry ice for three days while the community kept vigil, had a very hard time explaining to his teachers why he wanted to stay home from school during that time. Michael Fentin, who enjoyed the TV show *Six Feet Under*, talked about the room in the show's funeral home—and in real-life funeral homes—where people are ushered if they get "too emotional," where they can go to "collect themselves." When he saw Lydia and Lucy wailing over Jeanie's body, he described it as "the most pure emotion" he'd ever seen.

The conversation was rich, honest, and poignant—spanning favorite memories of Jeanie, fears about losing their own parents, thoughts about heaven and hell, and ideas about where and who Jeanie is now. Meanwhile, the adults were having a rare and courageous conversation of their own. They shared with one another what they had learned through Jeanie's dying and what they hope for in their own deaths—naming doubts as well as decisions, and fears along with faith.

On Saturday afternoon, we all came back together and shared ideas. Interest was expressed for writing a manual to help other people who want to do burials themselves, hands-on and simply. There was a desire to share lessons learned about how to navigate legal obstacles and physical challenges. There was talk of a "community coffin" that could be handmade and reused.

The young people asked of their parents and the other adults one thing over and over: "Tell us the stories." Ben Buetel-Gunn expressed that he didn't really know how special and important Jeanie was until she died, and he didn't want to feel that way about the others. Several of the other young people chimed in with a chorus of affirmation for that sentiment. They wanted to know what drew their parents together, how they came to be a community, what binds them together still. In their pleas, and in the telling of the stories that will come, Jeanie's legacy will indeed live on.

We ended our time together by sharing communion, being invited to the table with these words: "Let love be genuine; hate what is evil, hold fast to what is good; love one another with mutual affection; outdo one another in showing honor. Do not lag in zeal, be ardent in spirit, serve the Lord. Rejoice in hope, be patient in suffering, persevere in prayer. Contribute to the needs of the saints, extend hospitality to strangers. Bless those who persecute you; bless and do not curse them. Rejoice with those who rejoice, weep with those who weep. Live in harmony with one another" (Romans 12:9-16). Those words were both invitation and affirmation of what I had witnessed in this loving community.

Rescue

My heart was still warmed by the weekend and beating in sync with the rhythm of Julie's drum when Bill dropped me off at the Detroit airport late on the afternoon of December 31. It was hard to leave—in more ways than one. Reports were issued from the airline podium about heavy fog in Charlotte, then problems with our plane's auto-pilot mechanism. Airline agents sent us from gate A6 to A41. We made the long trek, dragging our carry-on luggage with our three-ounce containers of shampoo and toothpaste, expecting to find a plane there—but instead encountered a three-hour line as each of us was rebooked on other flights. Mine was scheduled to leave at 6:30 the next morning.

Bill rescued me, and I spent New Year's Eve with him, Lydia, Lucy, and several others I had met on the retreat, at Day House, Detroit's Catholic Worker house. There, a crowded room full of people shared the highlights and lowlights of 2006, then feasted

together. Sleep eluded me that night, as neighbors in that part
of Detroit ushered in the New Year by shooting off guns half
the night, and I had to be up long before dawn to catch my
early-morning flight.

Lydia, bless her heart, drove me back. Picture 5:30 a.m. on
New Year's Day at the Detroit airport, a planeload of people
mad that their New Year's Eve plans had been ruined, exhausted
and hung-over adults, cranky and crying children, a family of
Green Bay Packers fans wearing gigantic wedges of foam cheese
on their heads, and a plane blocking our destination gate in
Charlotte, North Carolina ... It wasn't pretty.

But beneath my exhaustion was a deep gratitude. The community that had gathered around Jeanie, and celebrated her life
on the edge of Lake Huron, had given me a gift and a reminder.
They had dug beneath their fears and doubts and found love
at the core. The thing they could count on was that they, like
Jeanie, would not be alone—come what may.

My friend Jeanie knew how to pick a community. I wish
everyone could be so fortunate. I almost wrote "when our time
comes." But the point is, Jeanie didn't pick her community
when her time came. She had picked it long before, and invested
her life in it. Her friends, when facing death, did what they had
done facing life: They sang and prayed, resisted and loved. The
extraordinary had become ordinary for them.

Most extraordinary of all were Bill, Lydia, and Lucy. (But
if you've read this far, you already know that.) They suffered
immeasurable, unspeakable loss without complaint, or self-pity,
and with a remarkable degree of both vulnerability and strength.

I was pondering these things as the sun peeked over the
eastern horizon, between the planes out on the tarmac, early on
New Year's Day. I wasn't at all where I had expected to be in the
first hours of 2007. It seems we're always being called upon to
rearrange things—the furniture, our plans ... our lives.

It is a source of aching sadness that Bill, Lydia, and Lucy have
had to rearrange theirs so dramatically. I wouldn't wish what
they have been through on anyone. But may I also dare to give

thanks that the lessons of this loss came to ones so generous and eloquent and brave? We could not ask for better teachers.

Author getting arrested on behalf of the Detroit Newspaper strikers in the mid '90s
Credit: Daymon J. Hartley.

About the Author

Bill Wylie-Kellermann is a non-violent community activist and United Methodist pastor recently retired from St. Peter's Episcopal Church Detroit. He remains connected to the Detroit Catholic Worker and its soup kitchen, Manna Community Meal. In addition to *Dying Well: The Resurrected Life of Jeanie Wylie-Kellermann*, he has authored five other books. He is co-founder of Word and World: A Peoples' School, adjunct faculty at Ecumenical Theological Seminary and Marygrove MA in Social Justice (Detroit). A graduate of Union Theological Seminary in NYC, he's been engaged in direct action for justice and peace for five decades, most recently as part of the Homrich 9, prosecuted for blocking water shut-off trucks. Presently, he is working hard with the New Poor Peoples Campaign. In Jesus, he bets his life on the gospel non-violence, good news to the poor, Word made flesh, and freedom from the power of death.

Other Books by Bill Wylie-Kellermann

Seasons of Faith and Conscience: Kairos, Confession, and Liturgy, (Maryknoll, NY: Orbis Books, 1991; Second Edition—Eugene OR: Wipf and Stock, 2008)

A Keeper of the Word: Selected Writings of William Stringfellow, (Grand Rapids: Eerdmans, 1994)

William Stringfellow: Essential Writings, (Maryknoll, NY: Orbis Books, 2013)

Where the Waters Go Around: Beloved Detroit (Eugene OR: Cascade Books, 2017)

Principalities in Particular: A Practical Theology of the Powers that Be (Minneapolis, MN: Fortress Press, 2017)

Bibliography

A Keeper of the Word: Selected Writings of William Stringfellow. Edited by Bill Wylie-Kellermann. Eerdmans, Grand Rapids, MI, 1994.

Atlee-Loudon, Jennifer. *Red Thread: a spiritual journey of accompaniment.* Epica Task Force, Washington, D.C., 2001.

Berrigan, Daniel. "A Letter to Vietnamese Prisoners." Illustrated by Tom Lewis. The Thomas Merton Center, New York, 1973. Radical Discipleship, https://radicaldiscipleship. net/2015/05/18/a-letter-to-vietnamese-prisoners/

---. *Block Island.* Unicorn Press, Greensboro, NC, 1985.

---. *Sorrow Built a Bridge: Friendship and AIDS.* Catholic Worker Books, New York, 1989. Wipf and Stock, 2009.

---. *We Die before We Live: Talking with the Very Ill.* Seabury Press, New York, 1980.

"Bill, the Bible, and the Seminary Underground." *Radical Christian and exemplary lawyer honoring William Stringfellow.* Edited by Andrew McThenia, Jr. Wm. B. Eerdmans Publishing Co., Grand Rapids, MI, 1994.

Boggs, Grace. *Living For Change: An Autobiography.* University of Minnesota Press, Minneapolis, MN, 1998.

Bury the Dead: Stories of Death and Dying, Resistance and Discipleship. Edited by Laurel Dykstra. Wipf and Stock, Eugene, OR, 2013.

Camus, Albert. *Neither Victims Nor Executioners.* Translated by Dwight McDonald. Liberation, New York, 1960.

---. *The Plague,* 1947. Vintage International, 1991.

Concentration camp Dachau, 1933-1945. Catalog and exhibition guide to the Dachau Memorial Museum. Edited by Barbara Distel and Ruth Jakusch. *Comité International de Dachau,* Munich, 1978.

"Contempt, Conscience, and Community." *Christianity and Crisis.* Aug. 13, 1984.

Crumm, David. Obituary. "Jeanie Wylie-Kellermann: Fought for Peace, Rights." *Detroit Free Press.* January 7, 2006.

Csastary, L.K., et al. "MTH-68/H oncolytic viral treatment in human high-grade gliomas." *Journal of Neuro-Oncology,* 67: 83–93, 2004. Recognize Jeanie in case No. 4.

dePaola, Tomie. *The Clown of God.* Harcourt, Brace & Company, New York, 1978.

Detroit Lives. Edited by Robert Mast. Especially: "City Life, Scenes, Feelings: Bill and Jeanie Wylie-Kellermann," Temple University Press, 1994.

"Dying in Community, Freedom, Decision." *Bury the Dead: Stories of Death and Dying, Resistance and Discipleship.* Edited by Laurel Dykstra, Wipf and Stock, Eugene, OR, 2013.

Eagles, Charles W. *Outside Agitator: Jon Daniels and the Civil Rights Movement in Alabama.* University of North Carolina Press, Chapel Hill, 1993.

Eliot, T.S. "Four Quartets," "The Hollow Men," "The Wasteland." *T.S. Eliot: The Complete Poems and Plays, 1909-1950.* Harcourt Brace & Company, New York, 1952.

Enns, Elaine and Myers, Ched. *Ambassadors of Reconciliation, vol. 2.* Orbis Books, Maryknoll, New York, 2009. Especially sections on Marietta Jaeger and the Greensboro Massacre: Nelson and Joyce Johnson.

Excerpts From the Diaries of the Late God. Edited by Anthony Towne. Harper & Row, New York, 1968.

Exorcism: The Report of a Commission Convened by the Bishop of Exeter. Edited by Dom Robert Petipierre. S.P.C.K., London, 1972.

Forest, Jim. *At Play in the Lions' Den: A Biography and Memoir of Daniel Berrigan.* Orbis Books, Maryknoll, NY, 2017.

Grahame, Kenneth. *The Wind in the Willows*. Charles Scribner's Sons ed., New York, 1960.

Harding, Vincent. *There is a River: The Black Struggle for Freedom in America*. Vantage Books, New York, 1983.

Hollyday, Joyce. *Clothed with the Sun: Biblical Women, Social Justice, and Us*. Westminster John Knox Press, Louisville, KY 1994.

"Homiletic Afterword: A Keeper of the Word." *William Stringfellow: Essential Writings*. Edited by Bill Wylie-Kellermann. Orbis Books, Maryknoll, NY, 2013.

Jaeger, Marietta. *The Lost Child*. Zondervan Publishing Company, Grand Rapids, MI, 1983.

Johnson, Nelson. "Reflections on an Attempt to Build 'Authentic Community' in the Greensboro Kmart Labor Struggle." *University of Pennsylvania Journal of Business Law*. Summer 2000.

Kaup, Paul Edwin. *The Lyles of Western Pennsylvania*. Closson Press, 1987.

King, Martin Luther Jr. "Beyond Vietnam, Breaking the Silence," and "Letter from a Birmingham Jail." *A Testament of Hope: the Essential Writings and Speeches of Martin Luther King, Jr.* Edited by James M. Washington. HarperSanFrancisco, San Francisco, 1991.

Kubler-Ross, Elizabeth. *On Death and Dying*. Scribner, New York, 2014.

Lauchlan, Michael. *And the business goes to pieces*. Fallen Angel Press, Detroit, MI, 1981.

Lewis, C.S. *A Grief Observed*. HarperCollins, New York, 1994.

---. *The Last Battle*. Collier Books, New York, 1956.

---. *The Lion, the Witch, and the Wardrobe*. Collier Books, New York, 1950.

Luzwick, Dierdre. *Endangered Species: Portraits of a Dying Millennium*. HarperCollins Publishers, New York, 1992.

Lyons, Wendy. "Family Embraces Life in Death." *The Messenger: A Publication of the Funeral Consumers Information Society of Greater Detroit*. Winter 2008.

McAlister, Elizabeth. "Is Marriage Obsolete? Sex, Fidelity, and Freedom." *Sojourners*, March-April, 1996.

Michigan Citizen. "America's most Progressive Newspaper" published variously from Benton Harbor, Detroit, Highland Park from 1974 to 2014.

Munsch, Robert. *Love You Forever.* Firefly Books Ltd., Canada, 2001.

Myers, Ched. *Binding the Strong Man.* Orbis Books, Maryknoll, NY, 1988.

---. "In the Baptism of Jesus: a Homily for Jeanie Wylie-Kellermann." *Sojourners*, 2006. Reprinted in this volume.

Orenstein, Gloria Feman. *Multi-cultural Celebrations: The Paintings of Betty La Duke 1972-1992.* Pomegranate Books, 1993.

Oyer, Gordon. *Pursuing the Spiritual Roots of Protest: Merton, Berrigan, Yoder, and Muste at the Gethsemani Abbey Peacemakers Retreat.* Cascade Books, Eugene, OR, 2014.

Rhomberg, Chris. *The Broken Table: The Detroit Newspaper Strike and the State of American Labor.* Russell Sage Foundation, New York, 2012.

"Samuel J. Wylie." *Modern Canterbury Pilgrims: Why They Chose the Episcopal Church.* Edited by James A. Pike. Morehouse-Gorham Co., New York, 1956.

Silverstein, Shel. *The Giving Tree.* Harper, New York, 1964.

Stringfellow, William. "Harlem, Rebellion, and Resurrection: How My Mind Has Changed." *The Christian Century.* December 11, 1970, pp. 1345-48.

---. *A Simplicity of Faith: My Experience in Mourning.* Abingdon Press, Nashville, TN, 1982. Wipf and Stock, 2005.

---. Introduction. *They Call Us Dead Men: Reflections on Life and Conscience,* by Daniel Berrigan, Macmillan, New York, 1966. Wipf and Stock, 2009.

---. *Second Birthday: A Personal Confrontation With Illness.* Doubleday & Company, Inc., Garden City, NY, 1970. Wipf and Stock, 2005.

Svoboda, Sandra, "Grave Debate." [Jeanie and the Funeral Industry], *Detroit Metro Times.* January 21, 2009.

The Surrealist's Bible. Jonathan David Publishers, Inc. Middle Village, NY, 1976.

Towne, Anthony. "God is Dead in Georgia: Eminent Deity Succumbs During Surgery—Succession in Doubt As All Creation Groans." *motive magazine*, 1966.

"Use of Money." *The Sermons of John Wesley.* Edited by Kenneth J. Collins and Jason E. Vickers. Abingdon Press, Nashville, 2013.

Voices of the Catholic Worker Movement. Edited by Rosalie Reigle Troester. Especially sections on the *Detroit Catholic Worker* and Father Tom Lumpkin. Temple University Press, Philadelphia, 1993.

Wagner, Jerome. *The Enneagram Spectrum of Personality Styles.* Metamorphosis Press, Portland, OR, 1996.

Welsh, Ann Morrison. *Held in the Light: Norman Morrison's Sacrifice for Peace and His Family's Journey of Healing.* Orbis Books, Maryknoll, NY, 2008.

Wesley, John. "Thoughts Upon Slavery." *Works of John Wesley, vol.* 2. Edited by Thomas Jackson. 1872.

Wylie, Samuel. *A Celebration of Smallness.* Forward Movement Publications, Cincinnati, OH, 1973. Republished with an introduction by Jeanie Wylie-Kellermann (Episcopal Diocese of Northern Michigan, 1995).

---. *Precede the Dawn: The Church in an Age of Change.* Morehouse-Barlow, New York, 1965.

---. *Sacramental Living.* The Seabury Press, New York, 1965.

Wylie-Kellermann, Bill. Foreword. *Minor Prophets, Major Themes*, by Daniel Berrigan, Fortcamp Press, 1995. Wipf and Stock, 2009.

---. Introduction. *An Ethic for Christians and Other Aliens in a Strange Land*, by William Stringfellow, Word, Inc., Waco, TX, 1973. Wipf and Stock, 2005.

---. Introduction. *Conscience and Obedience*, by William Stringfellow, Word, Inc., Waco, TX, 1977. Wipf and Stock, 2005.

---. Introduction. *Instead of Death*, by William Stringfellow, The Seabury Press, New York, 1963, 1976. Wipf and Stock, 2005.

---. "A Moveable Feast: the Underground Seminary," *The Other Side*, Vol. 35, No. 6. November/December, 1999, pp. 16-19.

---. "A People's School of Discipleship: Word and World." *The Witness*. June 2002.

---. *Principalities in Particular: A Practical Theology of the Powers that Be.* Fortress Press, Minneapolis, MN, 2017. Especially: "Death Shall Have No Dominion: Daniel Berrigan of the Resurrection," "Barbed Wire and Beyond: the Freedom to Unmake Nuclear Weapons," "Readers Before Profits: The Detroit Newspaper Strike," "Unholy Alliance: John Wesley and the Global Powers of Slavery," and "Lest Death Prevail: Harry Potter and the Principalities."

---. *Seasons of Faith and Conscience: Kairos, Confession, and Liturgy.* Orbis Books, Maryknoll, NY, 1991. Introduction, Wipf and Stock, 2008.

---. "Surveillance: Wise as Serpents, Gentle as Doves," *Sojourners*, February 1986.

---. "Taking the Book with Life and Death Seriousness.", *Apostle of Peace: Essays in Honor of Daniel Berrigan.* Edited by John Dear. Orbis Books, Maryknoll, NY, 1996.

---. "To Stir Up God's Good Trouble: John Wesley and the Methodist Revival Movement." Cover essay. *Sojourners,* Vol. 13, No.2. March 1984.

---. "Unholy Alliance: John Wesley and the Global Economy of Slavery." *Christian Social Action.* July/August 2003.

---. "Unions and Communities." *The Boston Review.* Summer 1996. XXI, No. 3/4.

---. *Where the Water Goes Around: Beloved Detroit.* Cascade Books, Eugene OR, 2017. Especially: "Discerning the Angel of Detroit," "Interview with Jeanie and Bill Wylie-Kellermann," "Reading the Building, Seeing the Powers," "Readers Before Profits," and "To the Hoop Dance: a Grieving Rite."

---. *William Stringfellow: Essential Writings.* Orbis Books, Mayknoll, NY, 2013.

Wylie-Kellermann, Jeanie. *Poletown: Community Betrayed.* University of Illinois Press, Chicago, 1989.

---. "Between Living And Dying: A Conversation With Anne Finger About Disability, Abortion, And Assisted Suicide." *The Sun Magazine.* December 1996.

---. "The Blood of the Ancients." *The Witness.* November 1993.

---. "A Celtic Passage: Conversation with Daniel Berrigan on storms, death, and healing." *The Witness.* March 1997.

---. "Challenging Two-Party Politics: An Interview with the Green Party's Ralph Nader" with Bill Wylie-Kellermann. *The Witness.* November 2000.

---. "The Contra War: Report of a Witness for Peace Delegation" with Bill Wylie-Kellermann, *The Record,* March 1986.

---. "The Eucharist at Williams International: Sacrament or Sacrilege?" *The Record.* January 1986.

---. Introduction. *Letters Home: Julie Beutel's Letters from Nicaragua, 1984-1985* by Julie Beutel, Sun Press, Detroit, MI, 1985.

---. "Lakotas' Camp Is Staying Put." *In These Times*. April 21, 1982.

---. "A Neighborhood Dies So GM Can Live." *Village Voice*. July 8, 1981.

---. "Old Gray Lady vs. Valley Girl." [*News* vs. *Free Press*] *The Detroit Metro Times*. July 7, 1983.

---. "On Death and Time." *The Witness*. January/February 2000.

---. *Poletown Lives!* Written and directed by Jeanie Wylie. Produced by George Corsetti. Available from Information Factory, 3512 Courville, Detroit, Michigan 48224. Released March 1983. First Prize Documentary, American Film Festival.

---. "Remaking the Motor City—and America" with Lawrence Walsh. *The Progressive*. July 1982.

---. "Respecting the Freedom of the Dead." *The Witness*. March 1997.

---. "Resurrection in Oscoda: How Seven Activists Spent Their Easter Morning at Wurtsmith Air Force Base." *The Michigan Voice*. May 1983.

---. "Squatters Protest Housing Programs in Three U.S. Cities." *In These Times*. October 7, 1981.

---. *St. Nicholas*. Unpublished children's book. Illustrated by Virginia Macsymowicz.

---. "Within a Communion of Children." *On the Edge*, Vol. 12, No. 1. Winter 1987.

Wylie-Kellermann, Lydia. "Learning it in My Bones: Holding Her body, Touching Nonviolence." *Bury the Dead: Essays on Death and Dying, Resistance and Discipleship*. Edited by Laurel Dykstra. Wipf and Stock, 2013.

Selected Index

Sojourners, 221.

Stilp, Gene, 292.

Stringfellow, William, 260, 282, 283, 375: and Anthony Towne, 121-122; and Anthony's death, 124; Berrigan's eulogy, 119; and Block Island, 124, 123; burial, 122; and the circus, 283-284; death of, 118-119; on surviving death, 260-261; as exorcist, 122-123; flags at half staff, 121; icon of, 306; mantle of, 229; marriage blessing, 30; on miracle, 229; on the powers, 22, 27, 81; and race, 27; on resurrection, 260-261; on Second Advent, 257; on theodicy, 354; and underground seminary, 126, 127; and Jeanie Wylie-Kellermann, 13, 16-17; 27, 28-29, 30, 120, 124, 283.

Theodicy, 354.

Towne, Anthony, 120, 122; death, 122; obituary of God, 125.

Ultrapheresis, 148, 152-153.

Underground seminary, 28, 126, 127. See also Word and World.

Wallis, Jim, 25, 119, 122, 237.

Wallis, Joy Carrol, 237.

Wallis, Luke, 237, 314.

Walters, Elizabeth, 24.

War tax resistance, 49, 92.

Weber, Peter, 101-107, 111, 116; cancer, 102; death, 106; and Rocky Flats action, 102.

Wesley, John, 73, 131-134; covenant prayer, 50; fear of death, 134; and justification, 134; and slave trade, 132.

Williams, Ron, 152.

Williams International, Inc., 21, 22, 297. See also Cruise missile.

Winterfeld, Josie, 328, 362, 374.

The Witness, magazine, xxi, 36, 69-72, 74, 75, 78, 90, 92-93, 112, 116, 149, 152, 157-160, 164, 169, 187, 190, 195, 198, 217, 225, 230-231, 367.